ESSENTIAL VIRTUES
MARKS OF THE CHRIST-CENTERED LIFE

JIM BERG

Jim Berg
Jer 9:23, 24

JOURNEYFORTH
Greenville, South Carolina

Library of Congress Cataloging-in-Publication Data
Berg, Jim, 1952-
  Essential virtues : marks of the Christ-centered life / Jim Berg.
     p. cm.
  Summary: "Essential virtues presents 2 Peter 1 as the portrait of what
christlikeness is"—Provided by publisher.
  Includes bibliographical references and index.
  ISBN 978-1-59166-883-1 (perfect bound pbk. : alk. paper)
  1. Bible. N.T. Peter, 1st , I—Criticism, interpretation, etc. 2. Virtues—Biblical
teaching. I. Title.
  BS2795.52.B47 2008
  227'.9306—dc22

                                                            2008016061

Cover Photo Credits: Cathedral Albert Barr; Wood Carving Ahmad Faizal Yahya;
Columns iStock; Scrolled Column Guy Sargent; Leather Bill Noll; Paper iStock

Train (p. 89) John Woodcock

ESV: Scripture quotations marked ESV are from The Holy Bible, English
Standard Version®, copyright © 2001 by Crossway Bibles, a publishing ministry
of Good News Publishers. Used by permission. All rights reserved.

NASB: Scripture taken from the NEW AMERICAN STANDARD BIBLE®,
Copyright © 1960, 1962, 1963, 1968, 1971, 1972, 1973, 1975, 1977, 1995 by The
Lockman Foundation. Used by permission.

The fact that materials produced by other publishers may be referred to in
this volume does not constitute an endorsement of the content or theological
position of materials produced by such publishers.

All Scripture is quoted from the Authorized King James Version unless otherwise
noted.

Essential Virtues: Marks of the Christ-Centered Life

Design by Craig Oesterling
Page layout by Kelley Moore

© 2008 by BJU Press
Greenville, South Carolina 29614
JourneyForth Books is a division of BJU Press

Printed in the United States of America
All rights reserved

ISBN 978-1-59166-883-1

15   14   13   12   11   10   9   8   7   6   5   4   3   2   1

With steadfast love to Darrell, Jeremy, and Paul, my sons-in-law.

May this study help you grow in commitment, courage, and compassion as you and your dear wives rear the next generation of disciple-makers for the Lord Jesus.

CONTENTS

FOREWORD

The destiny of every believer is Christlikeness, the enemy of Christlikeness is sin, and the root of every sin is nourished by some theological error. That's why such a remarkable amount of space in the New
Testament is devoted to combating false teaching. Galatians, Colossians, and the Pastoral Epistles of Paul, as well as the letters of James,
Jude, Peter, and John all confront the Hydra of heresy. Every head may
take a different form, but they are all connected to the same beast.

That so much false teaching surfaced so soon in the first century signifies
the reality and gravity of our spiritual warfare. The transfer of our citizen-
ship and allegiance from Satan's kingdom to God's (Colossians 1:13) has
cosmic consequences. "There is no prince that will thus lightly lose his
subjects," threatened Apollyon to Christian. Declaring himself the sworn
enemy of Christian's new King, he raged, "I hate his Person, his Laws, and
People; I am come out on purpose to withstand thee."

We are not ignorant of his schemes (2 Corinthians 2:11). Demoniza-
tion of submission to authority and elevation of personal freedom as an
ultimate virtue are the stock in trade of heresy, and as old as Eden. So
the ubiquity of false teaching and the susceptibility of Christians to it
are nothing new.

In a fallen world, every silver lining has a dark cloud. The profusion of
modern communication media that furnish instant access to a surfeit
of information also disseminate misinformation and disinformation.
Religious teachers promoting personal freedom and peddling self-
gratification from under a white and wooly exterior are as common as
clover. The battle would be more manageable if the enemy were only
external, but falsehood finds a ready ally in the fallen flesh indwelling
each of us (James 1:14–15).

This book focuses on Peter's call to cultivate essential Christian virtues (2 Peter 1). But what initially sounds like a peacetime proposal
to pursue Christian extras ("*add to your faith . . .*") is actually a call to
arms triggered by the threat of this very brand of false teaching. I can
think of no better preparation for beginning this book than to sit down
and attentively read straight through Peter's very brief second epistle (a

ten-minute task). It's not difficult to detect what drives the letter: an urgency to warn believers that false teaching is intellectually, morally, and spiritually corrupting to the unstable (2 Peter 2). That's why Peter is passionate about our stability in the knowledge of Christ (1:10, 12; 2:14; 3:16–17). Bare knowledge of Christ isn't enough to protect us from the dangers of false teaching and apostasy (2:20–22). Believers must become *established* in their knowledge of Christ. How? Peter's answer is the informing and transforming influence of the Scriptures (1:2–4, 12–21; 3:1–6, 14–18). What Peter urges upon us in 1:5–7, therefore, are *virtues essential* for advancing our call to Christlikeness (1:4), for assuring us that our relation to Christ is genuine and vital (1:8–10), and for defending us against false teaching that appeals to the mind while seducing the flesh (3:17–18).

Essential Virtues is scriptural therapy for mind and life. Like most therapy, it may sometimes be painful. But the stakes are high. So are the standards Peter raises. So is our calling. Just as Jesus commands us to be perfect like our Father in heaven (Matthew 5:45), Peter reminds us that we are called *to God's own glory and virtue* (1:3), to become *a partaker of God's own nature* (1:4). Christianity is not a call to a higher standard or a higher life; it is a call to the highest standard, to a life impossible for us alone because it cuts cross-grain to all our fallen instincts and desires. That's why God has provided all we need in terms of both power and promises (1:3–4) and, in the end, a reward as unimaginable as it is certain (1:11).

Jim Berg's systematic exploration of these essential virtues is practical in the finest sense of the word. He seeks to trail the exegetical data in the text, tracking the path of God's mind in the passage from what He says to what it means for us in terms of our daily choices and actions. His energetic, personable writing style is coupled with an unusual gift for helping the reader translate principle into practice. Best of all, what drives his thinking is not a commitment to morality as an end in itself, but an understanding that we as believers are part of a reality much bigger than what we see around us and a destiny far greater beyond this passing world. He understands that God has destined us to be changed into His image because He has created us for His glory.

Layton Talbert

PREFACE

G od has dug several single-chapter "watering holes" throughout the Scripture's terrain where thirsty sheep can get an especially long drink of one particular teaching. You are probably familiar with many of them. They would include 1 Corinthians 15, the resurrection chapter; 1 Corinthians 13, the love chapter; Hebrews 11, the faith chapter; and James 3, the chapter-length discussion on the tongue. Of course, other chapters in the Bible discuss these topics, but not to the same depth and breadth of these passages. God has seen fit to place a great deal of teaching in one place for certain topics.

The same is true for 2 Peter 1. Here God has dug the largest watering hole on the topic of Christian maturity. It shows us what it takes for us to have a mature knowledge of Christ and what the resulting likeness to Christ looks like in the midst of a morally corrupt culture.

Those of you familiar with *Changed into His Image* know that it sketched out the process of sanctification whereby we are made like Christ.[1] Think of the list of virtues presented in 2 Peter 1 as the portrait of what that Christlikeness looks like. Because of the strategic part these qualities play in our development and demonstration of Christlikeness, I call them *Essential Virtues: Marks of the Christ-Centered Life.*

A MINISTRY OF REPETITION TO FORGETFUL BELIEVERS

Peter's audience lived in a world very much like our own. Religious pluralism and cultural corruption abounded. The pagan culture was taking its toll on the believers to whom he was writing, and the church needed an apostolic admonition that called these believers to demonstrate their faith by living distinctively virtuous lives. He warns them— and us—against "any tendency to treat sin lightly, to suppose that an immoral lifestyle can be pursued without any penalty."[2]

Some who had slid into moral apostasy were now propagating the false teachings of libertine Christianity that justified their sensual lifestyles.[3] Commentator Richard J. Bauckham believes that the attitudes and ethical lapses of the false teachers, especially the immorality, were an "accommodation to the permissiveness of pagan society . . . especially when Christian morality impeded participation in the social life of the cities. . . . [Christian teaching] seemed to them an embarrassment in their cultural environment. . . . Perhaps [these false teachers] saw themselves as rather daring young radicals trying to clear a lot of traditional nonsense out of the church."[4] The parallel to today's climate among both fundamental and evangelical Bible believers is obvious.

The apostolic antidote to such moral corruption is a maturing, Christlike character; Peter commits himself to the task of promoting the development of that character in their lives for as long as he lives. He even promises that his teaching will reach beyond his earthly time with them through the epistle that we will be studying. Notice Peter's great burden, recorded in 1:12–15:

> Wherefore I will not be negligent to put you always in remembrance of these things, though ye know them, and be established in the present truth. Yea, I think it meet, as long as I am in this tabernacle, to stir you up by putting you in remembrance; knowing that shortly I must put off this my [body], even as our Lord Jesus Christ hath shewed me. Moreover I will endeavour that ye may be able after my decease to have these things always in remembrance.

Peter goes on to assure his readers in 1:16–21 that "these things" (verses 12, 15) of which he is reminding them are not of personal origin but are from God Himself. Libertines must reject authority in order to practice their self-centered and fleshly lifestyles, and Peter must reassert the authority of the Scriptures as messages from God Himself about these matters.

We would do well to take our cue from the apostle. We must never tire of reminding ourselves and one another of the importance of submitting ourselves to the inspired Word of God and to developing a mature Christian character, for "there can be no claims to Christian spirituality apart from possessing a virtuous lifestyle."[5] Such a personal pursuit of Christian character is not incidental to our Christian experience; it is a primary evidence that Christ does, indeed, dwell in us.

What we have here in 2 Peter 1 then is strategic for overcoming the pull of the ungodly world around us and for resisting the lure of similar libertine false teachings in the church today. Both the world and false teaching appeal to our fleshly nature, and Peter prescribes full-grown

Christian character as the cure to both. If we are to represent Christ well in this day, we need a generous dose of the antidote—a fuller likeness of Christ stamped on our souls.

So, are you ready for a good long drink from one of God's special watering holes? I hope so. You will be amazingly refreshed and strengthened by Peter's inspired instruction. The primary emphasis of the book you hold in your hand is descriptive. That is, it describes the target we should be aiming for in our Christian experience. The accompanying study guide is prescriptive; it tells you in more detail how to get there. Combined, they will give you the necessary tools you need to develop Christlike character in your own soul and to help you disciple others toward that end as well.

I pray that your study of this passage will be as invigorating and as rewarding as it has been to me. So, if you too are a thirsty sheep, get out your Bible, ask God to teach you His ways, and let's get going. For starters, right now stop to read through 2 Peter 1:1–15.

ACKNOWLEDGMENTS

Grace is God's undeserved favor and help to His fallen creatures. It takes many forms. Most notably it was displayed on a cross outside Jerusalem, where God's Lamb was sacrificed for the sins of the world. No gift is more superlative than salvation through Jesus Christ. But God's grace shows up in other forms as well.

God's undeserved help to His fallen creatures is evident in an inspired, written revelation of His will. It is evident in the stability and, therefore, predictability of His physical creation and in the gifts of the institutions of marriage, the home, and human government.

Paul revealed to us that another of God's gracious gifts to us is the church—that body of believers who are given to one another for mutual edification in the ways of Christ and for a witness to a lost world.

I see those men and women who have helped me in the development of *Essential Virtues* as more of God's gracious gifts. Special thanks go to my friends and colaborers in Christ's ministry: Jim Newcomer, Randy Leedy, Sam Horn, Stephen Hankins, and Layton Talbert for their theological input and personal encouragement during the project. Their insight and suggestions were invaluable.

Suzette Jordan, whose editorial skills shepherded the manuscript into its final form, has earned my highest respect and deepest thanks. She and the rest of the BJU Press team are a most gracious gift to the church. Their dedication and sacrifice for the edification of the body are unsurpassed in my estimation.

God's greatest gift to me, after His Son, is my beloved wife, Patty, whose life continues to affect me profoundly. Her love for Christ is lived out daily in our home and in her ministry to others. She more than anyone else I know evidences the *Essential Virtues* of which I write. I pray that this book will have as great a ministry to others as Patty has had to me.

Chapter One

THE PORTRAIT OF THE CHRIST-CENTERED LIFE

And beside this, giving all diligence, add to your faith virtue; and to virtue knowledge; and to knowledge [self-control], and to [self-control endurance]; and to [endurance] godliness; and to godliness brotherly kindness; and to brotherly kindness [love]. (2 Peter 1:5–7)[1]

WHY THIS LIST?

Have you ever wondered why the apostles and the Lord Himself present lists of virtues that don't seem to agree? For example, why does the list of virtues in 2 Peter 1 differ from the fruit of the Spirit in Galatians 5 and from the qualities of love in 1 Corinthians 13? Why do even the Lord's beatitudes in Matthew 5 contain elements that are not included in the qualities of wisdom in James 3? Why do some qualities of these various lists overlap while others are unique to one of the inspired lists?

Think of it this way. If you were buying groceries, your shopping list would look somewhat different from the list you would take to a hardware store, though both lists are necessary for the overall well-being of you and your family. There might even be some overlap because you could buy light bulbs or flashlight batteries at either store.

Similarly, the lists of the New Testament support the context in which they are given and the particular burden of the writer. In Matthew 5 Jesus accentuated the characteristics of His kingdom that contrasted with the Judaism His hearers had known. The list in James 3 describes the characteristics of wise speech. First Corinthians 13 is a prism that breaks the white light of love into its individual "colors," or manifestations. The fruit of the Spirit lies in direct contrast to the works of the

1

flesh in Galatians 5. We must ask ourselves then, what is the context of the list we are looking at in 2 Peter 1? (As you study through this book it will help you to refer to the chart printed on the inside back cover.)

A Portrait of the Christ-Centered Life

Peter is quite clear about his intent. He wants these dispersed former members of his congregation to whom he is writing to come to an intimate knowledge of Christ that will transform them into the likeness of Christ (2 Peter 1:3–4). He describes for them what full-grown maturity in Christ looks like and heralds that maturity as the only antidote to the sensual, lawless appeals of the world and to the libertine false teaching around them. It is also a character that will gain for them a rich welcome into the everlasting kingdom (2 Peter 1:11). In other words, it is a character that is honored much by Christ because it is so much like Him. D. Martyn Lloyd-Jones observes, "It is a perfect list; you cannot add to it. He deals with the whole of the Christian life."[2]

Author Gary Inrig says of this passage, "The character sketch Peter gives is a beautiful portrait of the mature Christian. . . . The qualities which Peter describes are fascinating and provide a powerful basis for personal character analysis."[3]

These men are right on target. The list of essential virtues provided for us in 2 Peter 1 presents a clear template for our own growth in Christ and for our discipleship of others in the midst of our own morally corrupt culture.

Simultaneous yet Sequential

The next question before us asks, "Is there a particular significance in the order of these traits, and if there is, must we develop the previous traits fully before we can proceed to the next trait in the list?"

The grammatical construction in this passage indicates there is, indeed, a sequence involved.[4] None of the other scriptural lists repeats the previous trait while exhorting the believer to build the next trait upon it. Notice how several Bible teachers and commentators speak of this arrangement.

Michael Green quotes J. A. Bengel, "Each step gives birth to and facilitates the next. Each subsequent quality balances and brings to perfection the one preceding."[5]

M. R. Vincent in his word studies comments, "The A.V. exhorts to add one virtue to another; but the Greek, to develop one virtue in the exercise of another; 'an increase by growth, not by external junction; each new grace springing out of, attempting, and perfecting the other.'"[6]

D. Edmond Hiebert further comments, "Peter lists seven qualities or traits of character in this moral development, and he introduces each new trait as being 'in' (en), 'in connection with,' the preceding. Each is inherent in its predecessor, which in turn is supplemented and perfected by the new quality, giving it more abundant fruitage."[7]

Commentator Stephen Paine says, "Their presentation here seems to observe an order from the most elemental to the more advanced, but they are all of them facets of the Spirit's work in the life of a believer, aspects of the glory of the indwelling Christ, His character shown in the Christian's character."[8]

J. Daryl Charles, whose work *Virtue Amidst Vice* provides one of the most detailed exegetical and historical examinations of 2 Peter 1, sees clearly in this list "an ethical progression that builds toward a climax in [love]." Charles rejects the idea that except for saving faith (the first virtue) and love (the last) the rest could have been stated in any order. He says,

> Each virtue, a fruit of the life of faith, facilitates the next; none is independent of the others; as is suggested by the . . . syntactical arrangement of vv. 5–7. These virtues cannot stand in unrelated or unconnected juxtaposition. Because of this organic unity, which is rooted in the spiritual realities of faith and the righteousness of Christ, the catalog of virtues in 2 Peter is not largely random; rather, it demonstrates from a Christian standpoint a logical interconnection of virtues, all of which move toward the highest virtue, [love].[9]

Perhaps a good illustration to show what is happening here is to think of how an embryo develops in a mother's womb. All the parts of the baby are developing simultaneously. The fingers are forming and growing while the lungs are developing along with the arms and torso, and so forth. Yet even though all the parts are developing at a certain rate all the time, there is a noticeable developmental sequence as well.

The first thing we notice in a picture of an embryo is the large head. The brain must develop before the rest of the baby because it will be regulating the growth and development of all the other parts. If the

3

brain is deformed in some way, we can expect that the rest of the body will show deformities and dysfunction. After the brain the heart begins to develop more fully. It must be prepared to sustain the rest of the body. It also must now supply the demands of a larger brain. We can say that the parts of the baby are developing simultaneously yet sequentially.

> These essential virtues must be cultivated in the power of the Spirit of God upon the foundation of saving faith.

Christlike character develops in much the same way. All the traits in 2 Peter 1:5–7 are commanded elsewhere in Scripture, but in this passage they form a chain in which every link is necessary. The sequence here teaches us that none of the traits can reach maturity unless the previous supporting traits are maturing well.

Look at the chart inside the back cover of this book and notice their sequence. Do you see how even though we must always show love, no one can really have a full-bodied *love* (the last trait in the list) that "endureth all things" (1 Corinthians 13:7) until he possesses a maturing *endurance*, an earlier trait in the list? Likewise, *brotherly kindness* in the face of the cruelty or thoughtlessness of others cannot be sustained without that same *endurance*.

In a similar manner, no one can have full-grown *endurance* who has not developed a strong measure of *self-control*. He will not endure mistreatment or pressure long if he has not learned first to say no to his own desires and passions. So it is with all the traits, as we shall see in the discussions to follow. Each trait supports the development of the next in the sequence, yet none can be ignored until the previous ones are developed since all are commanded elsewhere in Scripture.

CAREFULLY CHOSEN WORDS

The words Peter chose to include in this list under inspiration from God were, as mentioned earlier, Greek words in common use in his day. Many of these traits in Peter's epistle were also included in lists proposed by various Greek philosophers of the day.

For example, the word for *self-control* that Peter uses in this passage had a broad meaning in the first century. Some of that meaning is retained in the Scriptures, but the word took on a specific refined and narrowed meaning when the apostles used it.

The Stoics, a school of philosophy popular at the time of Peter's writing, also promoted self-control. But to them, it was purely a matter of controlling the passions by reason. The apostles taught, however, that control of the passions had to involve much interaction with God if it was to be, indeed, a fruit of the Spirit. The branch must abide in the Vine for fruit to be produced.

To be sure that his readers did not get the common understanding of these words confused with the more specific and intense Christian meaning, Peter introduces each quality with the definite article in the original language. Unfortunately, that word was not brought into most English translations. Verses 5–7 actually read,

> Add to your faith *the* virtue; and to *the* virtue *the* knowledge; and to *the* knowledge *the* self-control; and to *the* self-control *the* endurance; and to *the* endurance *the* godliness; and to *the* godliness *the* brotherly kindness; and to *the* brotherly kindness *the* love.

Why is that important? Let me explain it this way. When I was a young boy and needed to be warned about my behavior—which seemed all too often—my mother would remind me that if I disobeyed she would have to get "*the* stick." Now on our farm we had many kinds of sticks. We had stakes for tomato plants, battens used on barn siding, tree branch walking sticks we boys used when trudging through the shelterbelts, and so forth. Although we had many kinds of sticks, I never had any confusion about what Mom was referring to when she said "*the* stick." I knew it was the two-foot piece of one-by-two she kept on top of the refrigerator, which she used when necessary to correct one of her three boys when we were disobedient.[10] My point is that when she used the definite article *the*, she was singling out that particular stick from all the other sticks we might be familiar with.

In a similar fashion Peter uses the definite article to point out something unique about his list of virtues. While the Stoic virtues could be developed by sheer willpower, these essential virtues must be cultivated in the power of the Spirit of God upon the foundation of saving faith. He wants his readers to know that he is choosing his words carefully and that they have a specific quality and intensity that he does not want them to miss. We will look at their unique qualities and how they are developed as we investigate each trait.

The Harvest

After Peter lists these essential virtues, he describes the benefits we can expect to reap when we cultivate them. He lists them in verses 8–11. Notice them carefully in the text below.

> For if these things [these essential virtues] be in you, and abound, they make you that ye shall neither be barren nor unfruitful in the [full] knowledge of our Lord Jesus Christ. But he that lacketh these things is blind, and cannot see afar off, and hath forgotten that he was purged from his old sins. Wherefore, the rather, brethren, give diligence to make your calling and election sure: for if ye do these things, ye shall never fall: for so an entrance shall be ministered unto you abundantly into the everlasting kingdom of our Lord and Saviour Jesus Christ.

The goal is for these evidences of the Christ-centered life to be "in you and abound." That means they are to be personally yours and constantly growing more dominant. The result is several-fold.

The Cure for Apathy

The apostle says that progress in the cultivation of these virtues will mean we will not be "barren." The Greek word here translated "barren" means stalled or stuck, and therefore, ineffective.

An automobile whose engine has stalled isn't going anywhere. It will have to be pulled, pushed, or fixed on the spot by someone else if it is to move off the side of the road and get on with its journey.

Such is the spiritual condition of many in the church today. Immature believers who are not advancing in their growth in Christ often have to be pushed or pulled along by someone else. They cannot seem to get going on their own; they appear apathetic.

The stalled Christian may be a teenager with parents and youth pastor who are concerned about his spiritual direction. He may even resist their attempts to check up on him with regard to his devotions, his friends, his failure to keep up with household duties, and his entertainment choices.

The stalled Christian may be a spiritually lukewarm husband whose wife daily begs God to work in his heart to get him "back on the road" where he can lead her and the children in the ways of Christ. He may get irritated that other men in his church are always trying to encourage him to join them in small group studies to help him make some progress in his Christian life.

Peter is clear that a person who seems "stuck" in his growth is like the embryo that ceases to develop at some point in a pregnancy. A stalled condition is serious for the forming infant in the mother's womb and is a grave condition for the developing believer as well. It leads quite readily to moral and ethical decline as the stalled believer by default is sucked into the ways of the world around him.

The Path to Intimacy with Christ

Peter continues by saying that the growing believer will be neither stalled out "nor unfruitful in the [full] knowledge of our Lord Jesus Christ." Here is the most wonderful benefit of cultivating these essential virtues. In the process of working on them we will get to know God! For these traits to develop there will have to be much interaction between the believer and his Savior.

Today those who wish to have guidance on improving their physical condition will consult a personal trainer. He is hired to evaluate his client's current physical condition and map out an exercise, diet, and lifestyle routine that will enhance overall well-being. The trainer will interact with his client daily, if necessary, to insure that he stays on the right track. He provides periods of instruction about various disciplines that must become lifelong habits for long-term health. He is available to answer questions about how certain exercise routines are to be carried out and why certain parts of his trainee's diet are so strategic to his health. In the process of interacting with his personal trainer over the course of time, the trainee gets to know the trainer quite well. He learns much about the trainer's personality and interests. He may even become acquainted with the trainer's family, upbringing, and professional goals. It is quite possible that the trainer takes on more of the status of a close family member or of a personal friend over time.

A similar relationship develops between the believer and Jesus Christ as the believer diligently takes instruction from his Lord and seeks to faithfully carry it out for his own spiritual well-being and for Christ's glory. Christ is the perfect Trainer! He made us, so He understands our makeup, and He made us for a purpose, so He understands what we must become in order to fulfill that mission.

A believer, however, who stays home from the "gym" can never develop into a "healthy" Christian. But beyond that, he will never get to know the Trainer well if he seldom shows up. If he ignores the instructions and skips the exercise sessions, he can expect to get a call (i.e., a convicted conscience) from the Trainer holding him accountable for his lack of performance. He will begin to see the Trainer as a nuisance to avoid rather than an insightful Coach who really knows what is best. Unfortunately, the relationship will disintegrate.

The Christian, however, who faithfully seeks to develop these essential virtues, will see every circumstance of life as a "fitness station" upon which the Trainer has arranged another repetition of the necessary surrender, dependence, and obedience required to develop and manifest that virtue. As the believer interacts with his Lord, taking instruction, asking for help, receiving encouragement and grace, and so forth, he will learn much about his Trainer. As the relationship develops, the believer will find the Trainer revealing more and more about Himself and His disposition toward and plans for His child.

The Key to Discernment

The apostle reminds us, on the other hand, that the person who lacks these qualities will be "blind, and cannot see afar off." Like the church of Laodicea, believers who are stalled in their Christian experience (i.e., those who are lukewarm) are "blind" (Revelation 3:17). Peter qualifies the kind of blindness he addresses. The Greek word here translated "cannot see afar off" is the same word from which we get the word *myopic*. It literally means "to shut the eye."

Peter uses this metaphor of shutting the eye to show the purposeful refusal to look at life with full perception. This is a willful blindness to spiritual matters.

Believers who are not diligently cultivating these virtues of Christlikeness will be taking on the likeness of the world instead. They willingly focus only on the temporal things right in front of them. They are obsessed with the present—the latest recording hits, the summer's blockbuster movies, the fall's television lineup, the current superstars and celebrity fashions, the hottest electronic games, and the season's ball teams' standings. From an eternal perspective, these things are entirely irrelevant. Yet the nearsighted believer can't see anything beyond the present draw of the world—neither does he seem to want to.

Furthermore, when he faces a trial or temptation, he is focused only on the immediate situation and how he can get relief. He cannot see beyond the

> Believers who are not diligently cultivating these virtues of Christlikeness will be taking on the likeness of the world.

trial or temptation to what God wishes to do through it in perfecting Christlikeness—the essential virtues. All he sees is the immediate pain or misery in the trial or the enticing pleasure of the temptation. Consequently, he lives an earthbound and narrowly focused life. He is "blind and cannot see afar off" and has brought on the condition by turning away from the ways of Christ.

We do not live in an age of wisdom—neither did Peter. Though the philosophies of his day spoke much of wisdom, moral corruption abounded. Similarly today, there is much talk among Christians about exercising discernment, yet there is little difference between them and the sensual, pleasure-seeking culture of our day.

Never before in American religious history have we had more believers turning away from what they call "legalistic standards" in favor of exercising "discernment." Yet neither have we seen so much immorality and blatant worldliness in the church. Like the victims of false teaching in Peter's day, many in the church today have been promised Christian liberty but have instead become slaves of corruptions (2 Peter 2:18–19).

Wisdom, as we shall see, is essentially knowing the difference between right and wrong. Solomon understood this (1 Kings 3:6–9). Many, both in Peter's day and in ours, do not. Peter teaches us that cultivating these virtues will correct this spiritual myopia. The pursuit of Christlikeness is the path to wisdom.

The Basis for Assurance
Peter continues with another warning to the person who fails to cultivate these essential virtues. He says that he has "forgotten that he was purged from his old sins." Because the things of this world are so much the focus of his life, spiritual and eternal things grow dimmer and dimmer to the point that he forgets he is a redeemed child of God. He lives as if he were unsaved.

His choices are the same choices an unbeliever would make. His ethics, morals, and standards are borrowed from the world around him. He has no sense that he is a citizen of another country (Hebrews 11:13–16) and lives as if the world around him is all that matters. He is worldly—the exact opposite of godly.

Peter does not take this lightly. In fact, in verse 10 he admonishes us to "give diligence to make [our] calling and election sure." The word *sure* refers to a business transaction whereby the purchaser could show a receipt.

You have probably walked out of a superstore or other retail shop only to have the alarm go off as you exited the building. An alert store clerk may have approached you and asked to see your receipt. He was asking you to produce something that would demonstrate you truly did own the goods you were saying were yours.

Peter is doing the same thing in this passage, saying in effect, "If you do not have these virtues growing and developing in you, and you have no motivation to cultivate them, then you better check to see if you, indeed, possess any saving faith upon which these are built."

Do you remember in grade school when your teacher gave you a paper cup with potting soil in it, and you planted a bean or corn seed in the cup for a science experiment? You set your cups on the classroom windowsill, and in a few days some sprouts began to appear.

Suppose that nothing sprouted in your cup. Your teacher would say, "I'm sorry, but I guess your seed is dead." You might even protest, "No, it's not. I remember planting the seed."

Regardless of whether you remember planting the seed, your seed is dead. Many believers who show no evidence of growth in Christ still protest that they remember a time when they asked God to save them. Peter, however, wants them to understand that if there is no growth, there is no saving faith. The receipt that they possess salvation is the evidence of some measure of Christlikeness in their life. "Lack of spiritual growth is a sign of spiritual death."[11] *If there is no desire to develop and no evidence of these virtues, there is no saving faith.* The person has what James called a "dead faith" (James 2:14–26).[12] His greatest need is to bow in repentance before the God he has ignored and accept Christ as his Savior from his sins. He will then possess an eternal life that will sprout likeness to Christ in him.

The Requirement for Stability

In stark contrast, Peter says, "If ye do these things ye shall never fall." Of course, he is not teaching a sinless perfection. He is telling us that instead of the ups and downs of a double-minded person, who is "unstable in all his ways" and who is "driven by the wind and tossed" (James 1:6) in his culture, a believer who is pursuing Christlikeness will develop the stability characteristic of those who hear the Word of God and do it (Matthew 7:24–27). When the winds and rains of a depraved culture beat upon his house, it stands firm.

He will know the ways of his personal Trainer because he has spent much time with Him—listening to His lectures, responding to His rebukes and corrections, experiencing the joy of progress, and enjoying His approval and encouragement as well as a healthy life. He will be ready to meet unexpected challenges of life. These things will not set him back. He knows what to do. He is stable.

This is what God promises for the believer whose purpose in life is to know and imitate Jesus Christ. David said that because this man "walketh not in the counsel of the ungodly, nor standeth in the way of sinners, nor sitteth in the seat of the scornful" but rather "his delight is in the law of the Lord; and in his law doth he meditate day and night," "he shall be like a tree planted by the rivers of water, that bringeth forth his fruit in his season: his leaf also shall not wither; and whatsoever he doeth shall prosper" (Psalm 1:1–3). This is stability and productivity.

The Cause for Expectancy

Peter ends his exhortation with a wonderful hope! He says to those who cultivated the conditions for the growth of these virtues,

> For so an entrance shall be ministered unto you abundantly into the everlasting kingdom of our Lord and Saviour Jesus Christ. (2 Peter 1:11)

The Greek word *ministered* in this verse is the same word translated "add" in verse 5. To those who "add"—generously supply—these essential virtues to their faith, God will "minister"—generously supply—a

11

full and lavish welcome into His eternal presence upon death. He will most honor those who look most like His Son. He can honor what they are because He Himself produced it in them. They have diligently cultivated the conditions in their hearts—using the means He Himself has provided—for Him to do His work. Nothing pleases the Father more than likeness to His Son.

Most notable is the contrast between the "abundant entrance" promised to the virtuous believer in chapter 1 and the judgment awaiting the morally lax in chapter 3. *The entire exhortation of 2 Peter is toward moral responsibility and godliness in the midst of cultural depravity.* No warning is so chilling, however, as the reminder in chapter 3 that there is coming a moral reckoning when we all must stand before Christ. Peter reminds his hearers—and us—that God knows how to deliver the righteous from corruption in this life and how to deliver the unrighteous to judgment in the next. Consequently, there is no excuse for worldly living. In light of this judgment Peter asks the rhetorical question "What sort of people ought you to be in holiness and godliness?" (2 Peter 3:11 ESV).

This is what Christ offers to those who wish to pursue His likeness. The stakes are high and the assessment points of virtuous living are already established. So, join me as we enter the fitness center of spiritual growth, where we will sit ourselves down on many different workstations to develop the core "muscle groups" of our character. Let's learn from Christ Himself what repetitions at each workstation will produce in us these essential virtues He is trying to develop in us. Put on your exercise clothes, grab your towel, and let us head out to the floor. We've got much work to do.

Chapter Two

THE PROVISIONS FOR THE CHRIST-CENTERED LIFE

According as his divine power hath given unto us all things that pertain unto life and godliness, through the knowledge of him that hath called us to glory and virtue: whereby are given unto us exceeding great and precious promises: that by these ye might be partakers of the divine nature, having escaped the corruption that is in the world through lust. (2 Peter 1:3–4)

BACK TO THE FARM

During my early boyhood days my family lived in the central farm-house of my grandfather's three-thousand-acre cattle farm. Though farming is an honorable calling, God had other plans for my life.

Let's suppose, however, that it had been my boyhood dream to farm. As I grew up, it seemed that my dream would never come to pass. I did not have the startup capital to purchase and work a farm.

Let's further suppose that as I reached young adulthood I learned that someone had left me a fully functioning farm equal in size, equipment, and buildings to the one I grew up on. A city slicker might sell it and buy a fancy house in town along with a sports car and membership at an elite country club. But not me—I want to farm!

So what would I do next? I would, of course, survey my good fortune. I would explore the farm. I would examine the barn and the various out-buildings and check out the machinery and tools housed inside them. I would test every piece of machinery to see if it worked—the grain elevators and augers, the tractors, the combine, the silage wagons, and the stock truck. I would look at the hay baler, the plow, the side-delivery rake, the hay mower, the silage cutter, and the corn picker.

I would walk through the house, look inside all the closets and cupboards, check out the plumbing, wiring, and furnace, get the termite inspection, and make note of the condition of the carpets, the paint, and the wallpaper.

The properties would be next. I would drive around the five square miles of land, examining the condition of the fences and taking soil samples for the county agent to examine. I would walk through the shelterbelts and windbreaks and check out the field wells for the livestock.

I would find out all I could about what I have to work with. I don't want to buy a tool or implement if I already have it. As I said earlier, I would *explore the farm*.

But to be truly productive, I must also *work the farm*. Crops and livestock do not grow well unattended. I must get up early every day, get into the fields, tend the livestock, fix fences, pull calves, bale hay, harvest wheat, repair machinery, and buy and sell stock.[1]

While God is the only one that can make corn and wheat grow and the only one who can turn a calf into a healthy side of beef, He has so set up the world that I must do something with what He has provided—all the while depending upon Him to give me what I need to do what He asks me to do.

We have in the illustration of farming the dynamics of what is set before us in the opening verses of 2 Peter 1. Peter is going to tell us in verses 5–7 to "work the farm"—to give diligent effort to cultivate certain virtues in our Christian character. Before he does that, He tells us in the first four verses that we must "explore the farm"—to examine the provisions He has made available to us to work the farm. Take a moment to reflect carefully on them before we proceed with our study.

> Simon Peter, a servant and an apostle of Jesus Christ, to them that have obtained like precious faith with us through the righteousness of God and our Saviour Jesus Christ.

> Grace and peace be multiplied unto you through the knowledge of God, and of Jesus our Lord,

According as his divine power hath given unto us all things that pertain unto life and godliness, through the knowledge of him that hath called us to glory and virtue:

Whereby are given unto us exceeding great and precious promises, that by these ye might be partakers of the divine nature, having escaped the corruption that is in the world through lust.

THE PERSON OF JESUS CHRIST

God's first provision for us is His own Son. Throughout the Bible God puts Jesus Christ front and center of everything He does. It is no surprise, therefore, that Peter's thought throughout this epistle is that the knowledge of God and of Jesus Christ is central in our Christian growth. He tells us that grace—God's enabling help—and peace will be multiplied to us through the knowledge of Jesus Christ (verse 2).

There are several Greek words for "knowledge," just like there are several Greek words for "love." One kind of knowledge means "I know as an expert—absolute knowledge." Another means "I know accurately, as a scientific fact." The word here translated "knowledge of God" is ἐπίγνωσις transliterated *epignōsis* (pronounced ĕp-ĭ´-gnō-sĭs). The prefix *epi* shows that it is an intensified version of the word γνῶσις, transliterated *gnōsis* (pronounced gnō´-sĭs), which means "I know by experience." *Epignōsis* means "a deeper and more intimate knowledge and acquaintance."[2]

My wife, Pat, is a gifted soloist and a speaker to women's groups. Many people have been blessed by her singing and teaching through the years. We could say they have a *gnōsis* knowledge of my wife. They certainly have experienced a measure of her life and ministry, but her immediate family—her husband, daughters, their husbands, and our grandchildren—can say they have an *epignōsis* knowledge of her. We have a far more intimate and up-close knowledge of her life and character. We know from personal experience how she is devoted to her family and has an exemplary walk with Christ.

Peter is telling us that multiplied grace and multiplied peace come through a similar deeper, more intimate, personal relationship with the person of Jesus Christ. It is this deeper relationship that is the goal of this passage; it is the equivalent of spiritual maturity.[3]

Peter expands the apostolic greeting of verse 2 in verse 3. He says, in effect, that not just "grace and peace" but "all things that pertain to [eternal] life and godliness [in this life]" come through an intimate, full relationship with Jesus Christ.[4] Very clearly, salvation and all that comes after it are wrapped up in the person of Jesus Christ. Therefore, anything that keeps a believer from that fellowship with Christ must be considered the believer's enemy. We will look at this more fully in the next chapter when we look at the matter of worldliness, which is a serious hindrance to our fellowship with Christ, and therefore, to our Christian growth.

Peter presents this full relationship with Christ in chapter 1 as the antidote to the sensuality and the resulting false teaching that denies moral responsibility, which he describes in chapters 2 and 3 of this epistle. Nothing is more central in Peter's thinking, nor more crucial for the believer's stability and joy, than a personal, intimate relationship with Jesus Christ. We must become and remain Christ-centered in our Christian experience.

Paul felt the same way. He said in Philippians 3:7–8 (ESV),

> But whatever gain I had, I counted as loss for the sake of Christ. Indeed, I count everything as loss because of the surpassing worth of knowing Christ Jesus my Lord. For his sake I have suffered the loss of all things and count them as rubbish, in order that I may gain Christ.

This is powerfully instructive for us. We must see that this intimate, personal, experience-it-for-yourself knowledge of Jesus Christ is central to everything truly important in our Christian experience. The next question then is "How can I develop and experience this kind of personal, fuller knowledge of God?" Peter answers that in verse 4, where he introduces yet another gracious provision of God—His promises to us.

THE PROMISES OF GOD

Peter says that God has through Jesus Christ given to us "exceeding great and precious promises." These are for two purposes. First, to make us "partakers of the divine nature," referring to our initial salvation, and second, to assure us that we are escapers "of the corruption [disintegration] that is in the world through lust" (2 Peter 1:4). These two purposes are flip sides of the same coin. The salvation that God promises is designed to have certain sanctifying effects on our lives. "Peter sees our participation in the divine nature as consisting especially in the new ability to resist sin through our union with Christ and the indwelling of the Spirit."[5] Genuine saving faith moves us away from the world with its lusts and toward likeness to Christ.

> Genuine saving faith moves us away from the world with its lusts and toward likeness to Christ.

In the next three verses (verses 5–8) the apostle is going to lay out for us a portrait of what that divine nature working within the life of a believer looks like. It is a portrait of the essential virtues that help the believer escape the corruption.

The result of depending upon the promises of God to develop these virtues is that in the process the believer gets to know God. He is neither "barren [idle, apathetic] nor unfruitful in the [full] knowledge of God (verse 8)." "[Full] knowledge" here is again *epignōsis*.

The promises of God are statements from Christ about how He will relate to His children. They show us God's *intentions* for us. They set forth what He wants to do on our behalf. Furthermore, the promises of God show us God's *disposition* toward us. If He did not care for us, He would not bother to help us. The promises of God are a most wonderful provision for our Christian walk!

When I was a child, it was customary for many Christian families to have a "promise box" sitting on their kitchen table. It was a small wooden or plastic box—usually in the shape of a loaf of bread—with thirty-one promise cards in it, and often the phrase "Our Daily Bread" was inscribed on the side. Each day a family member would choose the next card in the box and read it before praying for a meal or during family devotions after the meal. They would go through the entire promise box in one month.

I must confess that as a child I thought the promise box was a little corny. My youthful ignorance kept me from seeing the enormous importance of being familiar with the promises of God. Peter reminds us here that it is through these promises that we have everything of value to us spiritually and otherwise.

It wasn't until I was in college and seriously pursuing a relationship with Christ on my own that I learned the value of those promises. Two statements riveted their importance in my mind at that time. The first was God's statement about Abraham in Romans 4:20–21.

> He staggered not at the promise of God through unbelief; but was strong in faith, giving glory to God; and being fully persuaded that, what he had promised, he was able also to perform.

The second was a chapel saying by Bob Jones Sr., founder of Bob Jones University. He would remind the students, "The future is as bright as the promises of God." These statements motivated me to notice and trust what God had said He would do.

Romans 4:20–21 became such a beacon of hope to my wife and me when we were first married and struggling financially while I was still in school that Patty did a calligraphy of this passage for an art class she was taking. It still hangs in our home as a reminder of the importance of God's promises.

THE PROMISES AT WORK

The promises are not magic bullets or secret code words that unlock some mystical power. As we have seen, they are statements of God's intentions and are revelations of His disposition toward us. They work hand in glove with His commands. For example, in this passage before us we will hear God command us to cultivate in our saving faith "virtue."

Promises for cultivating virtue. To "add to your faith virtue," as we shall see in the next chapter, is a command to pursue the likeness of Christ in our lives. Are there any promises of God to motivate and sustain us in that pursuit? There certainly are! Jesus Himself told us in Luke 9:23–24,

> If any man will come after me, let him deny himself, and take up his cross daily and follow me. For whosoever will save his life shall lose it: but whosoever will lose his life for my sake, the same shall save it.

That is a powerfully motivating and sustaining promise! We know by this promise that any sacrifices we make to follow Jesus Christ will not be unnoticed by Christ Himself. Though we will experience temporal losses as obedient disciples, the spiritual gains will be great.

He promises in John 12:24–26 (ESV) that such sacrifice will be rewarded with fruitfulness and eventual honor.

> Truly, truly, I say unto you, unless a grain of wheat falls into the earth and dies, it remains alone; but if it dies, it bears much fruit. Whoever loves his life loses it, and whoever hates his life in this world will keep it for eternal life.

Peter captures much of the same flavor in 2 Peter 1:11, when he promises that God will bring stability in this life and an "abundant entrance into the everlasting kingdom" in the next life.

Promises for cultivating knowledge. Furthermore, we are to cultivate in that pursuit of Christlike excellence a pursuit of the knowledge of Christ. Are there any promises that bear on this command? Again, there are many.

Christ promises that the search for Him will not be in vain.

> Ye shall seek me, and find me, when ye shall search for me with all your heart. (Jeremiah 29:13)

> But if from thence [from your troubling circumstances] thou shalt seek the Lord thy God, thou shalt find him, if thou seek him with all thy heart and with all thy soul. (Deuteronomy 4:29)

He promises that the search for the knowledge of God will bring direction and discernment into your life.

> Thy word is a lamp unto my feet, and a light unto my path. (Psalm 119:105)

> The entrance of thy words giveth light; it giveth understanding unto the simple. (Psalm 119:130)

Though the two verses above are not couched in typical "promise formula" (i.e., If you . . . I will), they are nonetheless statements of what we can expect God to do for us when we seek Him in His Word.

David taught earlier in Psalm 119 that we could count on God's Word to keep us from sin.

> Thy word have I [treasured] in mine heart, that I might not sin against thee. (Psalm 119:11)

Anything that God has stated as a certainty we can trust as a promise that He will order His universe according to that statement. In order to be able to obey His commands, we must believe His promises.

Therefore, we must know them and must act upon them as we give "all diligence" to cultivate these essential virtues in our character. God has to do the growing. We do not make Christian virtues grow anymore than farmers make corn grow. God does that, but He has so ordered His universe that we are to respond in God-dependent obedience to His commands that map out our duties in the process.

WORKING THE FARM

After telling us that God has made marvelous provisions for us in the person of Jesus Christ and in the promises Christ has given us, Peter commands, "And beside this, giving all diligence, add to your faith virtue . . ." (2 Peter 1:5).

The Greek word translated "diligence" in verse 5 means "to make haste, exert yourself, be zealous in." The phrase "giving all" means "to bring in by the side of: adding your diligence to the divine promises."[6]

Literally translated, verse 5 would read, "For this very reason make every effort to supply alongside [these provisions] virtue. . . ." This is a call to serious human effort—sustained and motivated by the grace of God—but wholehearted utilization of that grace in this venture. Notice Paul's testimony of this in 1 Corinthians 15:10 (ESV).

> But by the grace of God I am what I am, and his grace toward me was not in vain. On the contrary, I worked harder than any of them, though it was not I, but the grace of God that is with me.

Paul testified that God gave him the grace to become what he was but that he had a responsibility to labor in that grace. Even in that, though, God gave him grace to labor to use the grace. It is all of God ultimately, but He has laid certain responsibilities upon us in the process.

The believer cannot be casual about this growth. Popular culture—the main purveyor of worldliness—celebrates the carefree, laid-back, casual, entertainment-driven mindset that places pleasure over responsibility and diligence.

It is a brilliant strategy of Satan because it produces all the qualities of the Proverbs fool as it points the heart away from a serious pursuit of anything but personal pleasure. The tragedy is that his tactic is working quite well. The world, sadly, is having a far greater influence on the Christian church than the church is upon the world. The church is filled with those who are "lovers of pleasures more than lovers of God" (2 Timothy 3:4).

Peter is calling us by contrast to single-minded, wholehearted commitment to loving and becoming like Jesus Christ so that we can honor Christ by that likeness and can be useful to Him. There is nothing casual or flippant here, nothing laid-back or halfway. These virtues must "be in [us] and abound" if we are to live stable and fruitful lives.

Cultivating the Conditions

Verse 5 reminds us that we must maintain the proper perspective on how sanctification—the Bible doctrine about Christian growth—takes place. God has ordained it to be a joint venture between God and the believer. "Human effort is indispensable, even though it is inadequate."[7]

> The very strength of Peter's exhortation—to diligently cultivate these virtues—raises two related theological/practical questions in our minds. First, how does Peter's stress on our own effort to become godly (verse 5) fit with the New Testament emphasis on the Spirit as the one who sanctifies us? Does not Paul claim that the qualities of godliness are produced by the Spirit working within us (cf. Galatians 5:22–23)? To put it theologically, is not our sanctification something that God does in us by his Spirit? How can Peter, then, make it seem that our own effort is crucial?

> The answer to these questions comes in finding the right biblical balance between God's contribution and our own in the process of becoming holy. The New Testament makes crystal clear that both are necessary if we are going to make any progress at all in godly Christianity.[8]

Some would say that our part in this process is merely to do nothing. They would say we are to "let go and let God," emphasizing the divine component in this process. Others would go to the other extreme and through their self-effort end up with mere moralism, good deeds, and a disposition produced by human effort alone.

Peter reinforces that joint venture in this chapter. He describes all the provisions God has made for our change and growth in verses 1–4 and then in verses 5–7 gives us a command to "add" certain things to what God has done.[9]

Most likely Peter stresses the human contribution in this epistle because the libertine false teaching he is countering had so strongly emphasized the grace of God. The predictable result is that God's people were living like the world while defending their sin and disobedience in the name of "Christian liberty." Peter by no means ignores the gracious provisions of God as the source for all Christian "life and godliness" (verses 1–4) but must bring the pendulum back to the biblical center by emphasizing the believer's responsibility to diligently apply himself to the development of a virtuous life.

> God's people were living like the world while defending their sin and disobedience in the name of "Christian liberty."

The Greek word translated "add" in the KJV does not mean "add" in the mathematical sense. It is translated "supplement" in the ESV and "supply" in the NASB. "Abundantly or extravagantly supply" catches the flavor of this word, which comes from a Greek word having to do with a chorus.

The picture in this word translated "add" is of a rich patron of the arts supplying all that was necessary for a first-century theatre troupe to train and perform—lodging, food, costumes, wages, sets, and furnishings. He didn't do the acting, but he made it possible for the actors—the "chorus"—to do their work. He abundantly, lavishly supplied what they needed to put on an effective performance.[10]

In the same manner, Peter is teaching us that we are to supply (through the provisions God has granted us in verses 1–4) or set the stage through proper responses for God to do His work of producing these characteristics of Christ in us. We do not produce the fruit of sanctification ourselves, but we are to earnestly and wholeheartedly cultivate the conditions whereby God can and will work out these qualities in our lives. Commentators D. Edmond Hiebert and J. Daryl Charles agree:

> In the task of Christian character development, believers must contribute what God rightly demands of them.[11]

Christian discipleship, as it is to be properly grasped, does not take either divine or human factors lightly. Grace is not to be presumed upon, neither is the need to cultivate ethical and spiritual disciplines.

Grace received does not preclude the rigors of Christian discipleship, but neither does discipleship consist in perfectionistic human striving divorced from divine resources. Both elements are necessary at work; both constitute a unity. Because ethical lapse characterizes the community in the present situation [which Peter is addressing], what demands immediate attention is [an] exhortation to the rigors of virtuous living; hence, the appropriateness of a catalog of virtues as a foundational element . . . of 2 Peter.

Yet even the catalog is far from a perfectionistic or legalistic work ethic. On the contrary, it is predicated on a foundation of faith ('to those who received a faith', 1.1; 'make every effort to add to your faith', 1.5) and is motivated by love (1.7). Even in the catalog, the divine and the human merge.[12]

Jerry Bridges paraphrases John Owen, who addressed this concept of "the relationship of God's grace (God's divine enablement) and our responsibility, which Owen calls our duty":

Let us consider what regard we ought to have to our own duty and to the grace of God. Some would separate these things as inconsistent. If holiness be our duty, they would say, there is no room for grace; and if it be the result of grace there is no place for duty. But our duty and God's grace are nowhere opposed in the matter of sanctification; for the one absolutely supposes the other. We cannot perform our duty without the grace of God; nor does God give his grace for any other purpose than that we may perform our duty.[13]

We will see how this process of sanctification works as we go through the study. For now just keep in mind that God has given us the responsibility to "cultivate the conditions" whereby God produces this fruit in us. We must intentionally pursue their development; they are not produced accidentally when we aren't looking. We must *explore the farm*—survey His marvelous provisions in Christ and His promises to us—then we must *work the farm*—put forth diligent and whole-hearted effort to cultivate the conditions in which God has promised to do His work. God ultimately does it all, but He requires man to fulfill his responsibility with the provisions God has given.

Part One

THE GROUNDWORK OF CHRISTIAN CHARACTER

Chapter Three

CULTIVATING THE EXCELLENCE
OF CHRISTLIKENESS

Add to your faith virtue. (2 Peter 1:5)

By now you should have an overview of what Peter has set before us in chapter 1 of his second epistle. He has introduced us to the marvelous provisions God has made available to us in order for Christ's likeness to be formed in us. We have been *exploring the farm* and now it is time for us to roll up our sleeves and *work the farm*. Peter makes the transition with the command "add to your faith virtue" (verse 5).

We learned in the last chapter that "add" means to "abundantly supply." We captured the intent of that concept with the phrase "cultivating the conditions." So then, how do we cultivate the conditions to develop "virtue," and just as important, what is "virtue"?

The King James Version translates the first word in the list as "virtue." This can be a bit confusing because in the way we normally use the term today, all the items on this list are virtues. In fact, we are calling this complete list the "essential virtues" of the Christ-centered life.

The actual Greek word here translated "virtue" is ἀρετή, transliterated *aretē* (pronounced ăr-ĕ-tā´). You certainly don't have to know Greek to profit from this study, but it will help to know the origins of the particular words in this list because each had certain meanings to New Testament readers. These were words in common use during the first century, but most of them were given specialized meanings when the apostles brought them into their New Testament writings.

Aretē is particularly difficult to define because, while it was the most discussed virtue by the classical Greek philosophers, it is used very little in the New Testament. In fact, it is used only five times in the New Testament, and three of them are in this chapter—once in verse 3, where Peter says that God has called us to His own "glory and virtue [aretē]," and then twice in verse 5, where he tells us to "add to [our] faith virtue [aretē] and to virtue [aretē] knowledge." It is not quite clear from these three references in this first chapter exactly what Peter means by aretē.

We get a little more insight when we look in Philippians 4:8 at Paul's only use of the term in his writings.

> Finally, brethren, whatsoever things are true, . . . honest, . . . just, . . . pure, . . . lovely, . . . of good report; if there be any virtue [aretē], and if there be any praise, think on these things.

We understand from this passage that the word as it is used in the New Testament keeps much of the same flavor it had in the Greek culture at large. Green tells us that "[Aretē] means 'excellence,' and was used to denote the proper fulfillment of anything. The excellence of a knife is to cut, of a horse to run."[1] Something was excellent—virtuous—only if it fulfilled its purpose.[2]

Therefore, you could not consider that the sword at your side was excellent—an aretē sword—unless it could cut. It did not matter how beautiful the handle was nor how shiny the blade, if it could not fulfill its purpose to cut something, it could not be considered excellent—aretē.

Likewise, a warrior could be considered excellent only if he was brave and courageous in battle. It did not matter how many countries he had visited nor how carefully he polished his armor, if he ran from conflict, he was not an excellent—aretē—warrior. He had not fulfilled his purpose.

A fishing boat was considered excellent only if it floated. A straight mast, finely crafted sails, and beautiful paint were of no consequence if the boat could not do what boats were designed to do—float. Only then could the boat be considered an excellent—aretē—boat.

I think you can see why Peter would set this virtue first in his list. None of the other qualities will be used for the right purpose until we decide what our purpose is and commit our lives to it. What then is the ultimate purpose for the believer?

THE BELIEVER'S PURPOSE STATEMENT

Peter tells us our purpose in his previous epistle—to show forth the excellencies of God. He says,

> But ye are a chosen generation, a royal priesthood, an holy nation, a [people of his own]; that [and here begins his purpose statement] ye should shew forth the praises [*aretē*] of him who hath called you out of darkness into his marvellous light. (1 Peter 2:9)

And here we have the fifth use of *aretē* in the New Testament. It is translated "praises" in this passage. Both the ESV and NASB capture the sense of it by translating it "excellencies"—a translation we should expect after our brief study above.

So here Peter is telling us that God has *aretē*—something that should not surprise us since what makes Him God is that He is excellent in all things that make a being worthy of being God. But since this verse is a purpose statement for the believer, we find also what makes *us* excellent.

As we have seen, our excellence is related directly to how well we are fulfilling God's purpose for us. That purpose set forth clearly in this verse is to develop and display the excellencies of our God! This is one of the clearest calls to Christlikeness anywhere in the Bible!

Michael Green asks, "What is the excellence of a man? . . . In a word, his life must reflect something of the attractive character of Christ. For He is the man par excellence, the proper man. True human excellence, then . . . is Christlikeness."[3]

> Our excellence is related directly to how well we are fulfilling God's purpose for us.

Peter describes for us exactly what that Christlikeness looks like—displaying knowledge, self-control, endurance, godliness, brotherly kindness, and love. Peter will not let us think of Christlikeness as some sort of nebulous metaphysical concept. He defines it very specifically for us in this list of virtues.

We have one major purpose on this earth then. We are to become like Christ in our character and then by our manner of life to show others what Christ is like so that they will honor Him too. Here is how Jesus put it.

Let your light so shine before men, that they may see your good works, and glorify your Father which is in heaven. (Matthew 5:16)

It matters not how intelligent, wealthy, and successful in our field we are, or how many people admire or appreciate us. If we are not displaying the excellent character of our God by our lives, we cannot consider ourselves excellent. We do not possess *aretē*. On the other hand, it matters not how naturally limited, poor, or unappreciated we are. If we reflect the likeness of Christ, we possess true excellence.

Note the working definition of *aretē* on the chart on the inside back cover: "Cultivating a God-mandated purpose to develop and display the excellencies [character] of Jesus Christ." In short, we are to be "pursuing the excellence of Christlikeness."

This is what it means to "add to [our] faith *aretē.*" *We must come to the realization that we are on the earth for one reason and must wholeheartedly commit ourselves to that purpose.* This is what Paul is addressing in Romans 12:1–2 (ESV).

I appeal to you therefore, brothers, by the mercies of God, to present your bodies as a living sacrifice, holy and acceptable to God, which is your spiritual worship. Do not be conformed to this world, but be transformed by the renewal of your mind, that by testing you may discern what is the will of God, what is good and acceptable and perfect.

When Paul says that we are to "present [our] bodies" to God, we might ask, "Why is He asking for our bodies? Isn't He more concerned about our souls?" Paul is using the word *bodies* here to represent the whole person much like a mother might command her preschool boy to stop ignoring her call to come in from play. She might say, "Johnny, get your little body in here right this minute!" She doesn't just want his body. She wants Johnny, the person, to obediently leave what he is doing and immediately come in.

There will be no significant maturing in the Christian experience until a believer comes to the realization that because of Christ's work on the cross on his behalf, he belongs *entirely* to God to be used *entirely* for God's purpose. He must, furthermore, agree with that understanding and commit himself to living that way for the glory of God. This is where many contemporary believers stall.

To many in the modern church, this call to *aretē—single-minded* commitment to be like Christ—seems like pie-in-the-sky idealism that cannot be expected of mere mortals. The standard of the Scriptures is unquestionably high, but by the grace of God it is also possible. The blessing and stability of this kind of life will be realized only by the few who, in moments of quiet reflection upon God's purposes set forth for us in His Word, see glimmers of the possibilities during lightning flashes of illumination upon the darkened landscape of their souls.

God may use the testimony of some godly saint, young or old, a Scripture text from a sermon, or the obvious biblical wisdom of some statement like that of Jim Elliot: "He is no fool who gives up that which he cannot keep to gain that which he cannot lose."¹ Through similar means the Spirit of God will capture the heart of the tender believer who is truly seeking something more than the morass of his lukewarmness and the guilt-induced stupor, which have dominated his own life and the lives of most believers around him.

The promise of God to draw near to those who draw near to Him will breathe fresh hope into his soul, and God will meet with him if he will heed the Lord's admonition that follows. Listen carefully to the promise—and the prerequisite command.

> Draw nigh to God, and he will draw nigh to you. Cleanse your hands, ye sinners; and purify your hearts, ye double minded. Be [wretched], and mourn, and weep: let your laughter be turned to mourning, and your joy to heaviness. (James 4:8–9)

Here is a call to humility that is manifested in repentance for the double-mindedness that breeds spiritual mediocrity. It is a repentance characterized by brokenheartedness at the horrible affront against Christ that double-mindedness breeds. At the same time this is a call to experience contentment and joy from Christ Himself, which only a surrendered soul can know. It is an experience known only to those who will diligently search for Christ in His Word (Proverbs 2) and then respond in worship, prayer, and obedience (John 14:21).

A Call to Discipleship—Normal Christianity

This single-minded focus to be like Christ is *normal* Christianity when measured by Bible standards. It is a call to discipleship—to *hearing* the words of the Master and *doing* them in order to be like Him (Matthew 7:24–27). The lukewarmness that pervades the church today is normal according to the prevailing attitudes of the church but is subnormal according to the Scriptures. Full Christian maturity is built upon a foundation that begins with a wholehearted pursuit of Christ and His ways. We must let Christ's own words about this tragic state of the church form our opinions of what is normal in His mind, and we must let those words determine for us what is the remedy.

> I know your works: you are neither cold nor hot. Would that you were either cold or hot! So, because you are lukewarm, and neither hot nor cold, I will spit you out of my mouth. For you say, I am rich, I have prospered, and I need nothing, not realizing that you are wretched, pitiable, poor, blind, and naked. I counsel you to buy from me gold refined by fire, so that you may be rich, and white garments so that you may clothe yourself and the shame of your nakedness may not be seen, and salve to anoint your eyes, so that you may see. Those whom I love, I reprove and discipline, so be zealous and repent. (Revelation 3:15–19 ESV)

The call to discipleship—to cultivating a God-mandated purpose to develop and display the character of Christ—is *normal* for the Christ-centered life. Discipleship requires the humility to abandon personal ambitions and ways of handling life and demands daily yoking oneself to the will and teachings of Another. Paul says that to offer our whole persons as "living sacrifices" is merely our "reasonable service"—our spiritual response of worship to Christ for His mercies (Romans 12:1).

This single-minded purpose to become like Christ is the large head of the embryo. It is the "brain," which will regulate the growth of all the other parts of the "body." Without the humility and the commitment to follow Jesus Christ as His disciple, the rest of the believer's character will remain underdeveloped—and even deformed. This is why Peter puts the pursuit of the excellence of Christlikeness—*aretē*—first in the list of essential virtues. Is this your conscious, daily pursuit? If not, you will see very little progress in your spiritual growth. The development of Christian character depends upon the humility to wholeheartedly submit to the person of Jesus Christ.

THE ENEMY'S NOT-SO-SECRET WEAPON

The other interesting principle taught in Romans 12:1–2 is that Paul sets worldliness in direct opposition to the wholehearted dedication God is calling us to. While Christ is calling us to a single-minded resolve to be like Him, Satan has set up the world to entice us away from that resolve.

The life God offers the believer is an abundant life that makes a man feel truly *alive and real and fulfilled* (John 10:10). The world can offer only a counterfeit of that experience. The godless mindset of the world is Satan's means to remake man after his own image, all the while luring him to destruction with promises of pleasures, possessions, and power (1 John 2:15–17). These will make the man temporarily feel alive, and real, and fulfilled, but at the expense of his relationship with God.

The world seduces the believer away from fellowship with Christ with entertainment laced with blatant sensuality, violence, and materialism; addictive adrenaline rushes through drugs, alcohol, extreme sports, gambling, and electronic games; the lures of power, sex, and virtual relationships through pornography and alternative online realities; and the illusion of relational closeness through social networking and technological connectedness.

The result for most believers who pursue these offerings with any degree of earnestness is an ever-deepening entanglement in sin and an increasing desensitization to anything spiritual and godly. They are unwittingly being "conformed to this world" by embracing its ideals and answering its appeals. The world is offering them a smorgasbord of ways to feel *alive and real and fulfilled*—all without God, which is the essence of worldliness.

These means of the world only hasten the natural disintegration of the man who is not living a Christ-centered life. The natural processes of the sinful nature within his own soul will undo him if left to themselves. (See appendix 2, "The Puritan View of Sin," for a more accurate picture.) Figure 1 shows the default downward path of the heart of man if he is not wholeheartedly pursuing Christlikeness.

FIGURE 1

ESSENTIAL VIRTUES		
Groundwork → of Christlikeness	Backbone → of Christlikeness	Trademark of Christlikeness
Saving FAITH EXCELLENCE KNOWLEDGE ⊘	SELF-CONTROL ENDURANCE GODLINESS ⊘	Brotherly KINDNESS LOVE ⊘
The Simple Man **Weak/Worldly** →	The Fool **Willful/Wild** →	The Scorner **Wicked/Wasted**

Satan has his own progression of "essential vices," which form the portrait of one who is increasingly made into his diabolical image. We can note that progression by observing the three types of fools in Proverbs. (See appendix 1, "Fools by Default," for the biblical references and summary of the simple man, the fool, and the scorner.)

The Simple Man. This is the beginning, or kindergarten, fool. He is weak since he has little or no allegiance to God's ways. He is easily seduced by the lure of the sensuality and the adventure of worldly pursuits. He is not naïve about the appeals and ideals of the world; rather he is quite in tune with the culture around him. He is naïve, however, about the end of those pursuits. He unwittingly follows those lures as an ox to the slaughter (Proverbs 7:22).

This is the level of discernment you would expect in the average American junior high youth. His heart is easily captured by the latest fashions, pop and reality show idols, superheroes, electronic games, sports personalities, junk foods, sexual enticements—both real and virtual—chemical stimulants—both legal and illegal—and the crude and sensual humor and violence of the most popular video clips and blockbuster movies. He is easily bored and increasingly resistant to correction. Work and learning are endured as necessary evils between pursuits of pleasurable experiences offered on the midway of the world's carnival.

In the spiritual realm, this type of believer has little tolerance for preaching unless it is high in entertainment value. He considers anything else irrelevant—which generally means he does not "like" it. Paul speaks of this kind of person when he says, "For the time will come when they will not endure sound doctrine; but wanting to have their ears tickled, they will accumulate for themselves teachers in accordance to their own desires, and will turn away their ears from the truth" (2 Timothy 4:3–4 NASB). Consequently, he is weak and worldly.

The world is noticing that this mindset shows no signs of decline in most young men—and some women—even as they grow older. This new phenomenon of "extended adolescence" is not uncommon in thirty somethings. They not only shun responsibility because it interferes with their pursuit of pleasure but are genuinely afraid of it because they are woefully unprepared for such adult tasks as earning a living, marrying and raising a family, and embracing a life course of constructive impact. Their formative years of youth, which should have been spent in guided preparation for adult life, were wasted in the pursuit of personal pleasure.

Diana West, a syndicated columnist for the *Washington Times*, laments this cultural phenomenon in her book *The Death of the Grown-up*. Though not writing from a Christian standpoint whatsoever, with poignant clarity she shows the destructiveness the mindset we have been discussing here has upon the character of men and women today. These paragraphs from her first chapter show how damaging the concept of today's pleasure ethic is to society at large—and to the church in particular.

> Once there was a world without teenagers. Literally. "Teenager," the word itself, doesn't pop into the lexicon much before 1941. This speaks volumes about the last few millennia. In all those centuries, nobody thought to mention "teenagers" because there was nothing, apparently, to think of mentioning.
>
> In considering what I like to call "the death of the grown-up," it's important to keep a fix on this fact: that for all but this most recent episode of human history, there were children and there were adults. Children in their teen years aspired to adulthood; significantly, they didn't aspire to adolescence. Certainly, adults didn't aspire to remain teenagers.

A lot of things have changed. For one thing, turning thirteen [nowadays], instead of bringing children closer to the adult world, now launches them into a teen universe. For another, due to the permanent hold our culture has placed on the maturation process, that's where they're likely to find most adults.

The National Academy of Sciences has, in 2002, redefined adolescence as the period extending from the onset of puberty, around twelve, to thirty. . . . These are grown-ups who haven't left childhood.

What has also disappeared is an appreciation for what goes along with maturity: forbearance and honor, patience and responsibility, perspective and wisdom, sobriety, decorum, and manners—and the wisdom to know what is "appropriate," and when.

Etched into our consciousness, in the universal shorthand of Hollywood and Madison Avenue, is the notion that life is either wild or boring; cool or uncool; unzipped or straitlaced; at least secretly licentious or just plain dead.[5]

This is precisely the junior high mentality of Proverbs' simpleton. The teenager today is allowed, ironically by the adults in his life, to cultivate a pleasure ethic that leads to the further disintegration of the fool who is ruined by his desires. Of course, as West points out, most of the adults in his life haven't left adolescence either. They, too, have been seduced by the world's pleasure ethic.

The Fool. Proverbs tells us that "the simple inherit folly" (Proverbs 14:18). The naïve, beginning fool graduates to the next level of destructiveness. His continued indulgence in the activities described above is not without effect upon his soul. Sustained indulgence leaves him willful and wild. He bristles at restraint, freely shares his misguided opinions, undermines and deceives the authorities in his life, stubbornly insists on his own way, openly identifies by his fashions and habits with the godless attitudinal and cultural trendsetters and entertainers of his day—all of whom are stuck in the adolescent, pleasure-seeking mindset themselves—and avoids attempts to hold him personally responsible for his actions.

He is not merely wide-eyed about the culture around him as the simple-minded junior higher. The fool knows what he wants and is sneaky and deceptive in his pursuits. His unbridled opinions and rants against the authorities in his life often find their way into his cyberspace postings where most of the adults in his life will never find them. He has effectively avoided earthly accountability and in the process further corrupts others of like mind. No wonder Jesus so strongly warns us of the responsibility we have for our words.

> Most believers try to deal with worldly influences piecemeal and in the process lose the battle in their own souls.

> I tell you, on the day of judgment people will give account for every careless word they speak, for by your words you will be justified, and by your words you will be condemned. (Matthew 12:36–37 ESV; see also James 3:13–18)

In the process of all this his conscience is increasingly hardened, and his personality and values become more and more shaped by the world around him.

The Scorner. Proverbs presents the scorner as the end-product of this tragic decline. Sin will not leave its victim in a moderately worldly state. The fool eventually becomes aggressively wicked and in the end his life is wasted. Only strong judgments will reach his soul. He is full of anger and violence, and he expresses both when he can contain himself no longer.

Can you see why the writers of the New Testament were so adamant that believers "be not conformed to this world" (Romans 12:1–2), "love not the world" (1 John 2:15–17), and why we are exhorted to "keep oneself unspotted from the world" (James 1:27)? The influence of the world, which "lies in the power of the evil one" (1 John 5:19 NASB) and whose course is determined by the "prince of the power of the air" (Ephesians 2:2)—the Devil himself—is deadly to the soul. It is for this reason that Christ came—to "deliver us from this present evil world" (Galatians 1:4).

Can you also see why a wholehearted, single-minded resolve to become like Jesus Christ is the only remedy? Most believers try to deal with worldly influences piecemeal—fighting this or that temptation and arguing about this or that worldly element—and in the process lose the battle in their own souls. There is no standard to measure the influence of these elements unless one has determined to live an entirely Christ-centered life in the first place. It is amazing how clear lifestyle issues—often called gray areas by many believers—become when examined against the commitment to be thoroughly Christ-centered.

This is the start of the journey to full maturity in Christ. It will cost you everything—as Jesus said it would—but it is the only way to cultivate the likeness of Christ. If that seems too big a sacrifice, review again "The Harvest" in chapter one of this book. God has promised certain things to those who will make Jesus Christ central in all things.

Capturing the Heart for Christ

We could say that cultivating *aretē*—the pursuit of the excellence of Christlikeness—is "capturing the heart for Christ." It is the mindset that turns away from the allurements of the world and of our own sinful heart to cultivate the essential virtues Peter is going to lay out for us.

Some questions before you are

- Whom are you desiring to become like?
- Whom do you imitate?
- What virtues of that person do you try to emulate?
- In what ways do you "shew forth the excellencies" of that person to the people around you?
- Are the models you seek to emulate the celebrities of the day—either entertainment or athletic personalities?
- What is it about them that is attractive to you—their wealth, their fame, their skill at acting, singing, or sports?
- How does your lifestyle reflect that they have captured your heart? Is it by wearing clothes they would wear, using language they would use, putting their posters up in your bedroom, watching the movies or games in which they are playing, going to their concerts or buying the songs in which they perform, taking up hobbies they enjoy, or keeping up with their personal websites and blogs?

Maybe it isn't a particular person that captures your fancy but rather the general mindset of the culture itself. We discussed that mindset above when we looked at the three kinds of fools in Proverbs. Review that section carefully and note anything that characterizes you. A worldly mindset seeks to feel alive and real and fulfilled through the experiences of the culture—and through like-minded friends—in place of wholeheartedly seeking fellowship with, imitation of, and fulfillment in Christ.

The most fundamental question before you is "Who has your heart?" If Christ truly has your heart, then you will see the dangers of the world's mindset and reject that mindset. The most important things for a disciple of Jesus Christ will be spending time with Christ in His Word, soaking up preaching about Christ in a local, Bible-preaching assembly, seeking the company of Christ-centered friends whose direction of life is distinctively different from their peers in the world, spreading the good news of Christ's salvation to the lost around him, and diligently seeking to bring every area of life under the lordship of Jesus Christ. If your heart has been captured by the world, and you live for yourself, you must repent of the treacherous bent and actions of your heart. Christ must have your heart if He is to transform your character. Repentance involves a change of heart and direction and the confession of sin in order for God to extend forgiveness. Change and growth require humility. This is where we must all start, and where we must all return, every time we go back to pursuing our own way rather than the ways of Christ.

THE CORE VISION

Vision is what tells an individual or an organization why they exist. That vision is often articulated in a mission or purpose statement. It brings them back to what is really important.

I find it helpful every morning when my alarm goes off to sit up on the side of the bed and before I do anything else, commit myself to developing and displaying the excellencies of Jesus Christ that day. I want Christ to be central in all I do that day. I often fall short of that goal, but it helps me to remind myself daily of what I believe is the purpose for me as a disciple of Jesus Christ. I have crafted the following statement as a reminder of that core vision of putting Christ first in all things, and I frame the words of my daily prayer of commitment from it:

> Because of what He did in my place on the Cross,
> what He has said to me in His Word, and
> what He will require of me at the judgment,
> I must live all of life under the lordship of
> Jesus Christ today.

Living under the lordship of Jesus Christ means simply that Christ and what He wills for us must be first. This is the core vision of the Christ-centered life.

I hope this is the prayer of your heart. If the message of this core vision is unfamiliar—perhaps even strange—to you, please read this chapter repeatedly and seriously meditate upon the Scriptures introduced in this chapter until your heart is captured for Christ by the truth of these matters.

Can you truthfully say that Christ has captured your heart? Have you humbled yourself before Christ and pledged yourself to be His disciple? Is He lord over all your life—or does someone or something else rule in that place? The *aretē*—excellent—man has rejected anything that does not help him pursue the *telos*—the purpose—of "cultivating a God-mandated purpose to develop and display the excellencies (character) of Jesus Christ." He is wholeheartedly committed to Jesus Christ.

This is where we start. This is the first station in the fitness center where Christlike character is formed. Stay with the repetitions that develop this muscle group. Christ, your personal Trainer, will be pleased, and you will begin to feel *alive and real and fulfilled* because you are on your way to becoming what God intended you to be when He created you—a disciple like His Master.

Chapter Four

CULTIVATING KNOWLEDGE

Add to . . . virtue knowledge. (2 Peter 1:5)

YOUR PERSONAL SATELLITE

The global positioning system (GPS) receiver is a marvelous techno-logical assistant for pilots, hikers, drivers, boaters, and the military. It triangulates its position by taking readings from three to four satellites orbiting ten thousand miles above the earth. Using that data, the computer in the GPS unit can determine the latitude and longitude of its own position. When loaded with mapping software, the unit can give a driver turn-by-turn instructions from his present position to his destination.

This personal guidance is possible because the GPS receiver maintains continuous contact with outside reference points. That concept is not new to navigation. Ancient mariners navigated by the sun, the stars, wind and ocean currents, shoreline landmarks, and depth sounding. In fact, all navigation uses some sort of external reference point to determine position and plot courses. Scriptural knowledge functions in a similar fashion. It is like your personal satellite for navigating your way through life.

Peter, of course, didn't know anything about satellites. He did know, however, the absolute necessity of cultivating the proper kind of knowledge because he says, "Add to your *aretē* [your pursuit of the excellence of Christlikeness] knowledge" (2 Peter 1:5). Virtue, or *capturing the heart for Christ*, leads naturally to knowledge or *informing the heart about Christ*. Most commentators agree that this knowledge is not a broad understanding of the world in which we live but, more specifically, the knowledge of Christ and His ways. We know that Peter views

41

this knowledge as the knowledge of Christ because of how he closes this same epistle in 3:18. He says,

> But grow in grace, and in the knowledge *of our Lord and Saviour Jesus Christ.* To him be glory both now and for ever. Amen.

Christopher Green comments that Peter

> means information about Jesus Christ and what pleases him. It is the kind of knowledge that comes from reading, thinking, and discussing as a Christian. If we want to grow in Christ-like goodness we shall have a hunger and a desire to grow in our knowledge of Christ (cf. Eph. 5:17; Phil. 1:9; Heb. 5:14). The nineteenth century Scottish preacher John Brown, whose commentary covers only this chapter [2 Peter 1], said that this knowledge means, "making a distinction not only between what is true and what is false but also between what is right and wrong—what is becoming and unbecoming—what is advantageous and hurtful."[1]

The knowledge of Jesus Christ as it is revealed in the Scriptures is the only reliable external reference point for how we should live. It is a personal and experiential knowledge of Christ that provides us everything we need for "life and godliness" (2 Peter 1:3). This is why I have defined this knowledge on the Essential Virtues chart as a "God-taught understanding of the person, the work, and the ways of Jesus Christ."

The twelve disciples of Jesus Christ, by living with Him and listening to Him for three and a half years, learned His ways. He told them that if they would hear His words and do them they would become wise. In a similar fashion, any believer who determines to be like Christ (*aretē*) and spends much time with Jesus Christ in His Word gaining knowledge of Him and then living in light of that knowledge will also become wise. We should

> A believer who neglects his Bible and the regular preaching of God's Word simply will not make it.

note that wisdom and Christlikeness are regarded as the same in the Scriptures. That should not surprise us since Christ Himself is called "the wisdom of God" (1 Corinthians 1:24). Notice the Master's words concerning how a man becomes wise—Christlike—in the Sermon on the Mount. This passage also shows that a man who does not act upon the knowledge of God remains a fool.

Therefore whosoever heareth these sayings of mine, and doeth them, I will liken him unto a wise man, which built his house upon a rock: and the rain descended, and the floods came, and the winds blew, and beat upon that house; and it fell not: for it was founded upon a rock. And every one that heareth these sayings of mine, and doeth them not, shall be likened unto a foolish man, which built his house upon the sand: and the rain descended, and the floods came, and the winds blew, and beat upon that house; and it fell: and great was the fall of it. (Matthew 7:24–27)

HEARING HIS WORDS

This is a crucial point in the Master's teaching and implies several things. First, it teaches that the stability of wisdom begins by giving attention to His words. A believer who neglects his Bible and the regular preaching of God's Word simply will not make it. His neglect of the Word also reveals he is not cultivating a God-mandated purpose to become like Christ, as we saw in the last chapter. He has not answered the call to discipleship.

Notice the mindset toward the Word of God of men who are determined to seek God. Job said, "I have not departed from the command of His lips; I have treasured the words of His mouth more than my necessary food" (Job 23:12 NASB). The psalmist David devoted the longest chapter in the book of Psalms to the priority of the Scriptures in his life. He said, "I have rejoiced in the way of Your testimonies, as much as in all riches" (Psalm 119:14 NASB).

Proverbs 2 outlines the kind of purposeful and diligent attention that must be given to the words of God if one is to become wise. This is no casual take-it-or-leave-it or I'll-read-my-Bible-if-I-have-time attitude. The disciple who wishes to become wise—Christlike—makes the reading, memorization, meditation, and study of the Word a consistent part of his life. There is no godliness without this kind of serious-minded pursuit of the mind of God in His Word by a believer who is daily determining that he must become more like Christ.

Though a man might decide with all his heart that he wants to become like Christ, his resolve will be short-lived and his efforts will fail unless he is seriously "cultivating a God-taught understanding of the person, the work, and the ways of Jesus Christ." It is this failure to "add to [their] virtue knowledge" that explains why many well-intended surrenders and consecrations to Christ flounder within a few days or weeks. The commitment to Christlikeness must be continually fueled with the knowledge of Christ and His ways. A Christ-centered life is possible only for the Word-filled believer.

OBEYING HIS WORDS

Secondly, Jesus teaches that the man who hears His words must commit himself to obeying His words. He must act upon them. This is why the apostle James exhorts us to

> be doers of the word, and not hearers only, deceiving yourselves. . . . But the one who looks into the perfect law, the law of liberty, and perseveres, being no hearer who forgets but a doer who acts, he will be blessed in his doing. (James 1:22, 25 ESV)

Putting into practice the knowledge of God will be the subject of our study in chapter five, where we will learn what to "do" with what we "know." That is the obedience component—the doing of the Word—spoken of by Jesus in the Sermon on the Mount and by James in the passages above. Both "hearing" the Master's words and "doing" them require the humility that will come to characterize the disciple who is becoming like his Master, Jesus Christ.

I will not attempt in this book to provide the turn-by-turn instructions for life, but I do want, in the remaining portion of this chapter, to help you understand the crucial place that biblical knowledge plays in the life of a believer who is truly striving to be like Christ, and therefore, to become wise.

WORLDVIEW 101

A disciple who spends much time studying the Scriptures to learn the ways of his Master, Jesus Christ, will develop a biblical worldview. A worldview is a conceptual framework for thought and action. It helps us understand who we are, explains where we have come from, tells us where we are going, declares to us what is good and what is evil, dictates how we should act, and prescribes to us what is true and what is false. In short, it helps us make sense out of our world and gives meaning and direction to our existence and our morals.

A biblical worldview "views" everything in the "world" through the lens of God's person, purposes, and plans. It references the most important fixed truth in the universe—the existence and nature of God the Creator Himself. His person and work is the only "satellite in the sky" from which we can get our bearings. Paul said it this way,

> For of him, and through him, and to him, are all things: to whom be glory for ever. Amen. (Romans 11:36)

> For in him we live, and move, and have our being. (Acts 17:28a)

More specifically, a biblical worldview "views" everything in the "world" through the lens of God's person, purposes, and plans *as revealed through the person of Jesus Christ*. Notice in the passage below how God Himself puts Jesus Christ front and center of everything He has done and is doing from creation to ultimate redemption.

> For by [Jesus Christ] all things were created, both in the heavens and on earth, visible and invisible, whether thrones or dominions or rulers or authorities—all things have been created through Him and for Him. He is before all things, and in Him all things hold together. He is also the head of the body, the church; and he is the beginning, the firstborn from the dead, so that He Himself will come to have first place in everything. (Colossians 1:16–18 NASB)

The kind of Christ-centered worldview we are talking about is far more than WWJD (i.e., "What would Jesus do?"). It is rather, what is Jesus Christ like? What has He done? What has He said? What is He doing in the earth today? What role does He wish me to play? What kind of person does He wish me to become? How does He wish me to view *temporal* things? How does He wish me to view *eternal* things? And what will really matter in the end when I stand before Him as my Judge?

A biblical worldview starts with the knowledge of Christ and His ways and answers those questions by showing us the whole picture and revealing the vital relationship between eternal and temporal matters.

Almost every error in Christian living and character stems from either ignorance of or disobedience to the divine priority of the *eternal* over the *temporal*. A Christ-centered worldview puts these in their proper place and gives meaning and significance to our lives.

A classic illustration of the tension between the eternal and the temporal is found in the Renaissance painting "The School of Athens." It is a fresco painted in 1509 by Raphael (Raffaello Sanzio) in the Vatican at Rome. Raphael paints a great hall filled with philosophers and people of notoriety—each representing a different school of thought or position in society. Present in the picture are Pythagoras (philosopher, mathematician), Alexander the Great (king, military conqueror), Diogenes (philosopher), Heraclitus (philosopher), Euclid (mathematician), Ptolemy (mathematician, astronomer), and many others.

Most interesting are the two figures framed in the furthermost arch in the center of the picture. They are the elder Plato on the left in a discussion with his pupil Aristotle on the right. Plato walks along with his hand pointing up, symbolizing his belief that the meaning of life was to be found in examining the *universals*—the transcendent ideals and concepts that lie behind the things we see. Aristotle, on the other hand, motions downward with his hand, demonstrating that he believed the meaning of life was to be found in studying the *particulars*—the individual, visible components, the "stuff" of life.

What neither Plato nor Aristotle understood was that both are important. These philosophers needed an external reference point to show them how these two concepts are connected and which has priority. The scriptural parallels for the philisophical terms of *universals* and *particulars* are *eternal* and *temporal*. A man's understanding of how the eternal and the temporal relate and which gets priority will determine whether or not he functions in this world with wisdom—with Christlikeness.

The Grand Priority

Our culture is not known for its wisdom. This should not surprise us since the most important part of reality is ignored. A major piece of the puzzle is missing—the eternal perspective God wants us to bring to every decision. This is why Paul says,

> Whether therefore ye eat, or drink, or whatsoever ye do, do all to the glory of God. (1 Corinthians 10:31)

Notice that what we "eat, or drink" are the particulars, the temporal matters. The "do all to the glory of God" is the overarching universal, the eternal issue. Notice also how Paul subordinates the temporal to the universal. Christlike wisdom keeps these two issues in their proper order. *The eternal always trumps the temporal.* This is, in itself, an eternal universal principle. It cannot be ignored without great consequence to the creature.

You may be thinking by now that all this philosophical talk is too heavy. Actually, all of us have our own philosophy about temporal and eternal issues. We already believe which is the most important, and we act consistently with that belief.

For example, ask yourself, "When I suffer (i.e., physical pain or relational hurt from betrayal, persecution, or loneliness), which seems more real to me—my temporal pain or the eternal God and His purposes and plans for me?" Here's how Paul discusses it:

> Therefore we do not lose heart, but though our outer man is decaying, yet our inner man is being renewed day by day. For momentary, light affliction is producing for us an eternal weight of glory far beyond all comparison, while we look not at the things which are seen, but at the things which are not seen; for the things which are seen are temporal, but the things which are not seen are eternal. (2 Corinthians 4:16–18 NASB)

Or ask yourself, "When I face a decision, does the temporal object or situation seem more real to me than the eternal God and His purposes and plans for me?" I am speaking about decisions such as whom to marry, where to work, where to go to school, what vocation to pursue, how to spend our leisure time, whether to obey an authority, what to purchase with our money, how to respond to a referee's call, a roommate's or spouse's carelessness or personal attack, a coworker's insult, a sexual temptation, and so forth.

Again, when we are confronted with these kinds of decision-points, what seems more real to us—the temporal or the eternal—and do we in humility subordinate our temporal concerns to eternal concerns? The answer will reveal how truly Christ-centered we are—how much true wisdom we have.

MAKING LIFESTYLE DECISIONS WISELY

Many believers today are making extremely misguided decisions, particularly when it comes to lifestyle issues. As a result they do not live distinctively Christian lives. They live basically like the world though they avoid some of the world's excesses. They have come to believe in moderate drinking, moderate nudity and sensuality, moderate profanity, moderate greed, moderate immorality, and moderate materialism. How did they come to these positions? Christians have not always held to these "moderate" positions, even in American culture.

The world system, primarily through the media, desensitizes people—including God's people—to biblical universals while enticing them to an endless pursuit of particulars. Not only are they desensitized to the universals of truth, goodness, and beauty, but they are also robbed of the very habits of heart and mind necessary to even reflect upon universals. A believer saturating his life with entertainment cannot concentrate on his Bible without feeling great boredom and restlessness. He does not have the humility nor the mental discipline to do so. Consequently, he neglects his Bible and the solid preaching of the Word and fills his life with entertaining distractions made possible by the electronic, connected age in which we live.

His ignorance of or rejection of universal, eternal matters is evidenced in many of the discussions about Christian lifestyle issues today. Many try to argue the particulars of music styles, dress standards, alcohol use, and entertainment choices without seeing the *universals* to which these issues are connected. The result is great confusion and ineffectiveness for Christ's kingdom.

In addition, there are many believers today who have a wrong understanding of Christian liberty. They believe that unless the Bible specifically forbids something, they have the liberty to pursue it. Paul did not have that mindset. He hammered out for us the crucial principles of Christian liberty in his writings to the Romans and the second letter to the Corinthians.

Though the piece of meat—a particular—sitting on his plate was not evil in itself, Paul would not partake of it if eating it violated any universal principles. The concern for the spiritual well-being of others (1 Corinthians 8:9–13; 10:24; Romans 14:15–21) and the control that something might have over his life (1 Corinthians 6:12b; 9:24–27) trumped his liberty. Any hindrance to the effectiveness of the gospel (1 Corinthians 9:1–23; 10:31–33), the sheer uselessness of an activity (1 Corinthians 6:12a; 10:23a), or the failure of an activity to edify others (1 Corinthians 10:23b–24) was enough to eliminate it from his agenda as well. Paul lived by the great commandments—love God and your neighbor. Those commands embody universal principles, and Paul would not allow any particular of his temporal life to violate a universal—an eternal truth. Because he lived for eternal matters, he had complete liberty to eliminate from his life any temporal issue. He was not enslaved to his own desires. This is the meaning of Christian liberty.

> The world system desensitizes people to universals while enticing them to an endless pursuit of particulars.

This mindset is greatly lacking today. The primary reason is that many believers have not followed Peter's first admonition to add to their saving faith *aretē*—the pursuit of the excellence of Christlikeness. They are not navigating by an external satellite. They have not answered Christ's call to discipleship—to hear and do His words in order to be like Him. When becoming like Christ is not a priority, neither is cultivating the knowledge of the person, work, and ways of Jesus Christ.

Since they do not spend much time in the Word cultivating the knowledge of Christ, they do not possess an understanding of how eternal truths regulate our view and use of the temporal matters of life—which is the essence of wisdom. Neither will they submit to what they learn. The result is that their lives have little impact for Christ in our culture.

THE QUALIFICATIONS FOR BECOMING WISE

Wisdom is the possession of the one who wants to know Christ because he wants to be like Christ. In other words, he cultivates knowledge because he is cultivating the pursuit of the excellence of Christlikeness. This is important because God will not reveal knowledge about Himself with illuminated understanding to a person who is not intending to use that knowledge *of* Christ to become *like* Christ. Notice what Solomon says.

> For the Lord giveth wisdom: out of his mouth cometh knowledge and understanding. He layeth up sound wisdom for the [upright]. (Proverbs 2:6–7; see also Psalm 25:12)

Essentially, he states that there is a moral qualification to wisdom. Proverbs teaches that if a man will not be good, he cannot become wise (i.e., if he has no heart for what is holy, he has rejected the essence of wisdom). God gives wisdom to the "upright"—those who are willing to use what they learn from Him to represent Him better by walking in righteousness.

This is why a believer can attend a Christian school, graduate with honors, and yet qualify as one of Proverbs' fools. He has viewed the facts he has learned—even about God and His Word—as particulars. They were pieces of information he needed to pass tests and conform to a religious environment, but he did not embrace them as universals that were to regulate everything he did as a disciple of Jesus Christ. He did not "hear" the words of God with any committed intent to "do" them. Consequently, he never became wise. He will suffer the same disconnected frustration of the unbelieving world around him and will not know why.

He will think the problem is with the "legalistic system" of his Christian school or home, or with some deficiency in the church he has been attending. He does not understand that the trapped, restless, and empty feelings he is experiencing are the result of his own disconnection from the life God intended him to live as a hearer and doer of the Word.

God-fearing pastors imprisoned in Russian gulags before perestroika did not experience restless agitation though they were restricted in many inhumane ways. They longed to be with their families and to be worshiping with their believing comrades, but they were not frustrated with life nor experiencing the profound emptiness of the average Christian today. Their lives in prison testified that God has indeed provided "all things that pertain unto life and godliness through the knowledge" of Jesus Christ (2 Peter 1:3). Since their lives were continually connected to the external reference point of the eternal God, they were stable and joyful. The "imprisoned" feelings of the normal believer today are the result of the emptiness within him caused by his own obsession with the temporal. His emptiness is not the result of the structures, environment, and people around him. He has turned away from Jesus Christ and has sought satisfaction elsewhere (Jeremiah 2:13).

FELLOWSHIP-KNOWLEDGE

Wisdom is, therefore, "fellowship-knowledge." It is the product of the interaction between a God-seeking man and his Savior through the Word of God. A. W. Tozer put it this way:

For millions of Christians . . . God is no more real than He is to the non-Christian. They go through life trying to love an ideal and be loyal to a mere principle. . . . A loving Personality dominates the Bible, walking among the trees of the garden and breathing fragrance over every scene. Always a living Person is present, speaking, pleading, loving, working, and *manifesting Himself whenever and wherever His people have the receptivity necessary to receive the manifestations* (emphasis mine).[2]

It remains for us to think on [these truths] and pray over them *until they begin to glow in us* (emphasis mine).[3]

If we cooperate with Him in loving obedience, *God will manifest Himself to us, and that manifestation will be the difference between a nominal Christian and a life radiant with the light of His face* (emphasis mine).[4]

This is what Peter wants us to experience. He wants us to be fruitful in "the [full] knowledge of our Lord Jesus Christ" (2 Peter 1:8). This "full knowledge"—*epignōsis*—is the result of much interaction with Christ about the "knowledge"—*gnōsis*—of His person, work, and ways. This is the first step in sanctification: the process of becoming like Christ. All of this is implied in Christ's command to "hear" His words (Matthew 7:24–25). We will examine the "doing" of His words in chapter 5.

As you can see, the desire to pursue the excellence of Christlikeness will falter if it is not nurtured by cultivating the knowledge of the person, work, and ways of Jesus Christ through a consistent devotional life in God's Word. Without the eternal and external reference point of the Scriptures and the humility to obey them, our Christian experience will gravitate to the temporal particulars of the ungodly world around us. We must "add knowledge" to *aretē*.

Part Two

THE BACKBONE OF CHRISTIAN CHARACTER

Chapter Five

CULTIVATING SELF-CONTROL

Add to . . . knowledge self-control. (2 Peter 1:6)

I invite you to look at the chart in the back of this book and note where we are in our study. In the first column, the Foundation of Christian Character, we were in the "sanctuary" learning how to behold the greatness and majesty of God in His Word and how we must reject the allurements of the world to be transformed into His likeness. We saw that our reason for being on the earth was to display the excellencies of the One Who has called us out of darkness into His marvelous light.

We saw the overarching priority that *eternal* matters should have over the *temporal* and how everything in our lives must revolve around Jesus Christ. He must become and remain our "first love"—the essence of wholehearted commitment (Revelation 2:4).

But as we discover in earthly marriage, we do not naturally live for another even though we intend to initially. We have our own interests, our own ways of doing things, our own pet peeves and personal quirks, our own spending habits—in short, our own way. With time—usually a very short time—we strain at the constraints of commitment. We begin to see what is meant when we hear "the honeymoon is over." The reality of obligations, duties, and responsibilities—the need for increased restraint—has surfaced. The same dynamics can be at work in our relationship with Christ. While our heart *desires* an intimate relationship with the One we have chosen, our heart is not yet *trained* to live for Someone else, for it certainly is not natural for us to do so.

Thus, we see our need in column two to enter the "gymnasium," where the spiritual muscle needed to protect and reinforce our *commitment to Christ* is developed by repetitions on the workstations of daily responsibilities, trials, and temptations in the power of God's Spirit. Thoughts and words must be checked; reactions must be restrained; personal desires must sometimes be sacrificed; ideas and standard operating procedures must be blended into the ways of Another. Our well-intended and perhaps well-informed spiritual desires must be turned into reality. The backbone of our Christian character will be forged here in column two. Paul captures the reality of this:

> *Discipline yourself for the purpose of godliness*; for bodily discipline is only of little profit, but godliness is profitable for all things, since it holds promise for the present life and also for the life to come. (1 Timothy 4:7b-8 NASB, emphasis mine)

BACK TO PETER

Peter points us next, therefore, to cultivating self-control—"a God-empowered mastery of internal desires." While cultivating the pursuit of Christlikeness *captures the heart* and cultivating knowledge *informs the heart*, cultivating self-control *trains the heart*. There are many internal desires that pull the heart away from its commitment to the One it has determined to love. Proverbs speaks to this from several directions. Ponder these carefully:

> [Guard] thy heart with all diligence; for out of it are the issues of life. (4:23)

> He that hath no rule over his own spirit [i.e., he lacks self-control] is like a city that is broken down and without walls. (25:28)

> The desire of the slothful [i.e., the lazy] killeth him; for his hands refuse to labour. (21:25)

These are sobering statements. Solomon teaches that a man who is ruled by his desires will be destroyed, for he is like a city without walls. He has no defense against his enemies. Everything he holds dear is inside those walls—all the issues of his life. They all will be pillaged by the enemy if he does not have the defense of self-control. Richard Bauckham says,

> It is perhaps worth noting that in Gal. 5:23 [self-control] occurs in the context of warning against the misuse of Christian freedom in libertinism (Gal. 5:13), which is also the problem in 2 Peter (2:19).[1]

Peter's call to self-control in the first-century church speaks to a parallel need in the twenty-first-century church.

Before we look at the meaning of this word in New Testament times, we must remind ourselves of the truths we have seen in the first four verses of chapter 1 of Peter's letter. The apostle has instructed us that God has given us everything we need for life and godliness through an intimate relationship with Christ (1:3).

> Natural desires must be gratified only within scriptural boundaries, and sinful desires must be denied entirely.

He has imparted to us His divine nature and thereby equipped us to escape the corruption that comes to us in the world through our lusts (1:4). Sanctification, while requiring cooperation on our part, is not a do-it-yourself project. We do not simply ratchet up the self-control by human effort alone. The Christian who is truly seeing the excellencies of Christ in the Word will be humbled by his own inadequacy to produce these qualities on his own. He knows he needs Spirit-empowered help to "row against the current" of his own sinful heart.[2]

A Fruit of the Spirit

Self-control is listed as one aspect of the fruit of the Spirit of God in Galatians 5:22–23. The more spiritually mature a believer becomes, the more of this virtue he will possess. It is important to keep in mind that self-control is not control *by* the natural self but the control *of* the natural and often sinful self. Natural desires must be gratified only within scriptural boundaries, and sinful desires must be denied entirely.

Natural desires are those that come as a part of our make-up as humans: desire to eat when hungry, desire to breathe, desire to sleep when tired, desire for sex when puberty is reached. These are not sinful in themselves but can be gratified sinfully—wrong time, wrong place, wrong motivation, and so forth. For example, it is not wrong to desire food, but the Bible tells us it is wrong to be gluttonous or to steal to get our food. In the same way, the desire for sex is not wrong, but the Bible tells us it is wrong anytime outside the covenant of a heterosexual marriage. Whenever we are tempted to gratify a natural desire outside of biblical parameters, we must deny that sinful impulse of the flesh. This is what Peter means when he calls for self-control.

Beyond the natural desires there are desires we create by the way we think about something. We create a desire for a certain fashion of clothing, a particular possession, a certain position or recognition in life, or a particular relationship or experience by thinking about that thing or person. We think of all the benefits it would bring to us and imagine ourselves with that person, experience, or thing. As we think in this way, we create a mental desire for it. Again, this may not be sinful, but if the priority this desire takes in our life or the manner in which we pursue it is unbiblical, it becomes sinful and calls for self-control. This self-control is what Jesus called self-denial in Luke 9:23–24.[3]

> If any man will come after me, let him deny himself, and take up his cross daily, and follow me. For whosoever will save his life shall lose it: but whosoever will lose his life for my sake, the same shall save it.

The development process is pretty straightforward. At every crossroad where he must decide whether he will please himself or please Christ in order to manifest a Christlike quality, he must then die to himself (Luke 9:23–24; 1 Corinthians 9:24–27) in order to receive the divine help—the grace—to carry out the right choice (1 Peter 5:5; 2 Corinthians 9:8). If he has already failed to do so, he must repent of his sinful choice. *This Spirit-enabled self-denial fuels the discipline of his life toward the Christlike excellencies he seeks to emulate.*

For example, a college student who knows he needs to develop the virtue of self-control so that he can stick with his studies for the evening and not be distracted by the technology or friends around him cannot merely say to himself, "I'll fail this course if I don't study, and I've got to prove to Mom and Dad that I can make it. Therefore, I'm going to buckle down and study."

A student operating this way may, indeed, earn better grades and perhaps the commendation of his parents, but he won't have developed any *Christian* character in the process. He will have developed only a human virtue of self-discipline—something an unbeliever can do as well.

To develop Christlikeness, *he must interact with Christ Himself in response to what Christ has said in His Word.* His conversation with Christ might go something like this:

Lord Jesus, right now I'm tempted to shut my books and waste a lot of time doing something more pleasurable like surfing the Internet or hanging out with my friends. I know, however, that if I do, I would not be living to please You but myself. You've done so much for me at Calvary, and I want to become someone You can use in Your kingdom work here on the earth. Therefore, with Your help I'll buckle down and study tonight.

I acknowledge that I have wasted the last several evenings. I ask forgiveness for my self-indulgence and my failures to be a good steward of the time and opportunities You have given me.

I need Your grace to resist the distractions and to concentrate on what You want me to learn in these courses. Thank You in advance for fulfilling Your promise to me that "I can do all things through You—the One Who strengthens me." Help me to do right tonight. In Christ's name I pray. Amen.

He then must obey God by applying himself to his studies that evening. This student is cultivating Christlike self-control.

It is this kind of personal interaction with Jesus Christ while cultivating these various virtues of 2 Peter 1 that turns *gnōsis* (knowledge about Christ) into *epignōsis* (intimate, personal experience with Christ). Peter says this interchange produces believers who are not "unfruitful in the knowledge [*epignōsis*] of our Lord Jesus Christ" (2 Peter 1:8). With the reminder behind us that we must respond to Christ in Spirit-enabled self-denial, let's look more closely at what that self-denial looks like.

DEFINITION OF SELF-CONTROL

The root word (ἐγκράτεια, transliterated *enkrateia*, pronounced *ĕng-krăt´-ā-ah*) from which the word for self-control comes means "to take hold of, to grip." We might say to someone who is out of control in some way, "Get a grip, friend." This is exactly the meaning of this word. It is "that strength of soul by which a man takes hold of himself, takes a grip of himself, is in full control and possession of himself, so that he can restrain every evil desire."[4]

Hiebert comments that "self-control points to the inner power to control one's own desires and cravings, the fruit resulting from true knowledge. While the term often connoted restraint from the fulfillment of sexual desires, it extends to all areas of life where the discernment between good and evil is important. . . . It is another thrust at the false teachers whose claim to liberty through knowledge led them into licentious practices (2:2; 3:3)."[5] Charles agrees: "True knowledge, then, leads not to license, but rather to self-control."[6]

The Greek philosophers always used this word—and they spoke of it often—to mean a victory over internal desires. They used it often in tandem with the next virtue in Peter's list—endurance—which is victory over external circumstances. Self-control for the Greeks, however, was achieved strictly by human reason over passion. Their rationale followed closely the first scenario we saw of the student battling with his need to study. He would talk himself into disciplined behavior based upon logical outcomes.

No one would discount the need for us to lecture ourselves. Psalm 42 is a good example of a man talking to himself in order to help himself come to the right position.[7] He does so because he has surrendered his will to what he knows God wants. *The believer can and will say no to any wrong desires when he has said a bigger yes to Christ's will for him.* It is this surrender to God Himself and to His will to which the Spirit of God responds with enabling grace and through which Christlikeness is formed. This is the missing component in the system of the ancient Greeks and in much character development today both inside and outside the church.

SELF-CONTROL: THE DIFFERENCE
BETWEEN A BOY AND A MAN

David DeWitt opens his book *The Mature Man* with the following paragraphs:

> A man is an increasingly hard thing to find. We live in a society of boys—twenty-, thirty-, forty-, fifty-, and sixty-year-old boys. Many guys today seem to have the goal of maintaining a junior-high mentality all the way through life. The ultimate in life seems to be to retire, still a boy. I suggest there is virtually no difference between the shuffle board courts of St. Petersburg, Florida, and the parties at Daytona Beach. The proof of my suggestion is that those playing shuffleboard would be at Daytona Beach if they

were fifty years younger. They've not developed into men at all; they've just gotten older.[8]

There are at least three major stages in the development of a male: boy, man, and patriarch. This means there are two major transitions he must make if he is to fulfill the character God gave him. As a boy he must decide to be a man, and as a man he must decide to be a patriarch.

IMPORTANT DEFINITIONS

A *boy* is a male who is generally chaotic; not yet having personally established order for his life.

A *man* is a male who has taken on the responsibility for establishing order for himself and that of his immediate family. . . .

A *patriarch* is a man who has taken on the responsibility for establishing maturity for himself and applying it to his extended family. . . .[9]

What makes a boy a boy is that he pursues chaos. He has not ordered his life. His life is not yet headed in a direction. He lacks discipline to accomplish tasks. He has not taken significant ownership of values or virtues.

A Boy → A Man → A Patriarch

Chaos → Order → Maturity[10]

"What turns a boy into a man?" This is the most important and most basic transition in the life of a male—and it is where most of us fail. If a boy does not become a man, all future development is merely a fabrication of the real thing. Of course, a boy will get bigger and older, but size and age do not make a man. Manhood is a spiritual decision a boy must make. If he doesn't make this decision, he will remain a boy all his life.

Definition: A BOY is a male who is generally chaotic, not yet having personally established order for his life. A boy is chaotic. His challenge is to become orderly.[11]

DeWitt has captured the essence of manhood. *A man is a male who is exercising self-control to bring order into his life.* A major distinction be-

61

tween adulthood and childhood is the cultivated habit of saying "no" to disorder.

Order is an important concept in biblical thinking. It is to the development of wisdom and character what the alphabet is to language and what notes are to music. Godly wisdom is essentially knowing the proper order of things in God's mind and then ordering one's life accordingly. You cannot build a wise life without order anymore than you can build a written language without an alphabet or a musical score without notes.

As DeWitt says, a boy must take on the discipline of himself under God and embrace order as a way of life. This is the goal of Peter's call to self-control—control of self. We cannot become God-like, nor can we develop adult maturity, while rejecting order. Lloyd-Jones is quite straightforward on this point:

> I defy you to read the life of any saint that has ever adorned the life of the Church without seeing at once that the greatest characteristic in the life of that saint was discipline and order. Invariably it is the universal characteristic of all the outstanding men and women of God. Read about Henry Martyn, David Brainerd, Jonathan Edwards, the brothers Wesley, and Whitefield—read their journals. It does not matter what branch of the Church they belonged to, they have all disciplined their lives and have insisted upon the need for this; and obviously it is something that is thoroughly scriptural and absolutely essential.[12]

THE GOD OF ORDER

Until recent days man has valued order, and human society has reaped the benefits of it. Order is the source of all that we enjoy and cherish in a productive and free civilization. To get a flavor of its scope and meaning, consider the term itself and some of its derivatives.

The word *order* means that something is properly arranged—ranked by degree of quality or importance. Military personnel who receive their orders are put on notice that they must arrange their lives for the next several months according to the dictates of their superiors. A city ordinance is an authoritative command telling the citizenry how they must regulate themselves. In biological taxonomy an order is a higher category of characteristics. Civilizations function best when law and order are maintained by fair courts, adequate enforcement, and cooperative citizens. An uncooperative person in a courtroom is out of order.

All these terms point to a systematic and proper arrangement of things—a ranking by degree of importance or quality. They imply that there is priority to certain things. In other words, certain things must precede others in terms of urgency or importance for something to function as intended. Order, however, is not man's idea. Order is the fingerprint of God upon all His works. It reveals His nature. Consequently, if we are to imitate Him we too must value and cultivate order. Much of this divine order is seen in how God commands that the *particulars* of life are to be regulated by revealed *universal* principles, as we have already seen. God has revealed His nature of order in several other ways.

> Godly wisdom is essentially knowing the proper order of things in God's mind and then ordering one's life accordingly.

The Created Order. The orderliness of God's physical creation stuns even the most casual observer. The heavens speak of God's power and intelligence. Every galaxy spins in its own predetermined path. The sun's distance from our planet and our planet's orbit are skillfully coordinated to sustain life on Earth. The gravitational pull of our planet provides the necessary attraction to keep our bodies from flying into space.

The molecular, atomic, and subatomic world joins the chorus. The periodic table of the elements testifies to God's order. The atomic weight and other properties of each element remain consistent whether that element is found in South Africa or South Carolina or discovered in the ocean or on the Alps. It is the predictability of order within the creation that allows scientists to theorize, research, and experiment. It is this predictability that is the foundation of the creation's stability. *It is the predictability of a well-ordered life that is the source of personal stability and trustworthiness as well.*

The Ceremonial and Civil Order. Much of the Old Testament is devoted to teaching man the importance of order as he relates to God in God's world. The ceremonial laws established that God could be approached only with a certain orderliness. The priests were instructed to place the wood "in order" on the altar (Leviticus 1:7). The sacrifice to follow was to be laid "in order upon the wood" (Leviticus 1:8ff.). God established procedures for setting up the tabernacle and its furniture. The proper order for the priestly dress and purification and for offering sacrifices was spelled out in great detail. There was a particular order of procession for travel through the wilderness and for setting up camp when they stopped.

Through all this, God was teaching the children of Israel—and us by extension[13]—that He cannot be approached haphazardly or carelessly. The order taught and established an aura of reverence that befits His holiness.

The civil laws of the Old Testament taught the same lesson. Whether a man was arranging for the sale of a piece of land or the return of his neighbor's lost ox or seeking justice for wrongs done to him, there was a certain procedure—an order—for him to follow. Those laws taught that love for God and love for neighbor were given the highest consideration. Personal desires must give way to these transcendent considerations.

The instructions given in the New Testament epistles for the church have the same flavor and purpose. Paul wrote his epistles to the Corinthian church because certain things were out of order in their assembly. They were fighting among themselves, tolerating immorality within the church, taking each other to court before unbelievers, mixed up about marriage issues, misusing their Christian liberty, disregarding the apostles themselves, confused about spiritual gifts, misdirected about the resurrection, and neglecting the collection for the poor they had promised.

Galatians, Colossians, the Thessalonian epistles, 2 Peter and Jude addressed doctrinal disorders that were infiltrating the church. The pastoral epistles dealt more directly with practical matters of church operation that needed to be "set in order" (Titus 1:5). The theme of order permeates the inspired writings. *God's people must know the order God has established for their lives and must follow it in the power of His Spirit. To do so requires self-control.*

The Commanded Moral Order. God's fingerprint of order is seen upon the moral realm as well. Every moral command is an order—a statement about how something must be subordinated to a standard God has fixed for His creatures.

The Ten Commandments in Exodus 20 illustrate how order is at the root of God's moral edicts. The first four teach man that God must always be first—a statement of order. The second six commands instruct how others must be placed above self—again, a statement of order. *It is this proper subordination under God and proper regard for others above self that is at the heart of ethical behavior.* When this order is abandoned or ignored, personal and social chaos and disorder flourish. God's commanded order displays His marvelous wisdom, protects His fallen, rational creatures from disintegration, and allows His children to live stable and satisfying lives.

THE ENEMY OF ORDER

Lucifer at one time enjoyed the special favor of God as "the anointed cherub." He was a being created with superpowers of unimaginable magnitude, and with those powers he served his Creator—to the delight of his Creator and to the joy of his own soul.

But eventually he was lifted up in pride and wanted to sit on the throne of the Most High God (Isaiah 14:12–14). His rebellion was the first disorder in all God's creation. Lucifer led a mutiny of angelic legions who also broke rank, abandoning the created order. Lucifer became "the god of disorder."

He peddled his disorder to Adam and Eve, corrupting their natures with a desire to rule themselves. So now God's highest earthly creatures carried with them a propensity to live dis-orderly lives.

We must not miss the point that disorder is an attack on the character and purposes of God. Today's terrorism, corporate scandal, sexual promiscuity, materialism, deceit, rebellion to authority, pop culture's rock idiom, and other assaults in the arts all are reflections of disorderly hearts and breed chaos among men to the glory of Lucifer and the dishonor of the God of order.

All history is an account of God's design to restore the order lost in the fall. One day it will be restored completely, and Lucifer will be forced to recognize his place again as a creature under the Creator. All mankind—redeemed and damned—will acknowledge that "Jesus Christ is

Lord [Ruler over all] to the glory of God the Father" (Philippians 2:11). Everything will be put back in order.

THE PENALTY OF DISORDER

Ultimately, a man who rejects God's priorities will pay the price of his rebellion—temporally or eternally. Self-will—the disorder of a man asserting his will against God's—in all its forms of stubbornness and rebellion is an imitation of Lucifer's original disorderliness. Unless pardoned by the Creator, it will bring the same doom that awaits Lucifer. The seriousness of the penalty for disorder should instruct us as to the seriousness of the crime of disorder.

Late penalties, parental scoldings and spankings, traffic points, fines, suspensions, and prison sentences are all human "disorder indexes" by which a person can measure the degree to which his life is out of order. They show the extent of a man's lack of self-control.

Of course, these interventions can be misused by officials who themselves have a "disordered" view of the purpose of law or of the use of authorized powers, but in themselves, none of these penalties should be looked upon as unnecessary or detrimental. They are essential to fostering and maintaining order in a fallen world.

THE AIDS TO ORDER

From a human standpoint accountability to courageous and compassionate human authorities and peers is God's means of helping fallen man achieve order. After Paul exhorts Timothy to flee youthful passions—the lack of restraint characterized by immaturity—he instructs Timothy to get involved helping others who are captured in the snares of their passions. He says in 2 Timothy 2:24–26 (ESV),

> And the Lord's servant must not be quarrelsome but kind to everyone, able to teach, patiently enduring evil, *correcting his opponents with gentleness.* God may perhaps grant them repentance leading to a knowledge of the truth, and they may . . . escape from the snare of the devil, after being captured by him to do his will.

A disorderly brother is weak and perhaps willful. Accountability to authorities exposes the willful in their defiance and supports the weak in their struggle. The compassionate brother in Christ, like the Good

Samaritan in John 10, sees the one alongside the road that has been taken advantage of by the Devil, crosses to his side of the road, and gives assistance often at his own risk and expense.

Unfortunately, not every willful believer wants help. The compassionate believer sees beyond the stubbornness to the heart that needs help to "escape from the snare of the devil." Like a lifeguard who must bring in a drowning swimmer who is fighting his efforts, he still must do what he can to help. He must have enough strength for both of them—and the willingness to use it—if both are to come out alive. We are our brother's keeper, and we must have the courage to get involved helping a brother be restored to usefulness to Christ once he has fallen (Galatians 6:1–2).

UNDERSTANDING OUR TIMES

Our society is increasingly disorderly because it has rejected God's rule over it and scorns self-control. The pipe dream of personal autonomy has replaced personal responsibility. The future of our country as we have known it does not look good.

But what is even more grievous is that this cultural disorderliness has infected the church and the Christian family. Permissive parenting on the one hand and mean-spirited authoritarianism on the other hand are both evidences of disorderly living. Maxed-out credit cards, obesity, laziness, dysfunctional marriages, the prevalence of sensuality in language, dress, and entertainment choices, outright immorality, unfaithful employees, and the disrespect to authority so commonplace today all testify to the disorderliness of God's people.

Parents who tolerate in their children behaviors that indicate and promote self-indulgence—hours watching television, playing video games, or surfing the Internet; purposeless hanging out with friends, whether online, on the phone, or in person; disrespectful body language and words; childhood obesity; and sloppiness in dress or living environments—are part of the problem. Such parental failures often reveal their own disorderliness. They are either too busy with their own activities, too afraid of their child's reactions, or too blind to spiritual things to see the need to actively disciple their children in the first place.

The root problem is obvious. *Most who know Christ live for themselves rather than wholeheartedly for Jesus Christ.* Their failure to pursue the excellence of Christlikeness and the knowledge of Christ—column-one virtues—is obvious by their failure to exercise self-control. They are ruled by their passions. In addition, unbiblical teaching on grace and Christian liberty has authorized the slide into self-indulgence. *Temporal* matters have been given priority over *eternal* concerns.

We must repent of any conformity to the world and of our indulgence in sinful passions. We must cultivate the pursuit of Christlikeness, knowledge, and self-control.

Self-control was not optional for the apostle Paul. He rightly saw it as his protection from disqualification of usefulness for Christ. He gave all diligence to add to his saving faith self-control. Listen to his words.

> Every athlete exercises self-control in all things. They do it to receive a perishable wreath, but we an imperishable. So I do not run aimlessly; I do not box as one beating the air. But I discipline my body and keep it under control, lest after preaching to others I myself should be disqualified. (1 Corinthians 9:25–27 ESV)

Paul admonished Titus to instruct every social group within the church to live disciplined lives. That is the meaning of the words in italics in the following passages. They are all various derivatives of the Greek word *sōphrōn* (σώφρων, pronounced sō´-frōn), another Greek word that means self-controlled or disciplined.

> That the aged men be . . . *temperate* [self-controlled]. (2:2)

> [The aged women should] teach the young women to be *sober* [self-controlled]. (2:4)

> Young men likewise exhort to be *sober-minded* [self-controlled]. (2:6)

He then closes this portion of exhortation with a description of what should characterize the believer's lifestyle. He said in Titus 2:11–12,

> For the grace of God that bringeth salvation hath appeared to all men, teaching us that denying ungodliness and worldly lusts we should live soberly [in a self-controlled manner], righteously, and godly, in this present world.

The word *soberly* above is the adverb form of our word *sōphrōn* again. "Denying ungodliness and worldly lusts" is the exercise of self-control for the purpose of bringing every part of life under the lordship of Jesus Christ—the essence of living a well-ordered life. Contrary to the libertine teaching of Peter's day—and ours—grace does not give a believer free reign to do anything he wishes as long as the Bible does not forbid it. Paul is clear here that grace does not produce license but rather teaches us to deny ourselves the worldliness that corrupts us and pursue the godliness that changes us for Christ.

These were not peripheral issues with the apostles. Self-control born of Spirit-enabled self-denial was a natural byproduct of the gospel. Anyone who had experienced the grace of God and was growing in that grace should have been experiencing greater measures of self-denial and should have been living an increasingly well-ordered life. God's priorities were becoming his in every area of life. If we are to become Christlike and wise, these must become our priorities as well.

Chapter Six

CULTIVATING ENDURANCE

Add to . . . self-control endurance. (2 Peter 1:6)

The twentieth century witnessed a continuous string of adventurers who in the face of seemingly insurmountable challenges conquered some yet-to-be-discovered portions of our planet.

Robert Edwin Peary planted an American flag at the North Pole on April 6, 1909. Previous expeditions through Greenland in efforts to find the most accessible route to the pole had cost him all but two toes due to frostbite and the best years of his life. Discouragement was a constant temptation—such as the time he had come within 174 miles of the pole but had to turn back because supplies had dwindled after several delays along the way. Though battling the prospects of yet another failure, he and his best friend, Matthew Henson, four Eskimos, and thirty-eight sled dogs finally reached the pole on his sixth expedition.

Roald Amundsen braved unpredictable ice floes, arctic temperatures amidst thirty-five-mile-per-hour winds, and unexpected delays when his sleds fell into hidden ice crevasses, but on December 14, 1911, he reached the South Pole. Edmund Hillary conquered Mount Everest's 29,028 feet on May 29, 1952, and Jacques Picard navigated his bathyscaph 35,800 feet below the surface of the Pacific Ocean to land at the bottom of the Mariana Trench on January 23, 1960.[1]

These were grueling journeys to the remote points of the earth. In addition to careful planning, extensive funding, and exceptional support teams, each explorer had to bring with him the quality of endurance. Hunger, frigid temperatures, uncharted territories, disease, and the death of comrades brought unexpected challenges to both body and soul. Despite these challenges these men did not quit. Years of preparation and the vision of accomplishment had forged the quality of perseverance into their character.

Most of us will never have our endurance tested by extreme arctic temperatures or the deadly water pressures on the ocean's floor seven miles below the surface, but all of us will face circumstances of other sorts that test our resolve to remain faithful to a task or to a mission God has given us to do.

The apostle Peter looked around him and saw that many believers who had started out right in their Christian experience were being sidetracked by the sensual appeals of the immoral culture around them. In addition, libertine false teachers had begun to convince them that they were free to live any way they wished. The professions of these believers to whom Peter was writing were being eclipsed by their immorality and worldliness. Outright persecution was not so much a threat as were the pressures of moral degradation.[2]

These people had begun well, but Peter wanted to insure that they finished well. He knew that in addition to a resolve to pursue Christlikeness (*arete*), they would need the *knowledge* of Christ. In addition, they would need *self-control* to keep their internal desires from sidetracking them. Furthermore, they would need *endurance*, the quality that guards the heart.

DEFINITION OF ENDURANCE

The word Peter uses for endurance (ὑπομονή, transliterated *hupomonē*, pronounced hū-pŏ-mŏ-nā´) is a compound word which reads "to remain under." In the literal sense of the word, Robert Peary's sled dogs illustrated endurance as they pulled his four supply sleds to the North Pole on a thirty-day trek. They "remained under" the burden of pulling the sleds across the frozen ice fields. They persevered at their task and were rewarded with a special dinner at the top of the world.

This picture captures the literal meaning of the original word, but the concept of endurance came to mean much more. "In its classical usage [the word] connotes courageous endurance that fully defies evil, and thus, is active rather than passive. In Plato, it is brave resistance that is honorable to a man."[3] Baukham agrees. "The word refers to a courageous and steadfast endurance in the face of suffering or evil."[4]

Though endurance means to be constant under external pressures, it does not mean merely controlling our temper, gritting our teeth, wait-

> Endurance is that ability to remain faithful to God under pressure because your heart looks continually to God in faith for strength and reward.

ing out the storm, or tying a knot in the end of our rope and hanging on. *There is often an ethical issue at stake in endurance—a principle to be courageously defended or advanced under pressure.* Barclay calls this "one of the noblest NT words." Because of its link with courage he calls it "the manly virtue."[5] Kittel comments that "there predominates in [this word] the concept of the courageous endurance which manfully defies evil. Unlike patience,[6] it thus has an active content. It includes active and energetic resistance to hostile power, though with no assertion of the success of this resistance."[7]

In the Scriptures the ethical principle at stake was maintaining a response that glorified God no matter what the external pressures. The pressures that could tempt a man away from God could be physical torture, natural affliction and disease, poverty, pressure from family or friends, or pressures from the external culture. These external situations can tempt a man to respond with anxiety, anger, or despair inside or to respond with outward sinful actions. The man with endurance would do nothing that dishonored God no matter how strong the external forces.

This steadfastness in the New Testament was accompanied by a look to the future for final resolution and to the God of the future for present strength. Thus,

> it is the spirit which can bear things, not simply with resignation, but with blazing hope; it is not the spirit which sits statically enduring in the one place, but the spirit which bears things because it knows that these things are leading to a goal of glory; it is not the patience which grimly waits for the end, but the patience which radiantly hopes for the dawn. It has been called "a manly constancy under trial." It has been said that always it has a background of *andreia*, which is courage. . . . It is the quality which keeps a man on his feet with his face to the wind. It is the virtue which can transmute the hardest trial into glory because beyond the pain it sees the goal. George Matheson, who was

stricken with blindness and disappointed in love, wrote a prayer in which he pleads that he might accept God's will, "not with dumb resignation, but with holy joy; not only with the absence of murmur, but with a song of praise." Only *hupomonē* can enable a man to do that."[8]

It is this courageous steadfastness that we admire in God's servants when we read missionary biographies and accounts of the martyrs or explore the circumstances behind many of the traditional hymns of the church.

Hebrews 11 catalogs many Bible heroes whose steadfast gaze upon God during adversity caused them to persevere under trial. These are men and women who

> through faith subdued kingdoms, wrought righteousness, obtained promises, stopped the mouths of lions, quenched the violence of fire, escaped the edge of the sword, out of weakness were made strong, waxed valiant in fight, turned to flight the armies of the aliens. Women received their dead raised again: and others were tortured, not accepting deliverance; that they might obtain a better resurrection: and others had trial of cruel mockings and scourgings, yea, moreover of bonds and imprisonment: they were stoned, they were sawn asunder, were tempted, were slain with the sword: they wandered about in sheepskins and goatskins; being destitute, afflicted, tormented; (of whom the world was not worthy:) they wandered in deserts, and in mountains, and in dens and caves of the earth. (Hebrews 11:33–38)

The commentary on Moses in this passage captures the dynamic at work here.

> By faith he forsook Egypt, not fearing the wrath of the king: *for he endured, as seeing him who is invisible.* (11:27)

Endurance is that ability to remain faithful to God under pressure because your heart looks continually to God in faith for strength and reward. This is the flavor of this word in the New Testament. "Adding to your faith . . . endurance" then is, as the chart in the back shows, cultivating "a God-sustained faithfulness under external pressure."

THE TEST OF YOUR CHARACTER

Bob Jones Sr. often reminded the students in his chapel messages of their need to endure. He captured the salient points of endurance with pithy, easy-to-remember "chapel sayings." Many of them are posted on placards over the chalkboards in the university's classrooms. They include,

Finish the job.

You can do anything you ought to do.

Go as far as you can on the right road.

The door to the room of success swings on the hinges of opposition.

Do not ask God to give you a light burden; ask Him to give you strong shoulders to carry a heavy burden.

The test of your character is what it takes to stop you.

I want us to further consider that last one. How much we are really committed to exhibiting a Christlike character is revealed by asking ourselves, "What does it take to make me stop doing the right thing?" Ask yourself,

- Do I stop being kind when another person offends me in some way or there is something about the person that does not appeal to me?

- Do I stop being obedient just because I don't agree with the policy or because it inconveniences me?

- Do I stop exercising self-control because I'm discouraged at the moment and want to do something that will make me feel better or because my friends are indulging sinfully in something and I don't want to be left out or thought of as a coward?

- Do I stop seeking God in my Bible and praying daily just because my schedule gets full or something doesn't go the way I want it to go and I'm upset with God?

- Do I stop maintaining pure thoughts and actions when I'm given the opportunity to feed my lusts undetected through the Internet, movies, or television or when I'm alone with a member of the opposite sex who is not my spouse?

- Do I stop being honest when shading the truth would keep me from being held responsible for wrongdoing or would bring me praise I didn't earn?
- Do I stop sacrificing for people when they don't seem to appreciate it or when no one seems to notice?
- Do I stop taking hope in the promises of God and become discouraged when I don't see circumstances working out the way I want them to or as fast as I want them to?
- Do I stop being a diligent worker when no one is present to hold me accountable for my work or when the work situation isn't what I had expected?

Every character quality is only as good as its steadfastness under pressure. "The mature Christian does not give up. There are few more reliable tests of faith than this; true faith endures (cf. Rom. v. 1–3, Mk. xiii.13)."[9]

CULTIVATING ENDURANCE

Before reading further, look again at the chart of Peter's virtues. I want you to see where Peter places endurance in his list. By looking at what precedes it, we can tell what fuels endurance. Think of endurance as the flavor of character you get when you put into a blender the pursuit of the excellence of Christlikeness, knowledge of Christ and His ways, and self-control. Combined and placed under pressure, these virtues develop endurance.

Cultivating endurance begins when we agree with God that our purpose on the earth is to display the excellencies of Jesus Christ. That is cultivating *aretē*. Next we must find out what that looks like. As we study about the person, works, and ways of Jesus Christ, we find what He is like, and thus, what we should be like. The standard is clear as we cultivate *knowledge*.

Now we must battle our own sinful impulses in order to respond like Christ in the particular challenges we face each day. We are often tempted to indulge ourselves in sexually immoral ways, protect or promote ourselves through dishonesty, pander to our laziness by time-wasting activities, feed our covetousness, express our contempt for someone, complain about our circumstances, waste our money, or ignore our time with God. We will face these temptations successfully

75

only by reaffirming our commitment to Jesus Christ Himself and then by Spirit-empowered self-denial bringing our impulses under control so that our lives reflect the order and priorities of Jesus Christ. Daily interaction with Christ Himself in prayer and in the Word keeps before us the coming day "when he shall appear" and "we shall be like him; for we shall see him as he is." It is "this hope" that causes us to "purify [ourselves] even as he is pure" (1 John 3:2–3).

As this becomes the habitual practice of our life, we develop *self-control* (control of self with the Spirit's grace). It is that cultivated self-control that is the foundation for endurance. *A man cannot effectively say no to the pressures outside himself until he is skilled at saying no to the pressures that come from within.*

For example, a woman facing her final months of life, suffering the excruciating pain of her cancer-ridden body and anticipating the soon separation from her faithful and loving spouse and from her children, might be tempted to give in to anger, fear, and, perhaps, despair. Though she may wince in pain or shed tears of sorrow at the thought of leaving her family behind, she can, by God's grace, "greatly rejoice though now for a season, if need be, [she is] in heaviness through [various trials]" (1 Peter 1:6).

This is possible because she knows from studying her Bible that she has a "living hope by the resurrection of Jesus Christ from the dead" (1:3) and throughout her Christian experience she has learned to "gird up the loins of [her] mind" and be "sober-minded"—another New Testament word for self-control—and has learned to "hope to the end for the grace that is to be brought unto [her] at the revelation of Jesus Christ" (1:13).

As a child she had been taught to say no to herself in order to obey her mother and dad. Coming from a home with limited financial means had taught her to resist impulse spending and to become consistent in her giving to the work of the Lord and in saving for her college education.

As a college student she had said no to herself in order to maintain a daily devotional life amid her busy schedule. She had developed the habit of saying no to her sinful desires to be popular when it was necessary to take an unpopular position on some worldly activity with her friends. Her leadership position in her resident hall had given her much practice in saying no to herself to minister to the girls on her hall and to enforce school policies when necessary.

She had resisted the temptation to dress and talk sensually in order to attract a husband, and when God brought the right man into her life, she said no to her desires to become physically involved with him before marriage. They agreed that it would be prudent to postpone marriage until both were out of school. The wait called for new levels of self-denial to stay in God's will for them.

Once married she had learned to make the necessary adjustments of living with a man she loved deeply but who was still a sinner, though saved by grace. She said no to herself many times as she learned to trust God while obeying her husband (1 Peter 3:1–6). Keeping up with the daily duties of running a household while holding down a full-time job before children came along meant that she often had to say no to herself when she thought of one of her girlfriends who didn't have to work so hard.

Later, the responsibilities of rearing children demanded new levels of self-denial. Late night feedings, early mornings, loads of laundry, dirty diapers, teething, grocery shopping, potty training, the challenges of disciplining disobedient children, and keeping the house in some semblance of order gave her much practice at saying no to what she would rather be doing at the moment as she sacrificially served Christ by serving her family. Having four children meant that she had to learn to do all of these over the long haul.

Now in hospice care for her final few weeks, she continues to bless others with an amazing joy and peace that confounds her doctors and comforts her family. There is no bitterness, no anger, no fear, no despair—only quiet confidence that God is doing all things well and will continue to give grace to her husband and each of her teenage children as He has given her grace all these years.

This kind of joyful, hope-filled, and courageous endurance does not break on the scene unexpectedly at a crucial time of need. *It is forged on the anvil of years of daily commitment to Jesus Christ followed by countless daily surrenders to Him as each new challenge and temptation arises that day.*

Endurance is cultivated in this way. It is the "trying of [our] faith that worketh [endurance]" (James 1:3).

PRISONS, PITS, AND PALACES

We can learn much about endurance from the Old Testament character Joseph (Genesis 37–50). He was the eleventh son of Jacob and firstborn son of Rachel, Jacob's second wife. Reuben, Jacob's firstborn son of his first wife, Leah, had forfeited his birthright by sleeping with one of his father's concubines (Genesis 35:22; 1 Chronicles 5:1–2). Joseph, being the firstborn son of Jacob's second wife, was granted the birthright in Reuben's stead. At the age of seventeen Joseph received from God the visions that confirmed him as God's choice to be his father's successor in Abraham's line of patriarchs.

Out of envy that Joseph was to be their ruler and because their father favored him, his brothers arranged for him to be sold into slavery. Ishmaelite slave traders bought him and sold him to Potiphar, the chief of the palace guards and chief executioner of Pharaoh, ruler of Egypt.

Imagine what this turn of events meant to Joseph. He was being groomed as the prince heir of his clan, and through the treachery of his brothers he was now someone else's property—no better than Egyptian livestock. He was placed in a job he didn't choose, forced to eat food he didn't have a taste for, compelled to dress as a slave, constrained to learn and speak a language not his own, and housed in the slaves' quarters. He was removed from everything he held dear—the support of his father, the freedom to do as he or his father pleased, and the community of people like himself. Everything was different in Egypt—religion, customs, lifestyle, and values. This was culture shock at its worst for a seventeen-year-old boy.

Yet there was a remarkable steadiness in this teenager's heart from the start. There was something distinctively different about him. Perhaps while other slaves were bitter at their lot in life, Joseph was unruffled by his change in circumstances. Perhaps while the others did as little work as possible, Joseph was throwing his whole heart into his labors. Perhaps while the other slaves cursed and mistreated each other, Joseph treated everyone with dignity and respect. We don't know the details, but we do know that Joseph "remained under" the yoke of bondage with a spirit that set him apart. He displayed a "God-sustained faithfulness under external pressure." He developed endurance.

There was something notable in his character and his work (39:2), and Potiphar himself "saw that the Lord was with him, and that the Lord made all that he did to prosper in his hand" (39:3). He didn't need supervision, and he didn't require emotional support from those around him to perform at his best. Joseph knew the Lord was with him (39:2) and that was all he needed.

Joseph probably started in the fields, an entry level slave position, but because of his character was soon brought into Potiphar's house (39:2) and finally promoted to chief steward of the house and of Potiphar's fields (39:5). His master's trust was so explicit that Joseph managed everything except Potiphar's kitchen; the Egyptians took great care to avoid ceremonial uncleanness, and Joseph, being an outsider, would defile the food.

Apparently, Potiphar wasn't the only one in the house who appreciated Joseph. Potiphar's wife repeatedly tempted Joseph to have sexual relations with her. Extrabiblical Jewish commentaries from the first century AD report that she seduced him for a period of a year.[10] Joseph not only had to fight his own sexual lusts but had to face the pressure of what this woman could do to his career if he didn't comply. Egyptian culture, as does ours, tolerated infidelity. No one would know, and no one would care. But Joseph endured; he exhibited "a God-sustained faithfulness under external pressure." He refused her advances, bringing God into the picture and reminding her that she did not belong to him but to Potiphar (39:2).

What a contrast Joseph's response was to that of his brother Judah in chapter 38! At the first opportunity to hire a prostitute, Judah had his credit card out. He would not have hesitated to be immoral with Potiphar's wife had he been in Joseph's place. Judah, like the rest of his brothers, had conformed to the lifestyle of the Canaanites around them. I believe that God gave us this steamy episode in Judah's life in chapter 38 to show us why God needed to get the children of Israel out of Canaan and isolated in Egypt. They were being secularized at breakneck speed. The story serves also to contrast the character of Joseph with that of his brothers.

Mrs. Potiphar retaliated, and Joseph was imprisoned by her husband on false charges of attempted rape. Most commentators agree that Potiphar knew Joseph was innocent because Potiphar did not have him executed. Instead, Joseph was given a position of trust in the prison once he had proved his character to the warden (39:21–23).

Once again Joseph was in a place he didn't choose, but now he was also charged with a crime he didn't commit. It was bad enough that he had gone from being the prince heir of his clan to becoming a slave. Now he was a slave in prison with a criminal record. He could go no lower. But here too "the Lord was with Joseph, and shewed him mercy, and gave him favour in the sight of the keeper of the prison" (39:21).

His steadfast spirit in his work got him the job of tending two royal prisoners under house arrest (40:1–4). One morning when he greeted them he noticed their troubled spirits and invited them to tell him the previous night's dreams that had unsettled them. God granted him the power to interpret their dreams, and he asked the butler to put in a good word for him before Pharaoh.

What is most instructive about this scene is that Joseph was so calmly confident of God's hand in his misfortunes that he came to work and noticed the needs of others. A bitter person steaming about the injustices of his own circumstances doesn't notice anxiety on the faces of others. Here again, Joseph demonstrated endurance—"a God-sustained faithfulness under external pressure." He had a ministry to others because he was not consumed with his own misery.

I believe the next two years in prison were perhaps the most difficult for Joseph. No matter how hard he tried to do right, life seemed to get harder. He had obeyed his father's command to check on his brothers, and he ended up in slavery. He had been faithful in the menial tasks of entry-level slaves, had been promoted to a place of trust, and then had been imprisoned for something he didn't do. In prison, he tried to attend to the needs of those in his charge, and the one he helped forgot him for another two years. These were hard times and inexplicable reversals, but Joseph endured. God had told him in a dream twice that he would be honored, and that had not yet happened. He knew that the final chapters had not been written. He remained steadfast knowing that God was at work.

Finally, after thirteen years of betrayal, hard labor, false accusations, and disappointment, God arranged for Joseph to stand before Pharaoh, interpret the king's dreams, and propose a plan for the coming famine that would be the salvation of Egypt and the surrounding countries. As a result he was promoted to prime minister of Egypt, second only to Pharaoh himself.

Though Joseph was in power, he did not use his power as prime minister to retaliate against Potiphar's wife nor against his brothers when given the chance. Once again he was steadfast. He was not corrupted by his newfound power. As the second in command of Egypt he used his power to advance the agendas of God and his master, Pharaoh. He did not become self-serving. Here, too, he demonstrated a "God-sustained faithfulness under external pressure."

Joseph eventually brought his entire family to Egypt to wait out the famine. Fearful that Joseph might take revenge upon them, his brothers begged him to forgive them in the final chapter of Genesis. I believe this is another test of Joseph's character. He had given them no reason to doubt his benevolence. The only motives they understood were those in their own hearts. And once again, Joseph did not waver from responding correctly. He comforted them, spoke kindly to them, and reassured them that he would continue to provide for them.

In his interchange with his brothers Joseph made clear what had sustained him during these years of hardship. He said to his brothers,

> But as for you, ye thought evil against me; but God meant it unto good, to bring to pass as it is this day, to save much people alive. (50:20)

Joseph was stable because his eye was upon his God. God had promised him something, and he, like Abraham,

> staggered not at the promise of God through unbelief; but was strong in faith, giving glory to God, and being fully persuaded that, what he had promised, he was able also to perform. (Romans 4:20–21)

Joseph knew God to be a certain kind of person—a Person Who would keep His word; a Person Who had a plan and was working that plan. He remained steadfast under pressure because he knew God would be

> Endurance is grounded in the knowledge of God and His ways.

faithful to His promises. This is our only true stability as well. If God is not our vision and His promises are not our confidence, we will fall when betrayed, seduced, mistreated, or promoted to power.

Endurance, as we have seen from the life of Joseph, is grounded in the *knowledge* of God and His ways. But it also draws upon a *self-control* that is able to keep the mind stayed upon the goal and the promises of God and not be distracted by unsettling events.

What is remarkable is that Joseph had only the oral teachings about God from his father and his own dreams to sustain him during these hard times. We have a "more sure word of prophecy," Peter tells us. We have the inspired words of the living God written down for us to meditate upon (2 Peter 1:19–21). What's more, those inspired words tell us of Jesus Christ, Who becomes not only our Savior but also our example of endurance.

CONSIDER HIM

One of the major themes of the book of Hebrews is endurance. The believers to whom the book was written were beginning to feel the pressure of persecution. After cataloging the heroes of the faith in chapter 11, the writer exhorts this first-century church—and us—with the following words in the first four verses of chapter 12:

> Wherefore seeing we also are compassed about with so great a cloud of witnesses, let us lay aside every weight, and the sin which doth so easily beset us, and let us run with [endurance] the race that is set before us, looking unto Jesus the author and [perfecter] of our faith; who for the joy that was set before him endured the cross, despising the shame, and is set down at the right hand of the throne of God. For consider him that endured such [hostility from] sinners against himself, lest ye be wearied and faint in your minds. Ye have not yet resisted unto blood, striving against sin.

Here is divine instruction and a divine example of endurance. We must carefully consider the life of the Lord Jesus. He endured because He kept before Him the result of His suffering—the smile of His Father and the redemption of His people. He knew what His Father was doing and what His Father had promised. It is this sort of commitment to an eternal goal and this kind of mental discipline that en-*courages* endurance. The opposite is to grow weary and faint-hearted—to become dis-*couraged*.

This "race that is set before us" is not a sprint but a marathon. Peter in the passage we have been studying and the writer of Hebrews both call us to diligent, sustained effort in our Christian walk. This is not a theme reinforced by the world around us. We are promised popularity, ease, and fun if we will pursue the lifestyles presented to us by the world. We are promised easy credit, 250 channels, unlimited minutes, all you can eat, no-fault divorce, free wireless, confidential abortions, and safe sex.

These are the "joys set before us" by the world, and most people trust these promises to deliver joy apart from God. But notice what is happening. The *pursuit of the excellence of Jesus Christ* is replaced by the pursuit of the lifestyles of the rich and famous. The *knowledge* of Jesus Christ is replaced with the ratings of what or who is most popular, and *self-control* is traded for self-indulgence. Consequently, there is no foundation for *endurance*. Even God's people quit jobs and marriages at the same rate as the world. More tragically, many of God's people quit trusting God. They have been stripped of Christian character.

It doesn't have to be this way. We have a model before us—Jesus Christ—Who authored our faith and Who promises to perfect it in us. As Peter has already taught us, we have been given marvelous provisions in the person and promises of Jesus Christ. It is now our duty in the daily affairs of life to be "giving all diligence to add to our faith . . . endurance."

Chapter Seven

CULTIVATING GODLINESS, PART 1

Add to . . . endurance godliness. (2 Peter 1:6)

William Wilberforce is revered for his tireless efforts before Parliament to abolish the slave trade in England during the late 1700s and early 1800s. He was born into a wealthy family but was plagued with physical weakness and infirmity from his youth. He indulged in the excesses of the university student life in his early adult years, and, though very intelligent, graduated without honors because his studies lacked purpose and motivation. Upon graduation he ran for Parliament since he had no desire to take up the family business.

At the age of twenty-five he came under the influence of Isaac Milner, whose friendship eventually led him to Christ. Once he became a child of God, his lifestyle changed and he sought the spiritual guidance of John Newton, author of "Amazing Grace." Newton, a former slave ship captain, discipled Wilberforce on the excellencies of Christ and the horrors of the slave trade.

Newton, along with his fellow parliamentarian, William Pitt, persuaded Wilberforce to use his political position to advance the antislavery movement in England. He lobbied tirelessly for twenty-four years before he saw the slave trade abolished in the British Empire in 1807. He would labor until 1833 to see Parliament pass an act freeing the slaves—three days before his death.

Ridding Britain of the inhumanity of slavery was not his only burden. He stated that "God Almighty has put before me two great objects—the abolition of the slave trade and the reformation of the manners [morals] of England."[1] While maintaining his impeccable personal testimony of godliness, he challenged the corruption and immorality around him, whether it was in his peers in government or in the gambling and drinking establishments of his day.

His crusade for a return to godliness resulted in a 450-page book entitled *A Practical View of the Prevailing Religious System of Professed Christians, in the Higher and Middle Classes in this Country, Contrasted with Real Christianity.* When I read an abridged version of the book—editor James Houston's *Real Christianity*—almost ten years ago, I was profoundly struck with the warm affection for Jesus Christ, the doctrinal soundness of his philosophy of life, and the bold outspokenness of his Christian testimony. He said of his countrymen,

> Take such people aside at an opportune time and lead the conversation to the matter of religion. The most that can be done is to get them to talk in general terms about religion. They appear lost in generalizations. There is nothing specific, nor determinate. There is nothing to suggest a mind that is used to contemplate on specific realities.

> Vainly you strive to bring them around to speak on this topic. One would expect the subject of God to be uppermost in the hearts of redeemed sinners. But they elude all your endeavors. If you make mention of it yourself, they do not give it a cordial welcome; indeed they greet it with unequivocal disgust. At best, the discussion remains forced and formal.[2]

He bemoaned the average upper-class Christian's lack of appreciation for the person of Christ. When speaking of their concern for holiness, he says,

> The bulk of the Christian world is too little conscious of the inability of their own unaided efforts to produce holiness of heart and life. Each day they are not accustomed to using humbly and diligently God's means for the reception and the cultivation of His help.[3]

He decried the self-indulgent, sensual lifestyles of the majority of God's people, which have replaced the self-sacrificing mindset that wholeheartedly serves Christ and others.

> [Nominal Christians] have avowedly established a system of decent selfishness. Recreation is its chief business. . . . Amusements

> Godliness is the crown and the summary of the four "personal virtues" of *aretē*, knowledge, self-control, and endurance

multiply, combined and varied, "to fill up the void of a listless and languid life."

Some take up with sensual pleasures. The chief happiness of their lives consists in one species or another of animal gratification. . . . "Mortify the flesh, with its affections and lusts" is the Christian *precept*. A soft luxurious course of habitual indulgence is the practice of the majority of modern Christians. That constant moderation, that wholesome discipline of restraint and self-denial—which are the requisite to prevent the unnoticed inroads of the bodily appetites—seem wholly unexercised.[4]

He was also concerned about the growing skepticism in religious young people as they came into adulthood. He notes the reason.

> How then did they become skeptics? Reason, thought, and inquiry have little to do with it. Having lived for many years careless and irreligious lives, they eventually matured into their faithlessness—not by force of irreligious strength but by lapse of time. . . . Unbelief is not so much the result of studious and controversial age as it is one of moral decline. It disperses itself in proportion as the general morals decline. People embrace it with less apprehension when all around are doing the same thing.[5]

He closes his book with an appeal to true Christians.

> To those who really deserve to be called true Christians, much has been said incidentally throughout this book. I have maintained that they are always most important members of the community. No sound or experienced politician would deny that. But we boldly assert that there never was a period when this was truer than of the present time. For wherever we look we see that religion and the standard of morals are everywhere declining, abroad more rapidly than in our own country.

> However, at home the progress of irreligion and the decline in morals is enough to alarm every thoughtful person and to fill us with foreboding about the growth of evil. We can only depend upon true Christians to give some remedy against its decline. . . . Singleness

of purpose, consistency of behavior, and perseverance in effort are needed. Only true Christians can provide these qualities.[6]

My purpose in highlighting this man's life and work is to give a brief portrait of what godliness looks like. What is important in this biographical sketch of a godly man is not merely *what he said*—though his content was thoroughly biblical—but the fact *that he said it*. A godly man will not remain silent when evil is present and good is under attack. He is not a coward in the Lord's cause.

He may be Christian, but a man is not godly if he will not open his mouth and put the weight of his influence and life into the cause of righteousness. He will not tolerate evil in himself, in his family, in the church, nor in his community. He knows the apostle's warning: "All that live godly in Christ Jesus shall suffer persecution" (2 Timothy 3:12). But that does not matter. Right must prevail at all costs.

ADD TO YOUR FAITH . . . GODLINESS

Wilberforce's lifestyle is the mindset Peter is calling for when he says, "Add to your faith . . . godliness." The apostle is not calling for a socially acceptable Christianity. Peter's audience knew what it would cost to move to this level of Christian testimony. They also knew why they must be maturing in the previous traits of *self-control* and *endurance* if they were to cultivate *godliness*. Godliness would require generous doses of both. As we look at this strategic virtue, prayerfully consider what it is that God is asking you to become when he calls us to godliness.

Once again look to the chart and let's see where we are in the process of forming Christlike character. *Godliness* is the third virtue in the center column. It follows self-control and endurance.

Godliness is the crown and the summary of the four "personal virtues" of *aretē*, knowledge, self-control, and endurance (verses 5–6). It is also the launching pad into the two "social virtues"—brotherly kindness and love (verse 7). As you can see by the label at the top of the first two columns on the chart, godliness completes the picture of what it means to love God with your whole heart. Column three, of course, will describe for us what it means to love our neighbor as ourselves.

Godliness is a frequent term in Peter's discussion of Christian character in this epistle. He first mentions it early in chapter 1 of this second epistle before he begins the list of virtues we are studying. He says,

> According as his divine power hath given unto us all things that pertain unto life and *godliness* through the knowledge of him that hath called us to glory and virtue. (2 Peter 1:3)

Peter in the verse above uses this word to summarize all that is important in our personal response to Christ. It is a great comprehensive term.

Godliness again appears in this first chapter in the list of virtues (verse 6) in a strategic position that marks what it means to have a mature relationship with God. It is from this position of maturity that *brotherly kindness* and *love*, the social virtues that follow it, can pour out in their fullest expression.

The apostle also closes this epistle with an appeal to godliness. He has reassured his readers that contrary to the libertine teaching of false teachers there will be a coming day of judgment when God will hold all of us accountable for the way we have lived in this ungodly world. He reveals that the world will be destroyed at that time of judgment, not by a flood as in Noah's days, but by a conflagration such as the world has never seen. Against that background of coming judgment Peter exclaims,

> Since all these things [of the physical world] are thus to be dissolved, what sort of people ought you to be in lives of holiness and godliness, waiting for and hastening the coming of the day of God, because of which the heavens will be set on fire and dissolved, and the heavenly bodies will melt as they burn! (2 Peter 3:11–12 ESV)

Notice again the importance and comprehensiveness of godliness. Peter does not say, "Since the Lord is coming in fiery judgment, be sure you are wise or compassionate or just or generous." He says, "In light of the coming judgment, be sure you are holy and godly." That should give us another clue as to the significance this virtue should hold in our thinking and lifestyle. So then, what is godliness?

Definition of Godliness
Though this Greek word for godliness (εὐσέβεια; transliterated *eusebeia*, pronounced yū-sě´-bā-ah) appears only fifteen times in the New Testament, it was the primary word used for "religion" in the ancient Greek

world. The word means worship that is worthy of God.[7] Barclay defines it as "awe in the presence of that which is more than human, worship which befits that awe, and a life of obedience which befits that reverence."[8]

It was the term for authentic piety or true religion—the kind that was consistently lived whether in the home, the church, or the market-place. It is this comprehensiveness of meaning that makes it the New Testament equivalent to "the fear of the Lord." The fear of the Lord is that awareness of God that evokes reverence for Him, departure from evil, and a life lived on His behalf. It is this similarity to the fear of the Lord that prompted me to define godliness as "a God-fearing lifestyle that promotes righteousness and opposes evil." Scottish preacher John Brown paints the portrait well:

> It is descriptive of the right state of the individual with regard to God—the right state of his mind, of his heart, and of his life—of his thoughts, his affections, and his conduct—the right way of thinking, feeling, and acting towards God.[9]

Godliness is a vibrant, personal relationship with God that manifests itself in actions consistent with Who God is and with what He is doing in the earth.

The Engine of Wholeheartedly Loving God

To put it all together, let's think of it this way. Godliness represents all that makes up the "engine" of loving God with all our heart [Figure 1]. Godliness is made up of devotion (*aretē* and knowledge) and discipline (self-control and endurance). It welds these four virtues of the first two columns together into a focused and powerful combination of spiritual commitment and strength engaged in the Lord's cause on the earth.

Figure 1

GODLINESS — GOOD WORKS

Devotion — *Areté* Knowledge — Discipline — Self-control Endurance — Brotherly Kindness — Love

LOVING GOD WITH ALL MY HEART — LOVING MY NEIGHBOR

The commitment—the *devotion*—to Jesus Christ of *aretē* and knowledge points the soul in the right direction and keeps it on track, but the believer will never go very far without the "horsepower"—the *discipline*—of self-control and endurance. Godliness molds all these together into a package of Christian maturity that captures what it means to love God with your whole heart.

Godliness as a way of life then becomes the force that pulls along the "cars" of good works (brotherly kindness and love). Good works will not get down the track very far without the strength of *discipline* and the Christ-centeredness of *devotion* pulling together. The "personal virtues" that make up columns one and two—the vertical dimension of a man's relationship with Christ—provide the core character for living the "social virtues" of column three—the horizontal dimension of a man's relationship with his neighbor. The "engine" of godliness must be "firing on all four cylinders" of *aretē*, knowledge, self-control, and endurance. Only then can it pull the sometimes heavy loads of brotherly kindness and love.

Like the harnesses for a pair of horses drawing a wagon, godliness keeps both devotion and discipline from galloping off by themselves. Devotion by itself can run off into emotional sentimentality and pietism, and discipline can veer off into hard-nosed self-confidence, legalism, or even arrogance. The harness of godliness keeps them together and hitched to the cause of being salt and light for Christ in the world.

When both steeds are maturing and pulling in tandem, they create a *God-fearing lifestyle* that is truly useful to the Master. They boldly and effectively advance the cause of Jesus Christ in the earth. This is what it means to be godly—to have a lifestyle that is distinctive from the world and useful to Christ. Here is how Paul described it:

> For the grace of God has appeared, bringing salvation for all people, training us to renounce ungodliness and worldly passions, and to live self-controlled, upright, and godly lives in the present age. (Titus 2:11–12 ESV)

As you can see, godliness is a crucial concept for us to understand—and to cultivate![10] *It is cultivated by continuing to develop the previous virtues in order to deploy them in the cause of Jesus Christ.*

So then we must ask ourselves, "What does a godly person look like? What are the marks of maturity? How can we tell when the engine is firing on all four cylinders?"

While entire books have been written on the marks of a godly man,[11] I want to concentrate on one mark in this chapter and two marks in the next chapter.

THE HEART OF A PSALMIST: THE GODLY MAN'S DEVOTION

Because of the virtues preceding it, we know that the godly man possesses a committed pursuit of *aretē* and a mature knowledge of the person, work, and ways of Jesus Christ. We could say that the godly man pursues a relationship with Christ fueled by the knowledge of Christ in order to become like Christ and to be used of Christ in His cause. As a man becomes more godly, he will have increasingly high and frequent thoughts of Christ.

As the godly man grows in godliness, Christ will become ever more dear to him because of His work on his behalf on Calvary's cross. He will see more clearly the utter horror of his sinfulness—that factory of self-centeredness within him that turns him away from God and draws him to the worldliness around him. He will be more stricken by the stinging guilt of his wayward thoughts, his self-serving ambitions, his injury to others, and his failure to keep the laws of God. He feels the burning shame before God when his selfishness is exposed. He knows the piercing conviction and painful chastening of his loving heavenly Father drawing him back to fellowship.[12]

But he has also increasingly experienced the exhilaration of reconciliation when in God-induced contrition he has, like the prodigal, seen the Father, Whom he has forsaken, searching for him "a great way off," running to him, embracing him, and welcoming him home. Through tears of remorse he will confess his stubborn waywardness and sob, "Father, I have sinned against heaven, and in thy sight, and am no more worthy to be called thy son." But his tears of repentance change to sobs of gratitude when the Father assures him, "Your transgression is forgiven; your sin is covered. You have confessed your sins, and I will be faithful and just to forgive your sins and cleanse you from all unrighteousness" (Luke 15:11–24; Psalm 32:1; 1 John 1:9).

Though it grieves him to wrong the One Who has loved him most, a man growing in godliness is not discouraged by his sin since he has often seen the amazing forgiveness of Christ to him time and again. Others who have not seen the amazing work on the cross as clearly are despondent when they find out that their actions have fallen "short of the glory of God" (Romans 3:23). The godly man is humbled more by the grace of God in the light of his sin than he is by his sins themselves.

The godly man never forgets that the Father "brought [him] up also out of an horrible pit, out of the miry clay, and set [his] feet upon a rock, and established [his] goings" (Psalm 40:2). He has known the burden of guilt, the defeat of repeated failures, yet continually marvels that the Father should have pity on him.

Others may misunderstand his thirst for the Savior's words and his love for preaching about his Savior's works. It is grievous to him to boast in anything except "the cross of our Lord Jesus Christ, by whom the world is crucified unto [him], and [he] unto the world" (Galatians 6:14). He is heavy-hearted—and sometimes angered—at the arrogance of a sex-crazed world, which places the sinner's pleasure above the pleasures of his Creator-Redeemer, Jesus Christ. He is likewise grieved when he takes to himself any glory that should rightly go to his Lord.

To him these are not merely poetic religious themes such as you might find in a hymn or a devotional book; they are the personal, heartfelt responses of a grateful, redeemed sinner who loves his God because his God first loved him (1 John 4:19). He has the heart of a psalmist who cries out,

> Bless the Lord, O my soul: and all that is within me, bless his holy name. Bless the Lord, O my soul, and forget not all his benefits: who forgiveth all thine iniquities.

> He hath not dealt with us after our sins, nor rewarded us according to our iniquities. For as the heaven is high above the earth, so great is his mercy toward them that fear him. As far as the east is from the west, so far hath he removed our transgressions from us. Like as a father pitieth his children, so the Lord pitieth them that fear him. For he knoweth our frame; he remembereth that we are dust. (Psalm 103:1–3a, 10–14)

Wilberforce lamented the lack of this kind of vigorous affection for Christ in the professing believers of his day. In chapter 3 of *Real Christianity*, entitled "Inadequate Conceptions of God and of Christian Behavior," he notes that in contrast to the lukewarmness of heart "which is the object of God's disgust and aversion," God "favors and delights in zeal and love." He describes the *devotion* of the godly.

> If we look to the most eminent of the Scripture characters, we find them warm, zealous, and affectionate. When engaged in their favorite work of celebrating the goodness of their Supreme Benefactor, their souls appear to burn within them, and their hearts kindle into rapture. The powers of language are inadequate to express their transports of delight. They call on all nature to swell the chorus, and to unite with them in hallelujahs of gratitude, joy, and praise.
>
> The man after God's own heart abounds in these glowing expressions more than any other writer. The psalmist's writings appear to have been given to us in order to set the tone, as it were, to all succeeding generations.[13]

Nothing erodes progress toward godliness more than today's entertainment mindset and the modern church's casual Christianity. Devotion to Christ, which characterizes the godly man, is cultivated not with a game console in hand by the hour but by gradually increased time spent with a Bible in hand. It does not grow by hours a week spent before a television, computer, or theater screen but by more and more understanding of the person, work, and ways of Jesus Christ through increased time spent in His Word. This is foundational. *Godliness is not accidental; it is intentional.* "The Lord hath set apart him that is godly for himself," (Psalm 4:3) and the godly man thrives on his personal time with God. The Christian who would be godly cannot fill his time with entertainments and recreations. They have their place but should be sampled more like salt sprinkled sparingly on a meal rather than a plate of salt consumed as the main course.

Furthermore, this devotion to Christ is not fueled by high-energy Christian pop concerts, sentimental Kumbaya campfire experiences, or emotional charismatic services. Energy, enthusiasm, and emotional experiences are no substitute for the daily, personal pursuit of Christ in the Word.

The believer must personally and regularly observe Christ in his Bible, meditate upon what he sees, and respond in contrition, commitment, and praise to his Lord and Savior. There is much going on between the godly man and his God, and his personal quiet time with God is measured, not by minutes a week but eventually by hours a week.[14]

Thus, the godly man's life is notably *Christ-centered* rather than *self-centered*. It is his chief distinction. It is this way because he has purposefully cultivated the pursuit of the excellence of Christlikeness and sought the knowledge of Christ in His Word. Godliness has the imprint of this kind of personal devotion to Jesus Christ as its hallmark. Many men today are Christian, but alarmingly few are godly.

GODLINESS TAKES TIME

Please do not get discouraged at this point when you see the high bar of godliness before you as described in this chapter. To be honest with you, studying this topic of godliness has been greatly convicting to my own soul. I am by no means where I want to be in this area, but studying it has increased my desire to increase in godliness.

So, this is the target; godliness grows by making the cultivation of the previous virtues your *lifestyle*. It is the byproduct of a maturing, personal knowledge (*epignōsis*) of Jesus Christ (2 Peter 1:3, 8). It is the fruit of a grace-filled and Word-filled life (2 Peter 3:18, Titus 2:11–12).

Do not be alarmed at the reference to "hours a week" in the descriptions above. This is the *eventual* habit of the one who is godly. He doesn't start out this way. He begins by turning away from the world and its amusements to spend more time in the Word. The more he learns about the person, work, and ways of Jesus Christ, the more time he wants to devote to the study of his Bible.

However, be forewarned. Anyone who decides he must turn off his television and computer—or whatever it is he must stop doing to spend more time with Christ and/or to quit feeding his flesh—will feel a strange awkwardness as he tries to manage his newfound time. His mind will seem strangely agitated as he sits down to read his Bible. Prayer will seem uncomfortable. He won't immediately be able to find a passage of Scripture that seems to speak to him. Even if he tries to read a Christian book or devotional, his efforts will feel clumsy and his brain will not engage quickly. Some of it may be that he does not know what to do with this increased time to be spent with God, but part of it is that he is now working against the inertia of his ingrained habits.

This awkwardness is the normal experience of those who are making major lifestyle adjustments. Habits are not easy to change—including mental habits—but can be changed nonetheless. Let me illustrate it this way. Pick up a pen and write your first name on a piece of paper.

> A man wanting to grow in godliness must cultivate the knowledge of Christ and His ways.

Did you do it? If not, please participate in this exercise. I want you to "feel" something about habitual activity. So, write your first name on a piece of paper.

OK, now that you have written your name with your normal writing hand, put the pen in your other hand and write your name again. Notice how uncomfortable and unnatural the new exercise feels? Did you notice how you had to deliberately think about every movement of your pen to form the letters? That deliberate, uncomfortable action tells you that writing with your other hand is not yet a habit. If you broke your normal writing hand and had to learn to write with the other hand, over a period of time you would find that using that hand would become comfortable and automatic. This explains some of the awkwardness of any change in lifestyle. Familiar habits feel comfortable and come automatically. *Actions that are not habitual feel awkward and require concentration.*

But there is another factor at work here as well. Our sinful nature does not want to give up its indulgences and submit itself to our King. It is easier for us to just go on living the way we are, hoping that we can ignore God and His Word and somehow still have a satisfied and useful life. This is spiritual warfare. This is where the lessons learned while cultivating self-control and endurance are of great value. In fact, many of those lessons are learned at the "fitness station" of establishing a personal time with God every day in the way I am describing in this chapter.

A man wanting to grow in godliness must cultivate the knowledge of Christ and His ways; he must open his Bible and study the words of God. The Word will increasingly expose more selfishness and lusts. He will sit down with paper and pen in hand ready to write down any sins that need to be "confessed and forsaken" (Proverbs 28:13) as he begs

God to "search" him and "try" him to see if there is "any wicked way" in him (Psalm 139:23–24).

He must continue to respond to the conviction of God's Spirit by repentance and resolve to escape the "corruption that is in the world through lust" (2 Peter 1:4). The Word applied in this manner has its cleansing effect. The more he takes nourishment from the Vine and responds to it, the more the Husbandman prunes him in order to bring forth more fruit (John 17:17; 15:1–8). The result is that he grows in Spirit-enabled self-control—the mastery of his passions and the proper ordering of his life around God's priorities.[15]

He continues to eliminate sinful indulgences, worldly companions, and time-wasting activities that draw him away from God. He finds that as he resists the Devil by submitting himself to God, confessing his sins to God, and forsaking his double-mindedness, he experiences more of God's grace. He joyfully finds that as he draws near to God, God draws near to him (James 4:6–8).

Trials will increase his desperation for the Word in which he finds the comforts, grace, and direction of the Savior entirely sufficient to bear up under the pressures of unfavorable circumstances. He sees those tests as God's way of perfecting his character. So, he "lets [endurance] have its [perfecting] work" and learns to "count it all joy" when he comes upon various trials (James 1:2–4).

This is the *normal* course of growth for the believer. Just like the relationship between a new bride and groom must be carefully and sacrificially cultivated to blend two essentially self-centered lives into one to the glory of Christ and the enjoyment of the couple, so the Christian's relationship with Christ is cultivated purposefully and progressively. Two sinners do not naturally and easily learn to live for the other. Good marriages are the result of much self-denial, hours of conversation, many tears of hurt and remorse, repeated times of reconciliation and renewal, and many moments of sheer ecstasy and delight as they give themselves to each other in wholehearted devotion—all of this over years of time. So it is with growth in Christ. It takes time and commitment to cultivate the kind of devotion that forms the foundation of godliness.

By the way, this isn't the *normal* course of growth just for believers who are *starting* to cultivate these essential virtues. It is the *normal* course for every believer who wishes to continue to grow in Christ. Even the mature believer's engine needs work on all four cylinders to keep the engine of godliness properly tuned and useful.

So, seriously ask yourself, "Am I purposing to become distinctively Christ-centered?" "Do I daily delight in the *person* of Christ?" "Would an actual, daily accounting of my time spent reading and meditating upon His words reveal that I am seriously seeking to know Christ and His ways?" "Do I see around me and in the Word the work of Christ?" "Is my mind filled with the ways of Christ?"

If not, are you willing to cultivate *aretē*—the pursuit of the excellence of Christlikeness—and knowledge: the points where this journey begins? If so, go back to chapters 3 and 4 and restudy what it means to "add to your faith virtue, and to virtue knowledge." The engine of godliness cannot run well when these two cylinders are not firing. There will be little power, little joy, and little wisdom in your Christian experience. *The godly man is known for his delight in God*, which is fueled by the process I have been describing.[16] *You may not be there yet, but this is the target, and by the grace of God you can become everything I have portrayed above.* This devotion is the first part of godliness. We will explore two other aspects of godliness in the next chapter.

Chapter Eight

CULTIVATING GODLINESS, PART 2

Add to . . . endurance godliness. (2 Peter 1:6)

THE STRENGTH OF A WARRIOR—
THE GODLY MAN'S DISCIPLINE

The train illustration in the last chapter shows the relationship these essential virtues have to one another. *Devotion* to Christ is first. It sets the direction of the believer's life as we have just seen. It turns his face away from the world and fills his heart with the proper affections for the person, work, and ways of Jesus Christ. Devotion is nurtured in the greenhouse of solitude with Christ in His Word. The Scriptures, however, teach us that there is a second component—*discipline*—that is developed in the gymnasium and displayed on the battlefield. Paul says,

> Discipline yourself for the purpose of godliness; for bodily discipline is only of little profit, but godliness is profitable for all things, since it holds promise for the present life and also for the life to come. (1 Timothy 4:7–8 NASB)

Peter agrees. He says that we must add to devotion (*aretē* and knowledge) the disciplines of Spirit-enabled self-control and endurance, which provide the "horsepower"—the strength—for the godly life. We saw in chapter 5 how the maturing believer must leave behind his chaotic and self-serving ways to bring his passions under control by the Spirit's power. He must be increasingly ruled not by his lusts but by the priorities of the Savior's commands and teachings. He must be developing self-control.

Furthermore, his heart must be learning to bear up under the external pressures of adult responsibilities and of spiritual attack from the world.

He must form a tested and courageous character that displays to others the sustaining grace of God.

The disciplines of self-control and endurance are key ingredients in the courage that characterizes godliness. A courageous man must have his passions under control and must be able to remain true to his commitments even under overwhelming outside pressure.

This is why these two qualities are so highly valued in military training. Military personnel in any branch of our armed forces, when protecting our country's interests, must be able to subordinate their personal passions in order to carry out the country's mission. Their bodies may be screaming for rest while on an extended march, and their hearts may be bursting with longing for those they love at home, but they say no to their desires—and they continue to say no to their desires over the long haul and under great pressure.

Paul understood the necessity of these disciplines in the lives of believers, who are to be actively engaged in the spiritual warfare of their time. He told Timothy—and us—in 2 Timothy 2:3–4,

> Thou therefore endure hardness as a good soldier of Jesus Christ. No man that warreth entangleth himself with the affairs of this life; that he may please him who hath chosen him to be a soldier.

Paul had in an earlier epistle told Timothy that the godly man has a certain mindset. He will first "flee" the covetous and corrupt lifestyle around him. Second, he will "follow after righteousness, godliness, faith, love, [endurance], [gentleness]." And last, "fight the good fight of faith" (1 Timothy 6:11–12). This command to "fight" is what prompted Barclay to say the following about godliness:

> [Godliness] is the *soldier's* word. The Christian is at once the *athlete* and the *soldier*. As the athlete trains himself for the contest so the Christian must train himself to be the follower of Christ. As the soldier must battle towards final victory, so the Christian must dauntlessly and tirelessly face the struggle of goodness.[1]

Imagine how effective a soldier would be if he exercised and trained only when he felt like it. How ready would he be for battle if he practiced his marksmanship and studied battle strategies only when he felt up to it? What if he put on twenty extra pounds by snacking on chips, soft drinks, and ice cream? What if he opted out of the long training hikes where he would have to walk and run for miles in full gear? Instead he stayed in the barracks surfing the Internet and communicating with his friends back home. Or what if he spent the majority of his time off the base partying and shopping?

Of course we cannot even imagine that his officers would let this happen. The reason is obvious. If they did, he would be utterly useless as a soldier. In battle he would be dangerous to himself and to his comrades. He would not possess the skills needed for warfare nor the will to endure hardship for a cause bigger than himself.

The whole purpose of boot camp is to transform a civilian from a life of self-indulgence and ease into a soldier of disciplined usefulness for his country. In a similar fashion, the believer who is not "giving all diligence" to cultivate self-control and endurance will have little usefulness in the kingdom of God. The engine of godliness must have the strength of these disciplines if it is to have an impact.

THE LOYALTY OF A PATRIOT—THE GODLY MAN'S DUTY

Godliness not only possesses great *devotion* and *discipline*, but it embraces a *cause*—"the kingdom of God and His righteousness" (Matthew 6:33). Growing in godliness is characterized by an increasing concern for the Lord's mission on the earth.

The godly man is not just *being good*; he is *doing good*. He realizes there is a battle against the Lord he loves. As his commitment for Christ grows, so does his courage to stand with Christ against the evil within him and the evil around him. He takes the cause of Christ as his own. He sees it as his joyful duty to serve the One he has grown to love and admire. He is a patriot for the kingdom of God. He loves, supports, and defends the cause and kingdom of his Sovereign. Like our men and women in uniform in our postmodern times, he remains a patriot though others may not understand his loyalty because they do not possess his devotion or his discipline.

David the shepherd-king evidenced the godly lifestyle of the psalmist-warrior-patriot. He was a master at proclaiming the excellencies of the God he loved. There is no question about the devotion of David's heart. He did not possess just column-one virtues, however. Throughout his youth he trained himself in column-two virtues. He cultivated self-control, endurance (i.e., discipline), and a concern for God's concerns—godliness.

He did not waste his time on the Judean hillsides while watching his father's sheep. He practiced his harp, wrote psalms of praise to God, practiced his rock slinging, and meditated much upon the nature of God and upon the role that God had called him to play as a king over Israel at some time in the future. As a *result he developed a reputation—even among the young men of his own age—of being a devoted and disciplined man.* When the need arose to find a musician to play for Saul during the king's fits of despondency,

> Growing in godliness is characterized by an increasing concern for the Lord's mission on the earth.

> One of the young men answered, "Behold, I have seen a son of Jesse the Behlehemite, who is skillful in playing, a man of valor, a man of war, prudent in speech, and a man of good presence, and the Lord is with him." (1 Samuel 16:18 ESV)

This was his testimony among his peers! They knew he had disciplined himself to play his instrument well, had prepared himself to be useful as a soldier, had a good control of his tongue, didn't let his appearance become sloppy, and evidenced the presence of the Lord. What a testimony! He had a reputation for both devotion and discipline—key elements in godliness.

But there is another element that made David stand out when his country faced a crisis. Like Wilberforce, he would not melt into the background and pretend he did not see the evil around him, which needed to be confronted—even at great personal risk. As a loyal patriot he would defend God's honor and advance His cause. *This sense of duty and loyalty is the response of godliness.*

David's confrontation of Goliath is a powerful testimony of godliness in action. While others were cowering at the size of the Philistine champion, David was enraged at the blasphemies the heathen warrior was hurling at Israel and Israel's God. David was not concerned about the giant's height; he was concerned about the Lord's name. This is the kind of heavenly perspective that sets the godly man apart from the armies of professing Christians who gather as mere spectators of the battle when they should be participants in the battle.

What is remarkable to me about this scene in 1 Samuel 17 is not only that a mere shepherd boy had the courage to fight a nine-foot giant with only a sling and a pouch full of stones in full view of the Philistine army. What is also astonishing is that one seventeen-year-old boy should step out in front of his own people and do the thing that needed to be done. Every member of Israel's army—including King Saul—had voted in one block: "We are not going to do anything about the evil before us; it is too dangerous."

David did not consider the risk too great to get involved; he considered the dishonor to God too great to go unchallenged. He was compelled to do something. This is where the heart and the strength of the godly man are evidenced in his actions. He will step out in full view of the enemies of his God—and in front of those who are supposed to be on God's side—and do what needs to be done for the name of God. *The godly man embraces God's causes.* The godly man is not passive, nor is he cowardly.

David said to Saul, "Let no man's heart fail because of him; thy servant will go and fight with this Philistine" (1 Samuel 17:32). That was not the boast of youthful recklessness or pride. It was the confidence of a man who had seen God work before on his behalf. He had seen God deliver him from lesser enemies—a lion, a bear, boredom, loneliness, and perhaps ridicule since he, as the youngest, had to take the most menial jobs of the family business—keeping sheep.

Because David knew and trusted God, he didn't fear men. He boldly met the giant in the valley of Elah, shouting in the hearing of both armies,

> Thou comest to me with a sword, and with a spear, and with a shield: but I come to thee in the name of the Lord of hosts, the God of the armies of Israel, whom thou hast defied. This day will the Lord deliver thee into mine hand . . . that all the earth may know that there is a God in Israel. And all this assembly [those Israelites who were too cowardly to fight and those Philistines who thought they had the battle wrapped up] shall know that the

Lord saveth not with sword and spear: for the battle is the Lord's, and he will give you into our hands. (1 Samuel 17:45–47)

The valley echoed with his words as he ran to the giant, depending upon the God of Israel to use his well-practiced rock slinging to do its intended work. The giant fell, and the name of God was vindicated before the heathen, but most notably before God's people—the ones who should have known better.

This is the godly man—the psalmist-warrior-patriot. This is the man who is so committed to his God that he will advance His cause no matter what the risk or loss to himself. *There is no genuine godliness if there is no heartfelt devotion and love for Jesus Christ. And there is no godliness if there is no brave-hearted engagement against the enemies of the Lord.*

David was not contemptuous of countrymen who would not risk their lives for the Lord. He was not arrogant and self-assured in proclaiming his courage and skill. He was focused on one thing—the honor of the One he loved most. He was willing to risk all. This is devotion; this is strength; this is loyalty; this is godliness.

It is this sort of godliness that Peter says we must diligently cultivate to have Christlike character. And sadly, as in the days of Israel, there are few today who will step out from the crowd of self-protective onlookers within the church and face the giants of evil that threaten the people of God and dishonor the name of God. Often it is because they do not truly love Christ. Others who have a measure of devotion to Christ have not cultivated enough self-control and endurance to take the heat of ridicule should they speak up. Oftentimes, however, there is little sense of the danger of evil itself. The enemy has penetrated the camp, and they don't think it is so bad. Their strategy has become peaceful coexistence with evil.

CORRUPTION IN THE CAMP

Wilberforce was greatly concerned about the insensitivity of God's people to the evil that lay within their own hearts and permeated their culture. He devoted an entire chapter to "Inadequate Conceptions of Human Nature." He says, "Most educated, professing Christians either overlook or deny the corruption and weakness of human nature."[2] Later he laments,

There appears in the minds of most nominal Christians a profoundly inadequate idea of the guilt and evil of sin. It is as if religion were supposed to be no more than an affair for the police. Offenses are seen only as injuries to society, but not as offensive to God. . . . But the Word of God estimates actions by a far less accommodating standard. There we read of no *little* sins. . . . Scripture considers sin' rebellion against the sovereignty of God. Every different act of sin equally violates His law.[3]

Sin is seen by the godly man as an intrusion of the enemy into territory that rightly belongs to God.[4] He sees himself as a warrior engaged in battle and thus must put on the "whole armor of God." He knows that he is not wrestling "against flesh and blood, but against the rulers, against the authorities, against the cosmic powers over this present darkness, against the spiritual forces of evil in the heavenly places" (Ephesians 6:11–18 ESV). He does not see himself as a tourist upon the earth, visiting all the exciting sites and collecting souvenirs; he sees himself as a soldier in occupied enemy territory. He knows he and his compatriots are targets the enemy wants to destroy. He keeps his eye watchful, his weapons ready, and his mission ever before him.

How does the godly man view evil and what actions does he insist must be taken against it? The Scriptures are replete with examples of godly men confronting evil in God's people. One such man was the apostle Paul.

When Paul wrote the Corinthian church, he boldly addressed many concerns. One particularly grievous offense was the church's toleration of sexual immorality among its members. One particular member was even cohabiting with his stepmother. The church, rather than removing this unrepentant member, boasted of their tolerance and open-mindedness. Paul forcefully addressed their attitude.

Ye are [arrogant], and have not rather mourned, that he that hath done this deed might be taken away from among you. . . . Your [boasting] is not good. Know ye not that a little leaven leaveneth the whole lump? Purge out therefore the old leaven. . . . Put away from among yourselves that wicked person. (1 Corinthians 5:2, 6–7, 13)

Corruption—in our own soul or in the souls of others—does not stay contained. Neither is evil benign. Like a cancer it grows and destroys. Because of the godly man's pursuit of God he knows what diligence against his own sinfulness he must maintain. He knows the awful darkness that soon covers his soul when he tolerates sin in his life. It robs him of his peace and joy, and more importantly, robs his King of His rightful honor. He knows the same corruptive process works in the hearts of others if they are allowed to continue in their sin unchallenged. Satan's cause flourishes and God's diminishes. When the godly man sees a brother "overtaken in a fault," he knows his duty is to "restore such an one in the spirit of meekness; considering [himself], lest [he] also be tempted" (Galatians 6:1–2). So he gets involved in the lives of others.

Paul's godliness compelled him to address the evil in this assembly. His view of immorality and his means of dealing with it were very different from those of the church today. Today believers who know that another believer is corrupting his life with immorality are silent about it. They open their mouths only to gossip. Not only does their tolerance of evil permit that evil to go unchecked but *their passivity corrupts their own souls as well.* They are being made indifferent to evil and are tampering with the sensitivity of their own consciences. This is exactly what happened with Lot. He is the polar opposite of godliness.

A LESSON FROM LOT

Abraham's nephew Lot struck off on his own and settled outside the city gates of Sodom, according to Genesis 13. While Lot saw the possibilities for financial gain, God commented that "the men of Sodom were wicked and sinners before the Lord exceedingly" (Genesis 13:13) and planned for the city's destruction. Genesis 18 informs us that God, as a result of Abraham's intercession, agreed to spare Lot and his immediate family before He brought judgment (Genesis 18–19).

Three angels—looking like normal travelers—entered Sodom to bring Lot out and lodged overnight with his family. A homosexual mob stormed the house demanding that the visitors be delivered over to them for abuse. Lot offered his two virgin daughters to the men in place of the strangers, but to no avail. The angels intervened by blinding the mob, which eventually dispersed.

That evening Lot tried to persuade the husbands of his married daughters to leave the city with him the next day, but Lot's words sounded like a big joke to them. Upon daybreak the angels compelled Lot, his wife, and his two single daughters to leave Sodom, commanding them not to look back.

> The testimony of passive believers who refuse to be salt and light is useless.

Lot's wife, as we know, disobeyed and was turned into a pillar of salt on the spot. God rained down fire and brimstone on the cities, and Abraham from a distance saw smoke billowing to the sky from Sodom and Gomorrah like "the smoke of a furnace" (Genesis 19:28). Lot and his daughters fled to a cave in the nearby mountains, where over the course of the next two days his daughters got him drunk and took turns sleeping with him in order to carry on the family name with sons.

There were many troubling outcomes from this man's bankrupt character. He had lost all influence with his married children and wife, which resulted in their deaths. Furthermore, Lot was so morally deranged that he offered his virgin daughters as playthings to placate the sex-crazed crowd at his door. Had he been a man of courage and valor, he would have died protecting both the visitors and his daughters. The values of his own daughters were so corrupted by Lot's Sodom-influenced ways that they resorted to incest to preserve the family line.

Though this story is horribly tragic, it was predictable. As a lesson to us, God tells us the process that led to this decline. Note carefully what God says was happening behind the scenes of Lot's daily life in Sodom.

> [God] delivered just Lot, [tortured] with the filthy [lifestyle] of the wicked: (for that righteous man dwelling among them, in seeing and hearing, [wore down] his righteous soul from day to day with their unlawful deeds). (2 Peter 2:7–8)

Don't miss the lesson God is laying out for us here: *a believing man's soul is tortured and worn down when he regularly sees and hears the wicked deeds of the world's filthy lifestyle and does not exercise his will against that evil.*

Lot's conscience—along with the consciences of his daughters—was so desensitized by the evil lifestyles they observed every day that they eventually became engaged in activities they would have never dreamed of being a part of before they entered Sodom. Most notably their morals about sexual matters were reprogrammed. We know that Lot did not resist the corruption around him because neither the townspeople nor his own sons-in-law took his words seriously when he finally did speak up (Genesis 19:9, 14).

So it is in the church today. The testimony of passive believers who refuse to be salt and light is similarly as useless. Like salt that has lost its flavor, their influence is "good for nothing" (Matthew 5:13). How do these believers get to the place that when they finally speak up about something, their words are dismissed as a joke?

These Christians try to fit in; they want to blend into the crowd. To do so they have to compromise their distinction as children of light. The more they conform in order to be accepted, the more they harden their own conscience against the evil they see and hear. The more their conscience is desensitized, the more they can partake of evil themselves without its "bothering" them. So it goes, until they have lost their Christian conscience and any significant Christian influence.

It is not a stretch at all to apply Peter's words to how God's people today wear down their souls with the filthy entertainment they see and hear. If the profanity, violence, materialism, and immorality were happening in real life in their family or in the lives of those they work with, they would have an opportunity to testify of their faith in order to reach these lost folks with the gospel.

They could intercede for them before the throne of heaven in prayer, begging God to save the souls of their loved ones and coworkers. They could daily read their Bibles, looking for direction from God about how to respond to the issues that come up every day. In short, they would not be passive; they would be actively engaged in kingdom warfare. They would know that the eternal souls of men and women are at stake if they sit by and do nothing.

None of that is possible when watching degenerate behavior on a movie or television program. The wickedness on the screen can stir no burden for the lost people living such debauched lives in the story. They cannot pray for them; they cannot search their Bibles for truth to present to them. They cannot ask their Christian friends to pray for the movie's antagonists and protagonists. They know the story line is make-believe but forget that the evil influence on their soul is real.

There is no way a believer can exercise his will against the evil he sees and hears onscreen except to turn away from it—leave the room or turn it off. If he doesn't leave, he cannot escape the results—a worn-down soul and a desensitized conscience. Believers who tolerate this kind of wickedness as entertainment begin to tolerate it in the lives of others they should be trying to influence away from ungodliness. Eventually, they tolerate it in their own lives, and their children learn their ways. The results are predictable—and preventable.

Lot was righteous—he was one of God's own—but he was not godly. A godly man speaks up. He knows what a little leaven does to the lump. He doesn't tolerate evil in his own life, and he lovingly but courageously addresses it in the lives of other believers. Evil left unaddressed corrupts both the evildoer and the evil tolerator.

The Old Testament prophets and the New Testament apostles provide ample examples of what godliness looks like. *Godly men and women are spokespersons for God.* They are His voice calling the vast majority of the church to leave their mediocrity and pursue full devotion to Jesus Christ and His cause in the earth. They are His voice in evangelizing the lost and then discipling those converts "to observe all things whatsoever [Christ has] commanded" (Matthew 28:19–20). Everything else is incidental to that mission. And they are willing to do that at any cost.

Listen to Paul's response to his companions when they warned him of the impending persecution that was sure to come his way if he persisted in his plans to minister in Jerusalem.

> But none of these things move me, neither count I my life dear unto myself, so that I might finish my course with joy, and the ministry, which I have received of the Lord Jesus, to testify the gospel of the grace of God . . . for I am ready not to be bound only, but also to die at Jerusalem for the name of the Lord Jesus. (Acts 20:24; 21:13)

This is the heartbeat of a Christian patriot—one who loves the Lord enough to advance His kingdom even if it means he loses his own life. This is the response of godliness.

How About an Endorsement?

Most of us will never run for political office, but each of us can use our influence to endorse someone who is stepping out and representing our concerns. We can put bumper stickers on our cars, display campaign signs in our yards, attend fundraising events, and help man the call center for our candidate.

In a similar manner, you may not be the point man for a righteous concern among your Christian friends or in your church because someone else has already spoken out against wrongdoing, but you can publicly endorse the person who is taking the right position. Unfortunately, when a pastor who is doing right gets resistance from church members, the only ones who speak up are those opposing him. They are quite ready to "plant yard signs" and volunteer to work "call centers" to get people on their side.

Godly believers will join with the roommate, the youth director, the student leader, the professor, or the parent who is taking the right position and will encourage him in his right cause. They will not let the opposition have the only voice. What a tragedy that those who agree with a righteous position remain silent! *God's people need to support righteousness whenever they see it and encourage the people who are sticking their necks out for what is right.*[5]

Paul told Titus to groom and deploy into church leadership men who would "be able to give instruction in sound doctrine and also to rebuke those who contradict it. For there are many who are insubordinate, empty talkers and deceivers. . . . They must be silenced. . . . Therefore, rebuke them sharply that they may be sound in the faith" (Titus 1:9–11, 13 ESV).

If no one else is speaking up, you may have to be the David and be the first to oppose what is wrong. If someone already has, join him. Don't let a David enter the battle against the Philistines alone. The godly man knows where God has drawn the line in the sand and gets on God's side of the line.

The Last Days

The warning is clear to those of us who live in the last days before the Lord's return. "Evil men and seducers shall wax worse and worse, deceiving and being deceived." We also know that "all that will live godly in Christ Jesus shall suffer persecution" as the times worsen (2 Timothy 3:13–12). Meditate upon Hebrews 11 and join the ranks of those who please God by living all of life for the sake of His name no matter what the cost.

It is this godliness that sets the Hebrews 11 Hall of Famers, the prophets, apostles, martyrs, and persecuted believers of the early church apart from the libertines and the casual, worldly Christians of Peter's day—and of ours.

Others may scorn the godly man's "narrowness" about worldly indulgences, mock his desire to do right, and ridicule his efforts to help others walk on the "narrow way," but his zeal for righteousness is fueled by his affection for his Savior.

He is a puzzle to the ungodly but also to the lukewarm Christians around him. "With respect to this they are surprised when [he does] not join them in the same flood of debauchery, and they malign [him]." But he knows that he "will give account to him who is ready to judge the living and the dead" (1 Peter 4:4–5 ESV). He cares not for the praise of men for he enjoys the smile of God.

In conclusion, consider Revelation 7:9–12 about how this battle will end. We will join the "great multitude, which no man could number, of all nations and kindreds, and people, and tongues" and will stand "before the throne and before the Lamb, clothed with white robes, and palms in their hands." And we will cry with a loud voice saying, "Salvation to our God which sitteth upon the throne, and unto the Lamb." We will join the angelic hosts saying, "Amen: Blessing, and glory, and wisdom, and thanksgiving, and honour, and power, and might, be unto our God for ever and ever. Amen."

Just so we don't miss who is speaking here, the apostle John tells us in verses 14–17,

> These are they which came out of great tribulation, and have washed their robes, and made them white in the blood of the Lamb. Therefore are they before the throne of God, and serve him day and night in his temple: and he that sitteth on the throne shall dwell among them. They shall hunger no more, neither thirst any more; neither shall the sun light on them, nor any heat. For

the Lamb which is in the midst of the throne shall feed them, and shall lead them unto living fountains of waters: and God shall wipe away all tears from their eyes.

These are those who lived a God-fearing lifestyle for the cause of Jesus Christ. This is why Peter says to you and me that if these virtues are abounding in us "an entrance shall be ministered unto you abundantly into the everlasting kingdom of our Lord and Saviour Jesus Christ" (2 Peter 1:11). This is what awaits the godly. Give all diligence to cultivate godliness!

Part Three

THE TRADEMARK OF CHRISTIAN CHARACTER

Chapter Nine

CULTIVATING BROTHERLY KINDNESS

Add to . . . godliness brotherly kindness. (2 Peter 1:7)

Maybe you've heard the following quip that has showed up in the humor sections of church bulletins for years.

> To dwell above with the Lord we love,
> O, that will be glory;
> To dwell below with those we know,
> Now that's another story.

We chuckle because we all recognize the dilemma we often find ourselves in—we know we should have fewer disagreements with and more affection for those within the body of Christ, but at times reality proves otherwise. Some Christians are just not easy to get along with.

In fact, sometimes it seems that nonbelievers can be easier to work with than those who claim to be brothers and sisters in Christ. Even though we are "partakers of the divine nature" with every other believer, we fall too quickly into relationship-destroying sins such as gossip, bitterness, anger, partiality, and envy—actions that bear marks of the "corruption that is in the world through lust" more than marks of the "divine nature" (2 Peter 1:4). It should not surprise us then that Peter commands us to cultivate brotherly kindness, for it is a virtue that does not come as naturally as we would like to suppose.

The apostle places this as the first of the two "social virtues" in his list—love being the second. (Once again notice on the chart the placement of these virtues in column 3.) The fact that he includes both brotherly kindness and love in his list of virtues tells us that there is some sort of distinction between them, and the fact that brotherly kindness appears in the catalog of lists *before* love indicates that it is somehow subordinate to the crowning virtue of love. We can expect, therefore, that brotherly kindness will have some elements in common with love but can expect as well that love will include much more than is demanded in brotherly kindness. Let's begin our study with a look at how the single Greek word translated here "brotherly kindness" was used in New Testament times.

DEFINITION OF BROTHERLY KINDNESS

Philadelphia (φιλαδελφία; transliterated *philadelphia*) is a compound word made up of two smaller words: *philia* meaning "affection" and *adelphos* meaning "brother." It is translated "brotherly kindness" in the KJV and NASB and "brotherly affection" in the ESV. Both of these renderings capture an important component of the word's meaning, but neither translation captures it all. The term is actually quite rich.

What is most interesting is that in the secular Greek world of New Testament times, the word was reserved only for blood relatives. The early church extended its use to those outside the natural family because they considered anyone in the body of Christ a "brother" or "sister" in Christ. Because of the rigid class and family distinctions maintained out of pride and competition, the unbelievers despised the Christian use of this term outside the natural family lines.[1] In fact, Green and Lucas comment that "the New Testament is the only place where the word has been found outside the context of the home. A first-century reader would therefore come across it here with a sense of shock."[2]

As I mentioned earlier in this book, the apostles often baptized common words with distinctively Christian meaning when they brought those words into the use of the church and the Scriptures. This is another example of that practice. That means that we will have to look more closely at the Scriptures themselves to learn exactly what the apostles meant since the word had a significantly different meaning to the Greek world around them.

The apostles are quite clear that this virtue was to be extended to all that are in the family of God. Listen to their commands to the church—to us.

> Love one another with brotherly affection [*philadelphia*]. Outdo one another in showing honor. (Romans 12:10 ESV)

Let brotherly love [*philadelphia*] continue. (Hebrews 13:1)

Seeing ye have purified your souls in obeying the truth through the Spirit unto [sincere] love of the brethren [*philadelphia*], see that ye love one another with a pure heart fervently. (1 Peter 1:22)

But as touching brotherly love [*philadelphia*] ye need not that I write unto you: for ye yourselves are taught of God to love one another. (1 Thessalonians 4:9)

We know from these commands and from the one in our text in 2 Peter 1, whereby we are commanded to "add . . . brotherly kindness," that God expects us to be developing and displaying this Christlike virtue. So how do we do that? What fuels this affection? What distinguishes brotherly affection from the next virtue—love?

Though we will develop the meaning of "love" in more detail in the next chapter, we should note here that brotherly affection, or kindness, points to a feeling of affection toward and a willingness to share with those who are members of the "family"—those who share something in common. Love, the final virtue in Peter's list, which we will contemplate in chapter 10, is a virtue exercised often toward those who are not like us and may even be repulsive to us. I have tried to capture the sense of *philadelphia* by defining it as "a God-engendered affection for and service to those in the 'household of faith.'"

Brotherly affection is cultivated by diligently cultivating the previous virtues and then reminding ourselves of what we have in common with the one who is our brother or sister in Christ. The redeemed church is made up of believers from "every kindred, and tongue, and people, and nation" (Revelation 5:9). We may be different in many ways, but we share "one Lord, one faith, one baptism, one God and Father of all" (Ephesians 4:5–6). We are different only in superficial ways; we are the same in essential ways. There is more that joins us than divides us.

> We are different only in superficial ways; we are the same in essential ways.

The world through its emphasis on multiculturalism—and its ally, political correctness—tries to achieve unity by forcing everyone to protect, tolerate, and even celebrate the distinctives of others; the Bible promotes unity by commanding us to reinforce what we have in common.

We are to see beyond—and even subordinate—our differences to our similarities. Christ has bought us all, sought us all, found us all, and claimed us all. We are all Christ's if we know Him as personal Savior.

It is actually this spiritual commonality between two believers that makes their bond closer than two natural brothers who do not know Christ. But this commonality must be cultivated because we naturally gravitate to those who are like us in more superficial ways—they share common interests or pursuits, hail from the same part of the country or the world, like the same music or fashions, come from the same ethnic or economic background, or support the same ball teams or race car driver we do. The essence of friendship and the essence of brotherly kindness are similar in that they both are grounded in the sharing of something in common.

CYBER-FRIENDS

Consider with me for a moment how this commonality functions in the cyberspace of social networking. This medium allows us to pursue similarities to an almost obsessive degree. We can remain connected with hundreds of people "like us" in forums, threads, and groups dedicated to our interests. Consequently, we can develop a very strong bond—even an identity—by continually interacting only with those who share our personal preferences, tastes, experiences, or struggles. That can be helpful; it can also be destructive and self-limiting. While this kind of cocooning provides us with the security of the familiar, it shields us from the experiences that God intends to use to stretch us. In addition, when the similarity that links us to others is a superficial one, linking with more people with superficial interests only further entrenches that superficiality into our identity—making it harder for us to abandon it to become a person with higher priorities in life.

Long before social networking was a possibility, Leon Morris in his classic work on love commented on C. S. Lewis's discussion of friendship in Lewis's book *The Four Loves*. The discussion is germane to our study since the affection of friendship is similar to the affection among brethren.

> Friendship, as Lewis understands it, is built on common insight or interest or taste, something that friends have in common but that other people do not share (p. 70; p. 84).

Friendship is a stimulating affair, bringing out the best in each of
the friends. But, even though each is strengthened by the contribution of the others, this very strength can be a danger. . . .
"[Friendship] is ambivalent. It makes good men better and bad
men worse" (94f). Just as the group strengthens the friends' good
points, so it serves as a justification for their weaknesses. The
friends refuse to be controlled by outside opinion, because this is
part of what friendship means. This means that when outsiders
are wrong, friends strengthen one another in the right. But it also
means that when those outside are right, the friends may well
encourage one another to continue in a wrong way. Their very
friendship hinders them from seeing what is right in the conten-
tions of outsiders. Further, their bond may lead to pride, which
despises those not admitted to the intimacy of the circle.[3]

We see that warm feelings toward someone can be a positive or a negative depending upon whether the thing we hold in common is truly
important in God's scheme of things[4] and whether it is being used to
promote the glory of God or our own pleasure (1 Corinthians 10:31).
We must understand then that brotherly affection is built by focusing
on the things we share in common.

I find great delight in walking across the campus of Bob Jones University, consciously looking at each group of students I pass and thinking
that these are my brothers and sisters in Christ. They may be dressed
differently, be from another culture, or be of a different ethnic background than I, but my heart is warmed toward them as I think of them
as children of my own Father in heaven. No matter what differences appear on the surface, our stronger identity is in our union with Christ.

It is this conscious effort to remind ourselves of our common family
origins and common family goals that forms the foundation of brotherly
affection. This is a natural outgrowth for the one who has been cultivating godliness and the virtues before it. He has been growing in loving God with all his heart, building commitment to Jesus Christ, and
subordinating all his life under the lordship of Christ. The godly man's
goal is to love what God loves and hate what God hates. Since he has
grown in love for the Father and His Son, he does not find it hard to
love the rest of the Father's children in the way the Father loves them.

ONE-ANOTHER PASSAGES

To discover what brotherly affection looks like, we don't have to look any further than a collection of Scripture passages that feature another Greek term ἀλλήλων (transliterated *allēlōn*)—commonly translated "one another" in the New Testament. It actually appears over ninety times in the New Testament, but only a handful apply to our study here. By examining these passages, we can come to a pretty clear understanding of how we are to treat one another in the family of God; we will know what brotherly kindness/affection looks like.

The first thing we need to note is the "one another" passages that teach us that we are all part of the body of Christ. Note how Paul presents this idea in Romans 12:3–5:

> For I say, through the grace given unto me, to every man that is among you, not to think of himself more highly than he ought to think; but to think soberly, according as God hath dealt to every man the measure of faith. For as we have many members in one body, and all members have not the same office: so we, being many, are one body in Christ, and every one members one of another [*allēlōn*].

Paul points out in this passage that at the heart of this kind of unity is humility—the mindset whereby a man sees himself as he really is. Later in verse 16 of this passage he says, "Be of the same mind one toward another. . . . be not wise in your own conceits." He warns us against the pride that will divide us (see also Proverbs 13:10).

Every one of us plays a part that is important in the body, but none of us is more important than anyone else in the body. Everyone is needed. Paul points this out in even greater detail in 1 Corinthians 12:14–20.

> For the body is not one member, but many. If the foot shall say, Because I am not the hand, I am not of the body; is it therefore not of the body? And if the ear shall say, Because I am not the eye, I am not of the body; is it therefore not of the body? If the whole body were an eye, where were the hearing? If the whole were hearing, where were the smelling? But now hath God set the members every one of them in the body, as it hath pleased him. And if they were all one member, where were the body? But now are they many members, yet but one body.

Paul further teaches us in verses 21–24 that the parts of the physical body naturally care for one another. If we get a splinter in a finger or a speck of dust in our eye, stub our toe, or cut ourselves with a steak knife, our whole body rallies to the emergency in order to bring relief. In a similar fashion Paul tells us "that the members [of the body of Christ] should have the same care one for another. And [if] one member suffer, all the members suffer with it; or one member be honoured, all the members rejoice with it. Now ye are the body of Christ, and members in particular" (1 Corinthians 12:25–27).

This is not merely an illustration of how we ought to treat each other; we are *actually* members one of another in the same manner that Christ is *actually* the head of us all. It is upon this foundation of body life that all the other "one another" instructions rest.

We will look at those instructions in two categories—the *dispositions* (or attitudes) we are to have toward one another as a result of this unity and the *duties* we are to perform toward each other. We cannot look at every "one another" passage in the New Testament, but we can get a good sense of what brotherly kindness/affection looks like by examining a representative sampling.

DISPOSITIONS TO ONE ANOTHER

First, let's consider the dispositions—the attitudes—that show we recognize our unity as members of Christ's family. Take a moment to reflect upon the following instructions about the attitudes we are to have toward one another in the "household of faith."

Be warm-hearted	Be kindly affectioned one to another [*allēlōn*] with brotherly love [*philadelphia*]. (Romans 12:10)
Be others-focused	In honour preferring one another [*allēlōn*]. (Romans 12:10)
Be like-minded	Now the God of [endurance and encouragement] grant you to be like-minded one toward another [*allēlōn*] according to Christ Jesus. (Romans 15:5)

Be kind	Let all bitterness, and wrath, and anger . . . and evil speaking be put away from you, with all malice: and be ye kind one to another [*allēlōn*]. (Ephesians 4:31–32)
Be tenderhearted	Be . . . tenderhearted . . . [to] one another [*allēlōn*]. (Ephesians 4:32)
Be humble	Likewise, ye younger, submit yourselves unto the elder. Yea, all of you be subject one to another [*allēlōn*], and be clothed with humility: for God resisteth the proud, and giveth grace to the humble. (1 Peter 5:5)

Ask yourself, "Am I known to be a warm-hearted, others-focused, like-minded, kind, tenderhearted, and humble person to all believers? Are these my dominant *character*-istics? In other words, is this my *character*?"

If you answered yes, ask yourself, "Am I this way only with people who like me or with people whom I like, or am I also this way with all believers—*because* they are believers?" In other words, "Is this truly the character of my life—the fruit of godliness—or is kindness and acceptance just another way for me to get what I want with certain people? People who can offer me nothing don't get red-carpet treatment." This kind of relational selectivity is not the "brotherly kindness" Peter is speaking about. It is merely self-serving manipulation to get what I want.

At the heart of each of these attitudes is humility—the attitude that truly "esteem[s] other better than themselves" (Philippians 2:3). Even if this next passage in Philippians 2 is familiar to you, stop to consider it reflectively in light of the things we have been talking about. This kind of humility is at the heart of what it means to be Christlike.

Do nothing from rivalry or conceit, but in humility count others more significant than yourselves. Let each of you look not only to his own interests, but also to the interests of others. Have this mind among yourselves, which is yours in Christ Jesus, who, though he was in the form of God, did not count equality with God a thing to be grasped, but made himself nothing, taking the form of a servant, being born in the likeness of men. And being found in human form, he humbled himself by becoming obedient to the point of death, even death on a cross. Therefore God has highly exalted him and bestowed on him the name that is above every name, so that at the name of Jesus every knee should bow, in heaven and on earth and under the earth, and every tongue confess that Jesus Christ is Lord, to the glory of God the Father. (Philippians 2:3–11 ESV)

The kind of others-focused attitude we have been seeing in the "one another" passages is not possible without the kind of humility seen in Jesus Christ. He considered Himself a servant—someone Who existed for the benefit of someone else. This is the mind of Christ.

You can see this attitude in how He patiently put up with the foibles of His disciples, tenderly spoke with the woman at the well, kindly dealt with the questions of Nicodemus, tenderly touched blind eyes and healed lame beggars, accepted Samaritans, and submitted Himself to Pilate and the Jewish leaders. He was no pacifist or wimp, however. He could make powerful statements of righteousness when the temple needed to be cleansed or Pharisees needed to be rebuked. Though these leaders eventually crucified Him, He looked upon them with pity from the cross and begged His Father to bring them at some time to repentance whereby the Father could forgive them of the things they were doing in their darkness and ignorance.

Overall, there was something about His disposition that set Him apart from other leaders of His time. He was humble, and it affected his relationships. You and I must ask ourselves and answer honestly, "Do we have the mind of Christ; is this our mindset toward others; is this our disposition?"

This Christlike disposition—this essential virtue of brotherly kindness—is the fruit of cultivating the previous virtues. A believer who daily is pursuing *aretē*—the excellence of Christlikeness—daily seeking the *knowledge* of the person, work, and ways of Jesus Christ in His Word; daily subordinating his personal desires to what he has discovered in the Word (*self-control*); daily remaining faithful to those things that are right no matter what pressure is upon him (*endurance*); and daily committed to advancing the kingdom of God even at risk to himself (*godliness*) will have what it takes to look tenderly and compassionately on others. Loving his neighbor in this way is the natural outgrowth of loving God with his whole heart.

The others-centered disposition of brotherly kindness cannot be built upon a self-centered mindset. A self-centered mindset cannot be overcome except by a pursuit of a Christ-centered lifestyle as outlined in the previous virtues. Column-one and column-two virtues must be maturing if brotherly kindness is to flourish.

DUTIES TO ONE ANOTHER

Loving our neighbor is not just a matter of attitudes—of dispositions. It involves duties—actions and deeds that come from the right kind of heart attitude. The Scriptures give us several in the "one another" passages. You can substitute the words *brothers and sisters* for the word *others* in the headings below.

Edify others	Let us therefore follow after the things which make for peace, and things wherewith one may edify another [*allēlōn*]. (Romans 14:19)
Accept others	Wherefore [accept] one another [*allēlōn*], as Christ also [accepted] us to the glory of God. (Romans 15:7)
Forbear others	With all lowliness and meekness, with long-suffering, forbearing one another [*allēlōn*] in love. (Ephesians 4:2)
Obey others in authority	Submitting yourselves one to another [*allēlōn*] in the fear of God. (Ephesians 5:21)[5]
Caution/reprove others	And I myself also am [satisfied about] you, my brethren, that ye also are full of goodness, filled with all knowledge, able also to admonish one another [*allēlōn*]. (Romans 15:14)
Forgive others	Be . . . forgiving one another [*allēlōn*], even as God for Christ's sake hath forgiven you. (Ephesians 4:32)

	Forgiving one another [allēlōn], if any man have a quarrel against any: even as Christ forgave you, so also do ye. (Colossians 3:13)
Forbear others	Forbearing one another [allēlōn]. (Colossians 3:13)
Tell the truth to others	Lie not one to another [allēlōn], seeing that ye have put off the old man with his deeds. (Colossians 3:9)
Comfort others	Wherefore comfort one another [allēlōn] with these words. (1 Thessalonians 4:18)
Motivate others	And let us consider how to stir up one another [allēlōn] to love and good works. (Hebrews 10:24 ESV)
Confess sins to others	Confess your faults one to another [allēlōn]. (James 5:16)
Pray for others	Pray for one another [allēlōn]. (James 5:16)
Give to others	[Show] hospitality one to another [allēlōn] without [complaining]. (1 Peter 4:9)

In addition, there are several passages that simply say "love one another" (allēlōn): Romans 13:8; 1 Thessalonians 3:12; 1 Peter 1:22; 1 John 3:11; 3:23; 4:7, 11–12; 2 John 5). I won't comment on them here since the entire next chapter will be devoted to the topic of love. These instructions of what we can do in a positive way to others are accompanied by a couple of instructions of things that we should not do to one another.

| Don't badmouth others | Speak not evil one of another [allēlōn], brethren. (James 4:11) |
| Don't grumble about others | Do not grumble against one another [allēlōn], brothers. (James 5:9 ESV) |

A prayerful consideration of these passages reveals that cultivating brotherly kindness/affection requires a robust maturity since it is so others-centered, and our natures are naturally self-centered. The apostle John raises the bar especially high in 1 John 2:9–11.

> He that saith he is in the light, and hateth his brother, is in darkness even until now. He that loveth his brother abideth in the light, and there is none occasion of stumbling in him. But he that hateth his brother is in darkness, and walketh in darkness, and knoweth not whither he goeth, because that darkness hath blinded his eyes.

> We know that we have passed from death unto life, because we love the brethren. He that loveth not his brother abideth in death. (1 John 3:14)

> If a man say, I love God, and hateth his brother, he is a liar: for he that loveth not his brother whom he hath seen, how can he love God whom he hath not seen? And this commandment have we from him, That he who loveth God love his brother also. (1 John 4:20–21)

So you see, this matter of loving our brother by cultivating "a God-engendered affection for and service to those in the 'household of faith'" is not a trivial thing with God. It strikes at the very center of who we are. If we hate the Father's children, God says we have no love for the Father.

The Little Member That Destroys the Members

Before we leave this topic of brotherly kindness/affection, it is necessary to speak briefly about the one thing that destroys relationships with others more than anything else—an unbridled tongue. James says that "the tongue is a little member" but easily destroys other believers—members of Christ's body. He says,

> If anyone does not stumble in what he says, he is a [mature] man, able also to bridle his whole body. If we put bits into the mouths of horses so that they obey us, we guide their whole bodies as well. Look at the ships also: though they are so large and are driven by strong winds, they are guided by a very small rudder wherever the will of the pilot directs. So also the tongue is a small member, yet it boasts of great things.

CULTIVATING BROTHERLY KINDNESS

How great a forest is set ablaze by such a small fire! And the tongue is a fire, a world of unrighteousness. The tongue is set among our members, staining the whole body, setting on fire the entire course of life, and set on fire by hell. For every kind of beast and bird, of reptile and sea creature, can be tamed and has been tamed by mankind, but no human being can tame the tongue. It is a restless evil, full of deadly poison. With it we bless our Lord and Father, and with it we curse people who are made in the likeness of God. From the same mouth come blessing and cursing. My brothers, these things ought not to be so. Does a spring pour forth from the same opening both fresh and salt water? Can a fig tree, my brothers, bear olives, or a grapevine produce figs? Neither can a salt pond yield fresh water.

> People who are not kind lack Christian character.

Who is wise and understanding among you? By his good conduct let him show his works in the meekness of wisdom. But if you have bitter jealousy and selfish ambition in your hearts, do not boast and be false to the truth. This is not the wisdom that comes down from above, but is earthly, unspiritual, demonic. For where jealousy and selfish ambition exist, there will be disorder and every vile practice. But the wisdom from above is first pure, then peaceable, gentle, open to reason, full of mercy and good fruits, impartial and sincere. And a harvest of righteousness is sown in peace by them who make peace. (James 3:2–18 ESV, emphasis mine)

That is a sobering passage! There simply isn't any way to wiggle out from under the weight of responsibility God places upon our shoulders to use our tongues in constructive—not destructive—ways. Sadly, ball games and the airwaves are filled with "trash talk." Cyberspace postings and text messages are laced with gossip, sexual innuendo, filth, and contempt for others. Members of the body are slammed, ripped apart, shredded, and trounced upon at will by those who claim to be Christ's, and believers verbally seduce one another sexually as freely as unbelievers.

Do you see why Peter places brotherly kindness toward the end of his list? It demands a robust commitment to Christlikeness (*aretē*), a knowledge of Jesus Christ and His ways, a well-developed self-control, and much endurance. People who are not kind lack Christian character, and that lack of character is revealed by how they use their tongues.

Marriages go up in smoke because of unrestrained tongues; children and students are demoralized and embittered because of a parent's or a teacher's unrestrained tongue; roommates are hurt and wounded by an unrestrained tongue; parents and teachers are saddened and discouraged because of a child's or student's unrestrained tongue. The fire of the tongue kindles an enormous forest fire of destruction.

This is why James states so emphatically, "My brothers, these things ought not to be so!" And John makes it clear, as we have seen, that persistent behavior like this brings the professing believer's salvation into serious question. These behaviors are certainly the polar opposite of brotherly kindness/affection. So, what must we do? How do we cultivate brotherly kindness/affection?

First, we must reflect seriously on the actual union that we have with other believers because of the gospel. Jesus Christ has made us children of the Father and brothers and sisters of one another. Check out Romans 6 and 1 Corinthians 12.

Secondly, we must honestly evaluate our attitudes and actions toward others—especially toward other believers—to see if we are violating the commands God has given us about how to treat "one another." We must meditate upon the truth until our heart rejoices in it. Review the list of "one another" statements. Pick out the ones you need to work on the most and meditate upon the Scripture passages.

Thirdly, we must repent of where we have violated the will of our Father about these matters. We must be reconciled to the Father, Who is hurt when we, His children, disobey His commands about how to treat the other children in the family. Meditate upon Psalms 32, 38, 51, and Isaiah 55:6–7.

Fourthly, we must be reconciled to those members of the body whom we have violated, hurt, or otherwise wronged. We must approach them in line with Matthew 5:23–24 and seek to restore the relationship we have damaged. We must make it our goal—as did Paul—to "have always a conscience void of offence toward God, and toward men" (Acts 24:16). I remember hearing a child's prayer one time that captured some of the sentiment in brotherly kindness: "Dear God, Make all the bad people good, and all the good people nice." We need to be good people who are nice to others, especially those who are of the "household of faith" (Galatians 6:10).

Lastly, we must meditate upon these "one another" passages that detail for us how we ought to be interacting with each other. James 3 is another passage that should become very familiar ground to us. We must make the admonitions of the Scriptures our meditation until they become our practice.

Before we publish anything about our brethren in the blogosphere or on our social networking site—or in any other medium—or before we repeat something negative to someone who is neither a part of the problem nor a part of the solution, we should run our comments through the grid of the "one another" passages. We must live the Bible, not just salute it as we walk by. If we are chafing under Peter's exhortation to cultivate brotherly kindness, how will we ever be able to manifest the self-sacrificing virtue of the kind of love demanded in the next virtue?

BRINGING JOY TO THE FATHER BY HOW WE TREAT THE BRETHREN

If we love the Father, we want to please Him, and we know it brings great joy to the Father when His children live together in peace. The psalmist describes it this way in Psalm 133:1:

Behold, how good and how pleasant it is for brethren to dwell together in unity!

The Father is pleased, we ourselves are pleased, and the brethren around us are pleased. What could be more satisfying or gratifying than this? Let's seriously cultivate brotherly kindness! Not only will it be a universal blessing but will lay the groundwork for the robust demands of love—the final virtue in Peter's list and the topic of our next chapter.

Chapter Ten

CULTIVATING LOVE

Add to . . . brotherly kindness love. (2 Peter 1:7)

L ike the many movements of a symphony, all the virtues in Peter's list culminate in this final glorious crescendo. Everything has been moving to this end. While a rudimentary possession of this love is common to all believers, for we are "rooted and grounded in love" (Ephesians 3:17), it cannot exist in its mature 1 Corinthians 13 form without the supporting virtues before it in Peter's list.

Love cannot "endure all things" without *endurance*. It cannot "hope all things" and "believe all things" without *knowledge*. It cannot be "kind" and "suffer long" without *self-control*. In the same way that a sonnet cannot be penned without a command of grammar, diction, and poetic devices, so love cannot perform without its supporting cast of virtues.

It hardly needs to be said—but must be said anyway—that the *agapē* love of the Bible is not the Hollywood, turbocharged eroticism of today's world. Neither is it a mere affection or romantic attachment. There is far more strength and purpose in this kind of love.

DEFINITION OF LOVE

Much has been made through the years about the distinctions between the various Greek words for love: *agapē* (ἀγάπη, transliterated *agapē*, pronounced ah-gah´-pā), *philia* (friendship), *eros* (sexual love), and *storgē* (family love).[1] But we probably cannot cut these distinctions as finely as we would like to suppose. Each word does, indeed, have its particular flavor, but to make *agapē* refer exclusively to a self-sacrificing, willed benevolence to meet the needs of others doesn't always fit in various biblical contexts.

For example, when Paul grieves over the loss of a comrade, he says, "Demas hath forsaken me, having loved this present world" (2 Timothy 4:10); he uses here a form of *agapē* to describe the affection Demas has for the world, yet there was no self-denying sacrifice in the defector's heart. Similarly, John commands believers not to love (*agapaō*) the world (1 John 2:15–17). He certainly is not implying that disobedient brethren who do love the world are sacrificing themselves in some way to meet the genuine needs of a godless world system. Clearly, John uses *agapē* to refer to the will-directed wholeheartedness with which some pursue the world—as did Demas.

Likewise, Jesus speaks of the Father's love for Him using forms of our word *agapē* (John 17:23). Yet the Son is complete and has no needs to be met. Furthermore, there is no sacrifice involved in the Father's love for the Son.

Leon Morris cautions against rigid distinction among the various Greek words for love: "But it must be borne in mind that there is considerable overlap [among these words] as B. B. Warfield showed long ago. . . . It would be a mistake to think that any of these terms is used in a narrow sense."[2] D. A. Carson agrees. "Not for a moment am I suggesting that there are not different kinds of love. All I am denying is that specific kinds of love can be reliably tied to particular Greek words. Context and other factors will decide, not mere vocabulary."[3]

The cautions are necessary lest we misinterpret the words of the Scriptures. The meaning must come not from the word's etymology exclusively but from the word's use in the Scriptures themselves and from the overall themes of the Scriptures being expressed in parallel passages that don't even use those words.

I am not trying to be highly technical here; but if we are to be able students of the Scriptures, we must know how to interpret them correctly. If you are still with me this far, I congratulate you; if you agree with me, I'm also grateful. Now, what does all of this have to do with our definition of love?

Despite what I've already said about the overlap of meaning of these words for love in the New Testament, let's first consider that, generally, *agapē* is distinguished from most of the other Greek words for love by its deliberateness and focus. In fact, it is this wholehearted intentionality that describes the love we are to have toward God (Matthew 22:37–38). These statements by Barclay capture that intentionality.

> Agapē has to do with the mind: it is not simply an emotion which rises unbidden in our hearts;[4] it is a principle by which we deliberately live. Agapē has supremely to do with the will. It is a conquest, a victory, and achievement. No one ever naturally loved his enemies. To love one's enemies is a conquest of all our natural inclinations and emotions.[5]

> This agapē, this Christian love, is not merely an emotional experience which comes to us unbidden and unsought. . . . It is in fact the power to love the unlovable, to love people whom we do not like. Christianity does not have to ask us to love our enemies and to love men at large in the same way as we love our nearest and our dearest and those who are closest to us; that would be at one and the same time impossible and wrong. But it does demand that we have at all times a certain attitude of the mind and a certain direction of the will towards all men as they are.[6]

I think most Bible teachers and commentators would have a similar understanding about *agapē* love. We are to have a comprehensive attitude of mind toward all men that is willing to act on the behalf of their best interests even at personal sacrifice.

I want to show you in this study that according to biblical teaching those "best interests" are directed *primarily* at *spiritual* needs—though it does not exclude meeting material, social, and physical needs. It is for that reason that the definition I propose on the chart reads,

> Cultivating a God-imitating mindset that scripturally and sacrificially advances the spiritual welfare of others.

If casting the definition primarily in terms of *spiritual* needs puzzles you, please read carefully what follows. Understanding the entire flow of redemptive history is important if we are to love as God loves.

What's Going On?

When God killed an animal and covered the fallen Adam and Eve with skins and promised that one day her seed would crush the serpent's head, what was going on?

When daily animal sacrifices were offered upon an altar before the tabernacle and later before the temple, what was going on?

When a baby boy was born to a virgin named Mary in a stable in Bethlehem, what was going on?

When a young Jewish teacher, Jesus of Nazareth, walked on water, raised the dead, healed lepers, fed thousands with a boy's lunch, and broke the social barriers between Jew and Samaritan in order to witness to a fallen woman at a well, what was going on?

When that same Rabbi assembled around Him twelve followers who traveled with Him and listened to His unusual ideas of what the kingdom of heaven is like and Who took mission trips to the surrounding areas to spread His teachings, what was going on?

When Jesus was accosted by Roman officials, accused of blasphemy by Jewish religious leaders, tried by Pilate, and executed on a Roman cross outside Jerusalem, what was going on?

The answer is that we are seeing the love of God on a mission to redeem and restore fallen man. Jesus did not heal and feed people because there were too many beggars and hungry people on earth. That is not to say that He was not "touched with the feelings of [their] infirmities" (Hebrews 4:15), but He could have sent angels to do that job. There was something more going on.

Jesus performed miracles to testify of His deity and to prove Himself the One sent from the Father to be the Savior of the world—Israel's promised Messiah. His mission of love was to meet the spiritual needs of fallen man. His plan was to redeem them by atoning for their sin, calling them to repentance, and once restored to fellowship with Him, transforming them by His Spirit through His words into the God-satisfied, God-worshiping, God-imitating creatures they were designed to be from the beginning. This is what is going on.

THE STAGE IS SET

Suppose you were invited to chaperon a high school junior-senior banquet. As you enter the auditorium, you see tables spread with linen tablecloths, beautiful stemware, precisely placed flatware, and decoratively folded cloth napkins. The curtain onstage is open, anticipating a program that is to follow the dinner. Prominently placed in the center of the backdrop onstage is a silhouette of the Eiffel Tower. Upon closer examination of the menu and program on the table in front of you, you see that the words are printed in French with English translations supplied. The table decorations include a small replica of the Eiffel Tower. It wouldn't take much to conclude that the setting for the evening is Paris. The silhouette on the backdrop would be enough to give that away.

> The God of heaven is on a mission of love to redeem and restore His fallen man to the likeness of His Son to the praise of His glory.

If the silhouette on stage were of the Golden Gate Bridge, you would conclude that the setting is San Francisco. If it were of a riverboat, you would guess that you were somewhere on the Mississippi River. These icons immediately "set the stage" for what is to come. A symbol of the Eiffel Tower calls to mind a specific language, certain characteristics in food and fashion, certain political beliefs, morals, and aesthetics. Everything will revolve around the theme suggested by the silhouette on the backdrop.

When we study what God is doing from Genesis to Revelation, it is all about the sacrificial death of Jesus Christ for the redemption and restoration of fallen man to the likeness of God's Son to the praise of His glory. *The silhouette cast on the backdrop for the drama of the world is a cross.* The cross calls to mind a certain purpose for everything, a certain mission, a certain lifestyle, a certain coming reign upon the earth. It explains what God is doing for the good of men. The cross explains what is going on here.

GOD IS ON A MISSION

What is going on is that *the God of heaven is on a mission of love to redeem and restore His fallen man to the likeness of His Son to the praise of His glory* (see John 3:16; Galatians 2:20; Ephesians 2:1–7). His mission of love is about the salvation, sanctification, and eventual glorification of His people.

This is the purpose we embrace when we cultivate *aretē*—committing ourselves to participation in God's mission of restoring Christlikeness in our own souls. This mission is why we cultivate knowledge of the person, work, and ways of Jesus Christ and why we cultivate Spirit-empowered self-control and endurance. We cultivate godliness, which engages us in His cause—this same mission of redeeming and restoring to fallen man the likeness of the Son. Conversely, our attempts to reflect *agapē* love in our dealings with others actually forces us to develop the previous qualities in order to fulfill God's command to love. When we attempt to meet the standard of sacrificial intentionality of love, we see how much we still need to cultivate everything that comes before it on Peter's list.

If we do not keep in mind this mission of being both a disciple of Jesus Christ and a disciple-maker for Jesus Christ, we will lose sight of what it means to love. We will cast love in terms of merely doing good deeds.

The cross is the epitome of a "good deed." There was a *spiritual motive* behind the deed—Jesus' passion for His Father's glory. There was a *spiritual means* behind the deed—Jesus' obedience to the Father's will. There was also a *spiritual end* for the deed—Jesus' redemption and restoration of fallen man to His own likeness for the glory of the Father.

Good deeds are to be performed on the stage of daily life against the backdrop of a cross. Notice the spiritual motive in Jesus' command to us regarding *our* good works.

> Let your light so shine before men, that they may see your good works, and *glorify your Father which is in heaven*. (Matthew 5:16)

Of course, the absence of a conscious, ministry-minded motive does not invalidate benevolent efforts done for others (Matthew 25:35–40). Our works are incomplete in many ways. None of us this side of heaven can produce a flawless work or a pure motive. Often good deeds are both incomplete because of the limitations of our humanity and tainted because of our inherent sinfulness. The fact that God blesses any of the works of our hands is a testimony to the grace of God, not to the excellence of our works.

But our Father's works are always for our spiritual good (Matthew 25:35–40), so our works must be aimed at the spiritual good of others. When we begin to see the overall mission of the God of heaven, the things He has called us to do make sense. Speaking of Jesus' commitment to His Father's mission in His high priestly prayer, Leon Morris says,

[Jesus] prayed that [the world] might come to know that his mission was from God the Father and that the Father's love was wrapped up in that mission (John 17:23).[7]

Love is not full-bodied, God-imitating love unless it sacrifices for the advancement of what God is doing in the other person's life. We are called to be disciples of Jesus Christ to become like Him and then called to be disciple-makers like Jesus Christ to call others to be like Him. Everything we do in life must move to this end. This is the whole thrust of His "great commission" to us in Matthew 28:18–20 (ESV).

> And Jesus came and said to them, "All authority in heaven and on earth has been given to me. Go therefore and make disciples of all nations, baptizing them in the name of the Father and of the Son and of the Holy Spirit, teaching them to observe all that I have commanded you. And behold, I am with you always, to the end of the age."

Paul tells us in 1 Corinthians 13:1–4 that removed from this mission-mindedness of Calvary love, deeds of sacrifice and benevolence become useless for the kingdom of God. The gift of eloquence sounds like a noisy gong. The gifts of prophecy, knowledge, and faith amount to nothing without this love. Even extravagantly sacrificial deeds are unprofitable without mission-minded Calvary love. God's love is on a mission of redeeming and restoring in fallen man the likeness of His Son to the praise of His glory. This is what matters most and what gives significance to any deeds we do.

Why does Paul tell us that mission-minded Calvary love suffers long and is kind? Why is this love neither jealous nor proud? Why does it never behave inappropriately? Why is it neither self-seeking nor touchy? Why does it not keep accounts of wrong done to it? Why does it rejoice in truth and not in evil, and bear all things, believe the best about all things, and endure all things (1 Corinthians 13:4–8)?

Because to act contrary to these ways would be counterproductive to the mission of redeeming and restoring fallen man to the likeness of Christ to the praise of the glory of God! The unloving believer's actions would not advance the mission. Paul's concern is that we glorify God first by taking on the likeness of Christ ourselves by these actions—being His disciples. We then are in a position to glorify God by joining

Him in His mission of restoring the likeness of Christ in others by our disciple-making.

This mission of redemption and restoration is why it mattered to Paul when the Corinthians were fighting, condoning immorality, taking one another to court before unbelievers, mishandling the Lord's table, and neglecting their giving; God's mission of love is hindered by division and fleshliness.

This is why it mattered to Peter when the churches in Asia Minor were being infected by false-teaching libertines, who were turning the grace of God into a license for lust; God's mission of love is hindered by false teaching and fleshliness.

The apostle John shares the same concern that God's work not be hindered through unloving acts: "He that loveth his brother abideth in the light, and there is none occasion of stumbling in him" (1 John 2:10). Paul tells us that love will do no ill to its neighbor (Romans 13:10). Mature love always has spiritual impact at the forefront of the mind. Rather than "random acts of kindness," deliberate love acts to have an intentional spiritual impact.

It is this intentionality that allows mature love to continue even when it is not recognized or appreciated. Paul's ministry to the church of Corinth is a powerful example of unappreciated godly love in action. The church opposed him and called into question his motives. Yet he testified of a unilateral love for this church.

For all things are for your sakes. (2 Corinthians 4:15)

We have spoken freely to you, Corinthians; our heart is wide open. (2 Corinthians 6:11 ESV)

Ye are in our hearts to die and live with you. (2 Corinthians 7:3)

I wrote [hard things] unto you . . . that our care for you in the sight of God might appear unto you. (2 Corinthians 7:12)

In all things I have kept myself from being burdensome unto you, and so will I keep myself. (2 Corinthians 11:9)

I seek not yours, but you. . . . And I will very gladly spend and be spent for you; though the more abundantly I love you, the less I be loved. (2 Corinthians 12:14–15)

His ministry-minded, Calvary-love heartbeat is summarized in his powerful closing declaration:

We do all things, dearly beloved, for your edifying. (2 Corinthians 12:19)

This is godliness on a mission; this is *agape* love! It cares not if it is acknowledged or appreciated by its target. It cares only that the body of Christ is spiritually built up even if it means personal sacrifice.

The Dynamic of Love

Mission-minded Calvary love—*agape*—is self-evident, according to 1 Corinthians 13. Think of it this way. Every time a godly man intersects with another person the manifold "colors" of *agape* love are manifest to that person. Godliness on a mission manifests the same kind of love as when God is on a mission. If my intersection with others does not display this spectrum of characteristics when I meet the "prism" of a relationship, then I must honestly face the fact that there is little true godliness in me.

The Dynamic of Love

Love is godliness interacting with others

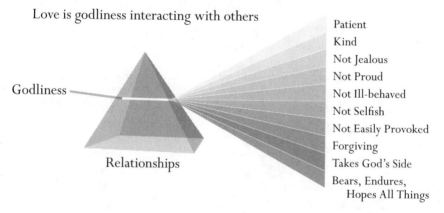

Godliness

Relationships

Patient
Kind
Not Jealous
Not Proud
Not Ill-behaved
Not Selfish
Not Easily Provoked
Forgiving
Takes God's Side
Bears, Endures, Hopes All Things

Paul announced that this kind of mission-minded Calvary love was of more value to the edification of the church than any other spiritual gift they could claim (1 Corinthians 12:31; 14:1). Imagine how our local churches would be transformed by the mutual edification of believers if every time a believer met another person, the white light of godliness was displayed in the 1 Corinthians 13 colors of love! The church would "turn the world upside down" as it did in the first century (Acts 17:6).

Do you see now why the previous virtues must be maturing before love can come to maturity? The first two columns on the chart are about becoming a certain kind of person—a *disciple* of Jesus Christ who loves God with his whole heart and will risk anything for His cause. The third column is about what it takes to effectively take that mission to people as a *disciple-maker*—evangelizing the world and edifying the church. Love is about being disciples and making disciples; it is about loving God and loving your neighbor as yourself.

CULTIVATING LOVE

This kind of love is not our natural tendency. We do not instinctively live for others, nor do we instinctively do good deeds out of concern for their spiritual needs. This is why it must be cultivated. Just like God, we must purposefully "set our affection" on others to meet their spiritual needs.

God's love is not the Hollywood version of love; God does not "fall in love" with us. He does not look down to the earth and see such beautiful creatures that He cannot restrain Himself from showering affection upon us. He does not watch any of us here on the earth and think, "I can't live without you." Rather He sets His affection on us deliberately (Ephesians 1:4–5).

Human beings are the crowning work of His creation; when "God saw everything that he had made [in the creation] . . . behold, it was very good" (Genesis 1:31). Yet it was not long before His rational creation mutinied against Him, and His love demanded that something be done to *redeem and restore His fallen man to the likeness of His Son to the praise of His glory*. This is where the deliberateness of *agapē* love enters in.

This kind of love is not only deliberately expressed; it must be deliberately cultivated. The question is how?

Agapē love, as we have already seen in passing, is created in us at salvation. It is, of course, immature and undeveloped, but since it is a fruit

139

of the Spirit (Galatians 5:22), it is present in some degree in every believer. Note these passages.

> The love of God is shed abroad in our hearts by the Holy [Spirit] which is given unto us. (Romans 5:5)

> But as touching brotherly love ye need not that I write unto you: for ye yourselves are taught of God to love one another. (1 Thessalonians 4:9)

> Beloved, let us love one another: for love is of God; and every one that loveth is born of God, and knoweth God. He that loveth not knoweth not God; for God is love. (1 John 4:7–8)

It matures as we are motivated to love by *beholding the love of God at Calvary.* God's essence is love. He doesn't have love; God is love. He radiates it like a stovetop radiates heat. Anything close to the stovetop takes on its characteristic—heat. Calvary does not just model love for us; it compels it. When Paul spent time reflecting on the work of Jesus Christ at the cross, it motivated him to live a similar life of self-sacrifice for the good of others and the glory of the Father. He expressed it this way in 2 Corinthians 5:14–15:

> For the love of Christ [controls] us; because we thus [conclude], that if one died for all, then were all dead: and that he died for all, that they which live should not henceforth live unto themselves, but unto him which died for them and rose again.

Everything about God that can be communicated to a mortal, finite being is seen in its most complete portrait at the cross. At Calvary we see all that a man can know about mercy, justice, wrath, gentleness, humility, wisdom, power, forgiveness—and love.

Whatever virtue you need to cultivate, study it in Christ at the cross.[8] Get close to the white heat of divine character, and your soul will take on that character. While you behold His work in the Word, pray diligently that you would "be able to comprehend with all saints what is the breadth, and length, and depth, and height; and [be able] to know the love of Christ, which passeth knowledge, that ye might be filled with all the fulness of God" (Ephesians 3:18–19).

God delights to show His people His love for them, but He does not reveal Himself to the casual observer anymore than we do. We must seek Him in the Word and pray for God-taught understanding of what we read. We will be changed into His image as we behold Him in His Word (2 Corinthians 3:18). Barclay comments on this change within a man who has been conquered by gazing at Calvary.

> Christianity does not think of a man finally submitting to the power of God; it thinks of him as finally surrendering to the love of God. It is not that the man's will is crushed, but that man's heart is broken.[9]

I cannot in this brief chapter expand this thought further. I have developed it elsewhere[10] and so have many others, and I must leave you to your own study and meditation on this great work of our Lord.[11] I will close this brief chapter on love with an extended quote from Jonathan Edwards that summarizes well the dispositions of those who cultivate *agapē* love. There should be no doubt in our minds why this virtue is called "the greatest commandment" (Matthew 22:37–40), "the ultimate trademark" (John 13:34–35), "the apostle's goal" (1 Timothy 1:5), and "the essential qualifier" (1 Corinthians 13:1–4).

JONATHAN EDWARDS ON "CHARITY, OR LOVE, THE SUM OF ALL VIRTUE"[12]

As you read through the following excerpt from Jonathan Edwards's classic book on Christian charity—love—notice his comments on how love fulfills all its various duties. We may not use the word *duties* in exactly the same manner in which he did in the eighteenth century, but we dare not miss the point. Since love fulfills all the law (Galatians 5:14), it should not surprise us then to see that a person who cultivates love will be fulfilling his obligations to God and to his neighbor. Read these closing paragraphs slowly and reflectively. They are most instructive.

> A due consideration of the nature of love will show that it disposes men to all duties towards their neighbors. If men have a sincere love to their neighbors, it will dispose them to all acts of justice towards those neighbors—for real love and friendship always dispose us to give those we love their due, and never to wrong them (Rom. xiii. 10)—"Love worketh no ill to his neighbour." And the same love will dispose to truth toward neighbors, and will tend to prevent all lying and fraud and deceit. Men are not disposed to

exercise fraud and treachery toward those they love; for thus to treat men is to treat them like enemies, but love destroys enmity. Thus the apostle makes use of the oneness that there ought to be among Christians, as an argument to induce them to truth between man and man (Eph. iv. 25). Love will dispose to walk humbly amongst men; for a real and true love will incline us to high thoughts of others, and to think them better than ourselves. It will dispose men to honour one another, for all are naturally inclined to think highly of those they love, and give them honour; so that by love are fulfilled these precepts, 1 Pet. ii. 17—"Honour all men," and Phil. ii. 3—"Let nothing be done through strife or vain-glory, but in lowliness of mind let each esteem other better than themselves." Love will dispose to contentment in the sphere in which God hath placed us, without coveting any things that our neighbor possesses, or envying him on account of any good thing that he has. It will dispose men to meekness and gentleness in their carriage toward their neighbors, and not to treat them with passion or violence or heat of spirit, but with moderation and calmness and kindness. It will check and restrain everything like a bitter spirit; for love has no bitterness in it, but is a gentle and sweet disposition and affection of the soul. It will prevent broils and quarrels, and will dispose men to peaceableness, and to forgive injurious treatment received from others; as it is said in Proverbs x. 12, "Hatred stirreth up strifes, but love covereth all sins."

Love will dispose men to all acts of mercy toward their neighbors when they are under any affliction or calamity, for we are naturally disposed to pity those that we love, when they are afflicted. It will dispose men to give to the poor, to bear one another's burdens, and to weep with those that weep, as well as to rejoice with those that rejoice. It will dispose men to the duties they owe to one another in their several places and relations. It will dispose a people to all the duties they owe to their rulers, and to give them all that honour and subjection which are their due. And it will dispose rulers to rule the people over whom they are set, justly, seriously, and faithfully, seeking their good, and not any by-ends of their own. It will dispose a people to all proper duty to their ministers, to hearken to their counsels and instructions, and to submit to them in the house of God, and to support and sympathize with and pray for them, as those that watch for their souls; and it will dispose ministers faithfully and ceaselessly to seek the good of the souls of their people, watching for them as those that must give account. Love will dispose to suitable carriage between superiors and inferiors: it will dispose children to honour their parents, and servants to be obedient to their masters, not with eye-service, but in singleness of heart; and it will dispose masters to exercise gentleness and goodness toward their servants.

Thus love would dispose to all duties, both toward God and toward men. And if it will thus dispose to all duties, then it follows, that it is the root, and spring, and as it were a comprehension of all virtues. It is a principle which, if it is implanted in the heart, is alone sufficient to produce all good practice; and every right disposition toward God and man is summed up in it, and comes from it, as the fruit from the tree, or the stream from the fountain.

Truly, "the greatest of these is love" (1 Corinthians 13:13).

Part Four

INTEGRITY—
PUTTING IT ALL TOGETHER

Chapter Eleven

THE CORE VALUE OF
COMMITMENT TO CHRIST

I beseech you therefore, brethren, by the mercies of God, that ye present your bodies a living sacrifice, holy, acceptable unto God, which is your reasonable service. And be not conformed to this world: but be ye transformed by the renewing of your mind, that ye may prove what is that good, and acceptable, and perfect, will of God. (Romans 12:1–2)

We've come a long way! We've climbed from the bottom of the Grand Canyon to the upper rim. We have carefully followed the path of biblical exegesis and have arrived on top. It is now time to pause to take in the panoramic view in front of us to see where we have been. How can we best summarize the trip and what we have discovered?

CORE VALUES

To help with this overview, I have grouped Peter's essential virtues into three logical categories—*commitment, courage,* and *compassion*—that summarize the emphasis of the virtues in the three columns of the chart on the back inside cover. I call them values—*core* values.

Values are things we think are important, things we care about. This trio of values is easy to keep in the forefront of our minds, and when we see that we

147

need some help in one of them, we can easily go back to the essential virtues that support them. I have illustrated them by a Greek column.

Commitment to Christ forms the base of the column. As we have seen, cultivating the *excellence of Christlikeness* is first. The next logical and scriptural virtue to cultivate is *knowledge*. These two pursuits form the foundation for Christian character. You cannot have Christlikeness without first deciding what you are going to pursue and then discovering what that looks like. Commitment is the *wholeheartedness* of the Christian's life.

Courage for Christ is the center support—the strength, boldness, and virility of Christian character. Peter tells us that upon the foundations of *arete* and knowledge we must build *self-control, endurance,* and *godliness.* This trio of virtues forms the backbone of Christian character. Courage is the *brave-heartedness* of the Christian's life.

Compassion like Christ's is the capital of the column. It is the beauty and attractiveness of *brotherly kindness* and *love*—the crowning virtues in Peter's list. They form the trademark of Christian character. Compassion is the *tenderheartedness* of the Christian's life.

BECOMING A PERSON OF INTEGRITY

The title for Part Four of this book is "Integrity—Putting It All Together." You might guess that putting it all together has something to do with connecting the dots about what we have learned, but we naturally ask ourselves then, "What is integrity?"

To most of us a person has integrity if he is honest. Of course, being honest is part of integrity, but consider this. Suppose that a married man is sleeping with another woman but is honest with his wife about it. Can we say that he has integrity because he is honest about his actions? He may be honest, and maybe his wife, who may have problems of her own, doesn't mind; but he certainly has some serious character flaws. We certainly wouldn't call him a man of integrity.

Some people today believe that being authentic and true to what they feel and believe is what it means to possess integrity. A homosexual may use this kind of reasoning to justify pursuing a practice and lifestyle that God calls sinful. A teenage couple may insist they should marry against their parents' wishes because they feel they must be true to what they are feeling.

Suppose you are visiting a friend in the hospital who is recovering from extensive surgery. You have been with your friend many hours and excuse yourself to take a little walk and to get something to eat in the hospital cafeteria. You mindlessly stroll the corridors until you find yourself in an unfamiliar part of the hospital. You overhear a rather strange dialogue between two patients who are having a loud exchange behind the locked double doors before you.

One man is being quite firm with another as he insists, "I am too Napoleon! Now go get my horse!" To which the other protests, "You are NOT Napoleon! You are Hannibal, and I brought your elephant!"

Upon hearing this conversation you would immediately surmise that the psychiatric ward of the hospital is on the other side of the doors because these men are out of touch with reality. Both, however, would insist that they are being true to themselves. Obviously, integrity is more than just being honest and certainly more than being true to yourself. So then, what is integrity?

The word *integrity* comes from the Latin word *enteger*, from which we get our word *integer*. It means complete, entire, undivided, or whole. Thus, we call whole numbers integers.

A person with genuine integrity is one who is complete and whole. He is the one Peter is describing in this passage—the one in whom these essential virtues are "in you and abound" (2 Peter 1:8). These virtues must exist in us and be bountifully increasing for us to be moving toward wholeness. The person who is progressing in these virtues, fruitful in his personal walk with Christ, and stable is the person of integrity; this is the person with mature Christian character. We want to summarize what Christian integrity looks like. We will take this chapter to discuss *commitment* and will cover *courage* and *compassion* in the final chapters to follow.

WHO IS AT THE CENTER?
Since *aretē* and knowledge form the foundation of a mature Christian character, essentially they are the virtues that put Christ at the center of life.

149

It is the natural tendency for a man in his fallen condition to put *himself* at the center of his existence. This is a serious break with reality and the main cause of trouble in the world today. Because our self-centeredness is such a part of us and of our world, it is hard for us to even imagine what a Christ-centered life would·be like. The paradigm shift is a drastic one. In

COMMITMENT

some ways it is more drastic than a paradigm shift centuries ago when men were debating whether the earth or the sun was at the center of the universe.

In the sixteenth century Copernicus challenged the prevailing view that the earth was the center of the solar system—the geocentric view championed by Ptolemy and others centuries before. From our vantage point on the planet, Ptolemy's view certainly seems to be the most reasonable. After all, from where we stand, it certainly appears that the sun rotates around us, not the reverse.

Copernicus, however, supported his heliocentric (sun at the center) view with mathematical and astronomical observations that accounted for every phenomenon philosophers and scientists could present. His views possessed integrity—wholeness: everything fit into the picture perfectly.

In 1633 Galileo defended Copernicus's "sun-centered" view and was challenged by the sitting pope. He was forced to recant his writings, which he did, or face dire consequences from the church. Eventually, the heliocentric view became the prevailing view: the view we know to be true today.

In a similar fashion from where we stand as fallen creatures, it certainly seems natural that everything should revolve around us. We are born with this innate self-centeredness. It seems so natural to us that it hardly seems wrong. But that self-centeredness is more than just an irritation to those we live with; it is rebellion against God. It is a serious break with reality.

We have already seen that God has placed Jesus Christ at the center of everything He is doing since the creation of the world. Man's sin in the garden was a result of temptation for man to place his own thoughts and ways above God's. The result was disastrous, and man began the process of his own *dis*-integration[1], dysfunction, and eventual destruction.

The whole point of the gospel—the good news that Jesus Christ has died for our sins, was buried, and was raised to provide justification for sinners—is to pay the penalty for us who placed ourselves at the center of our universe and to restore Christ to the central place in our lives again. The gospel makes the Christ-centered life possible.

As long as a man lives as if he can call his own shots, pursue his own ambitions, use his time, money, and talents the way he wishes, he is out of touch with reality. He has placed his own planet at the center of the solar system. He is not whole; he has lost integrity because he has rejected his foundation. He will dis-integrate.

A man without this integrity will sense that something is missing in his life. He will feel agitated, incomplete, fractured, disjointed, and disconnected. He will feel as if he is missing some puzzle parts that will complete the picture of what life is about and how it is supposed to work. He may not even know what the puzzle piece he is searching for looks like, but he knows there are major holes in his life. This is the source of the frustration, guilt, anger, anxiety, and despair that are so prevalent today: self-centered people trying to make life work their own way.

People have always searched for satisfaction. Even the pre-Socratic Greek philosophers sought to discover what constitutes *eudaimonia* (pronounced yū-dī-mo´-nia)—the flourishing life; the life worth living. Aristotle, some years later, concluded that the flourishing life of *eudaimonia* was the result of a certain kind of character whose life contributes heavily to the well-being of others so that the world around him is improved in character in the same manner in which he as an individual has matured in character. *Eudaimonia*, therefore, was the contentment a man experienced because of a highly developed character and a genuine usefulness to the community of which he was a part.

Unfortunately, this state of contentment was out of reach for Aristotle and his followers. True contentment and usefulness to others cannot be achieved by any human who lacks integrity—who has not placed Jesus Christ at the center of everything he is and does.

Lovers of Pleasure

This incompleteness in the soul, signaled by discontentment, is especially dangerous in a culture where the worldly means to personal pleasure are so readily available for everyone. No one has to face his emptiness for long because he can mainline pleasurable experiences nonstop to fill the hole in his soul instead of turning to Christ in repentance and dependence.

Yale Divinity School professor Miroslav Volf has observed that today "the idea of flourishing as a human being has shriveled to mean no more than leading an experientially satisfying life."[2] The quest for personal and community improvement has been replaced with the pursuit of pleasurable experiences.

God predicted that it would be this way in the end times when men would become "lovers of pleasures, more than lovers of God" (2 Timothy 3:4). He further stated that those who know Christ but have embraced the culture's passion for experiences and personal pleasure would have "a form of godliness"—an outward image of spirituality—but would be spiritually powerless (2 Timothy 3:5). Paul was quick to admonish us to "turn away" from—avoid—such men (2 Timothy 3:6). They are particularly identifiable because they "resist the truth" (2 Timothy 3:8). They justify their actions even in the face of clear biblical teaching.

Second Peter 2–3 warns against this pleasure-addicted mindset as well. As I said earlier, Peter presents a maturing presence of the essential virtues in chapter 1 as the only antidote. The stakes are high, the problem is clear, and the remedy is available to those who will be committed to leaving self-centeredness and will wholeheartedly pursue Christ-centeredness.

Keep in mind as well, that no one is uncommitted. The biblical opposites are a commitment to loving God or a commitment to loving self (2 Timothy 3:1–5). Nothing significantly changes until there is a wholehearted pursuit of becoming Christ-centered in every part of life.

Our culture does not foster or celebrate any commitment except commitment to self. The tactic has worked. It is next to impossible to find willing and faithful laborers in the general workforce. Some executives exploit their people to pad outlandish salaries and benefits. Politicians are generally not known for their principled decisions, and even members of the clergy have brought scorn upon their positions because of their self-ish indiscretions. Marriages are entered into lightly—if entered into at all—and broken just as lightly when the personal responsibilities outweigh the benefits. People spend far more than they earn and default on their credit payments. They live for themselves—their own pleasure.

> Commitment to Jesus Christ is for the believer the gravitational force that keeps everything in his life in its proper orbit.

When everyone acts as if the planet of his own life is at the center of the universe, you can expect collisions with other self-centered planets. Everyone is out of order, and gradually the solar system implodes. Commitment to Jesus Christ is for the believer the gravitational force that keeps everything in his life in its proper orbit. It is absolutely foundational—the starting point for integrity.

Mark Bertrand speaks to this issue in his excellent work on developing a Christian worldview:

> The twin principles that tend to govern our daily existence are: *minimize suffering, maximize pleasure*. If you could study an inventory of your behavior over the past week, a log of decisions and actions, you would find that the motivation for most of the things you do is either to avoid pain, discomfort, and awkwardness or to achieve happiness, excitement, or pleasures. These impulses do not require a great deal of introspection. . . . They come naturally. . . .
>
> While the act of avoiding pain or seeking pleasure may be fault-less, the philosophy of seeking pleasure and avoiding pain is not. As a belief system—and I would argue that it is, by and large, *the* belief system of most people, whatever philosophical professions they make—it elevates as ends two experiences we are intended to absorb in passing.
>
> There are times when virtue demands that we experience pain. There are times when doing right means forgoing pleasure. Christian wisdom differs from that of the world in that it treats as means what others seek as ends. The end, for a Christian, is neither pain nor pleasure, but Christ. If to serve him we must suffer, it is good. If in serving him we find pleasure, it is good. But pain or pleasure aside, our lives are dedicated to service.[3]

Our culture assesses the rightness or wrongness of most things by their pleasure value. Friends, family relationships, entertainment options, churches, colleges, jobs, and material possessions are embraced or rejected based on the amount of pleasure they will bring rather than on biblical principles of what is right and wrong or wise and foolish.

No believer can follow Christ without learning to "deny himself, and take up his cross daily" (Luke 9:23–24) in order to follow Christ. He learns quickly that if he tries to save his life he loses it, but if he loses his life he saves it.

The Starting Line of Commitment to Christ

The right relationship with God begins, therefore, with acknowledging the centrality of Jesus Christ in all things. *The self-centered believer must repent of his unbelief and rebellion and then begin the process of integrating all his life under the lordship of Jesus Christ.* Notice this commitment in the lives of several biblical characters.

Moses' wholeheartedness. While Moses was on Mount Sinai receiving the tablets of the law from God, Aaron was helping the people build and worship a golden calf. Moses returned to the scene and drew a line in the sand forcing the people to commit themselves to one side or the other. He said, "Who is on the Lord's side? Let him come unto me" (Exodus 32:26). Tragically, only the tribe of Levi joined Moses and became instruments of God's judgment for three thousand Israelites.

Joshua's wholeheartedness. Joshua assembled the people of Israel at Shechem to deliver his farewell address. The land had been conquered for the most part. Joshua rehearsed for them the goodness of God in bringing them out of pre-Abrahamic paganism and then out of Egyptian bondage. He reminded them that God had "given you a land for which ye did not labour, and cities which ye built not, and ye dwell in them; of the vineyards and oliveyards which ye planted not do ye eat" (Joshua 24:13). He then laid before them a very powerful challenge.

> Now therefore fear the Lord, and serve him in sincerity and in truth: and put away the gods which your fathers served on the other side of the flood, and in Egypt; and serve ye the Lord. And if it seem evil unto you to serve the Lord, choose you this day whom ye will serve; whether the gods which your fathers served that were on the other side of the flood, or the gods of the Amorites,

in whose land ye dwell: but as for me and my house, we will serve the Lord. And the people answered and said, God forbid that we should forsake the Lord, to serve other gods . . . therefore will we also serve the Lord; for he is our God. (Joshua 24:14–16, 18)

And Israel served the Lord all the days of Joshua, and all the days of the elders that overlived Joshua, and which had known all the works of the Lord, that he had done for Israel. (Joshua 24:31)

Though Joshua's commitment never waned, the commitment of Israel was short-lived. The subsequent book of Judges unfolds the disintegration of the nation of Israel and of its citizens as "every man did that which was right in his own eyes" (Judges 21:25). They made an initial, sincere commitment to follow God but abandoned it in the pursuit of their own self-interests.

Elijah's wholeheartedness. Israel had languished spiritually under the influences of King Ahab and his pagan wife, Jezebel. The prophet Elijah challenged her prophets to a showdown on Mount Carmel. He laid before the children of Israel a challenge: "How long halt ye between two opinions? if the Lord be God, follow him: but if Baal, then follow him" (1 Kings 18:21). Tragically, "the people answered him not a word." They remained uncommitted.

David's wholeheartedness. Perhaps one of the most obvious examples of long-standing, wholehearted commitment is that of King David. We saw in chapter 8 that from his earliest years he took the right side of issues even at personal risk—whether it was defending his father's sheep against predators or defending the name of God against a blaspheming Philistine giant.

We get a glimpse of how David maintained that commitment in Psalm 119. I challenge you to stop your reading at this point and read Psalm 119. Underline or highlight every time you see David saying, "I will" or "I shall." These are statements of commitment. David repeatedly states his intention of pursuing the interests of God above his own.

David does not let his bearings drift in his spiritual journey. He constantly checks his compass for true north. He does not want to get off the path. The few times David drifted—his sin with Bathsheba and his numbering of the people—were times brought on because David had neglected to keep fresh his commitment to God and His ways.

David had learned to delight in the words of his God. And herein is the secret that we have already discussed. *The development of a Christian character and the subsequent usefulness to Christ are dependent upon saturating our minds with the words and ways of God.* Psalm 119 is David's testimony to that fact. As you prayerfully study that psalm, vow with David that you will seek His ways and obey them.

In contrast to the wholeheartedness of these men, God has recorded for us countless situations in the Word of God in which kings, priests, prophets, judges, and lay men and women initially consecrated themselves to God but then let that consecration waver in the interest of serving themselves. Those whom God used mightily were those who committed themselves to God and maintained that commitment throughout their whole life. *Commitment to Christ is the only groundwork upon which a Christian character and lifestyle can be built.*

This is why Jesus stated so emphatically that if anyone would be His disciple he must learn to live a life of self-denial and sacrificial service for God and others (Luke 9:23). The kernel of wheat must fall into the ground and die before it can bring forth any harvest (John 12:24). The person who tries to manipulate life for his own benefit will lose it all in the end, but the person who is living for God and others will have found the secret to real living (Luke 9:24).

THE PERFECT ILLUSTRATION

Nothing illustrates the nature of this commitment better than the institution of marriage. In fact, it was God Himself Who drew the parallels between what He intends for a couple within marriage and the relationship of the believer with Christ Himself (Ephesians 5:22–23).

Consider how a marriage between two Christians might begin. Two unmarried individuals notice each other and then begin to spend time together. They talk of topics of mutual interest and discover facets of each other's life that delight them. They eventually enjoy walks in the park and long conversations at their favorite coffee shop.

If they are growing believers, they freely share with each other the milestones on their own personal spiritual journey. They speak of how they have seen Christ working in their lives and answering prayer. Perhaps they even have opportunity to minister together in their local church, where they get to observe the hand of God upon each other's Christian service. They regularly pray together, and certain passages of Scripture take on special significance as God uses His Word to speak to them about one thing or another. They face the challenges of work, family, and temptations with the welcome support of one who points them to Christ and His Word in the midst of those challenges.

With time they become best friends. No sacrifice is too great. No request is too demanding. They face the normal temptations to express their affection sexually but meet those with the grace of God and a commitment to honor His command for them to wait. They carefully guard their hearts against the sensuality that will destroy their fellowship with Christ and, thus, their foundation for a successful relationship.

They invade each other's dreams at night, and when they awake, they are eager to be with each other as soon as possible. An early morning text message or phone call to that special person starts the day. If they cannot be together for some time, they count the hours—or days—until they can see each other again.

It becomes obvious at some point that God has brought them together and that neither can bear the thought of going through life without the other, and he proposes marriage. She accepts, and at some future date they stand before their pastor and pledge their lifelong commitment to each other before God and a congregation of well-wishing witnesses. They formally obligate themselves to live selflessly for the welfare of the other and the glory of Christ for as long as they both shall live.

Their honeymoon explores an entirely new level of intimacy and commitment to each other as they give themselves to each other in tenderness and devotion. They return from that experience ready to build a relationship whereby they grow to become increasingly of one mind. Paul calls it becoming "one flesh"—one person. And thus, a Christian home is established where Christ is the center of all they do.

Eventually, God may grant them children who will grow up in a home where it is *normal* to speak of Christ and His ways, where it is *normal* for offences against another to be resolved by requests for forgiveness and tears of reconciliation, and where it is *normal* to obey authority, get along with each other, and help other people. Biblical principles underlie every decision—whether it is a financial decision or an entertainment choice. Family prayer and age-appropriate devotions are the norm. These are evidences of Christ-centered living in the home.

Most importantly, the children see between Mom and Dad a commitment to the well-being of the other that not only brings immense security to the children but also teaches the children firsthand what commitment to Jesus Christ looks like. They have modeled in front of them what wholehearted, single-minded devotion to another person looks like. This is the picture of commitment to the next generation and to the watching world that God intended marriage to be.

The commitment to each other is frequently expressed, and the exclusiveness of the relationship is carefully guarded. Other interests and people—even the children—are not permitted to take the primary place each has for the other under God. She does not flirt with other men at work or spend time online with a virtual lover. He does not spend his lunch hours with a female coworker or maintain contact with a previous sweetheart. Neither one permits anything or anyone to undermine the commitment to put the other first under God.

This is how a Christian marriage can—and should—function. The details will be different in each case, but the commitment to growing in Christlikeness and an awareness of the person, the works, and the ways of Jesus Christ will be the sun around which all the planets revolve. It will happen like this in the marriage when it is happening like this with Christ in the lives of the husband and wife. It is clear that this kind of commitment is foundational to the integrity of the marriage as well as to their Christian experience.

To be truthful, most Christian marriage relationships do not begin and unfold as described above. The reason is that the participants lack the essential Christ-centeredness in their own lives either before or after marriage. They have been more influenced by the worldly culture around them as is betrayed by their speech, entertainment choices, work ethic, financial decisions, problem-solving efforts, and interpersonal conflicts.

Though there is some measure of devotion to the other person in a developing romance, the motivating factor is usually how good one person makes the other feel. The relationship is a sort of "tick-on-a-dog" relationship. After marriage—and maybe before—the couple comes to discover that there are two ticks and no dog. Neither wants to be the host for the other. If that self-centered orientation isn't quickly addressed, one or both "ticks" go looking for another "host."

The pleasure ethic, mentioned earlier, is especially fatal to marriage relationships. Prospective spouses are evaluated too often not upon their Christian character and devotion to Jesus Christ but upon how much pleasure they bring to each other. Marriage is "up-close living" at its maximum, however, and two sinners cannot live together long without bringing discomfort, if not pain, into each other's life. If they are not committed to something higher than their own pleasure, the relationship is doomed. If both had seriously pursued the proper relationship with Christ before starting their relationship with each other, they would have seen early on how pleasure and pain must take a back seat to what is good for the relationship.

Marriages begin dis-integrating before they are even finalized at the wedding altar because the individuals involved do not possess the necessary other-centeredness that marriage requires. It has not been evident in their walk with Christ, and therefore, is absent in the bonds of matrimony. They do not possess the necessary component of commitment to another person. Their commitment has been entirely to their own interests. They have no foundation upon which to build stability; they have no integrity.

We saw earlier how the false idea that the earth was the center of the universe had to be replaced with a view that brought integrity into scientific thought. Only a "sun-centered" view explained how things really worked.

So it is with marriage and with the Christian life itself. Only a spouse-centered marriage will be a blessing to both parties, and only a Christ-centered walk will bring blessing to both Christ and the believer. Both relationships require self-denial—the subordination of personal desires in accordance with biblical commands. *The idea that self-centeredness will work is as mythological as the belief that the earth is at the center of the universe.*

Gospel Motivation
Where does the motivation for this kind of spiritual and marital commitment come from? Paul taught that it is based upon the work of Christ for us on the cross.

For the love of Christ controls us, because we have concluded this: that one has died for all . . . that those who live might no longer live for themselves but for him who for their sake died and was raised. (2 Corinthians 5:14–15 ESV)

The cross shows us the hideousness of our sin, the helplessness of our condition, and the amazing depths of God's love for us. *Paul gazed upon the cross-work of Jesus Christ and concluded that God did not carry out this blood-stained event to leave believing creatures in their self-centeredness.* He died that "those who live might no longer live for themselves."

It is the height of arrogance to think that life should be lived for anyone else but Jesus Christ after the event of Calvary. Why do we love Him? "Because he first loved us" (1 John 4:19). Why do we "present [our] bodies a living sacrifice" to Him (Romans 12:1)? Because of the "mercies of God." Everything turns upon the hinge of the cross in the Christian life. It is the cross that should compel us to the pursuit of the *excellence of Christlikeness* and to *knowledge* of the person, the work, and the ways of Jesus Christ. It will compel us to commitment—the foundation of Christlike character.

Chapter Twelve

THE CORE VALUE OF
COURAGE FOR CHRIST

*This book of the law shall not depart out of thy mouth; but thou
shalt meditate therein day and night, that thou mayest observe to do
according to all that is written therein: for then thou shalt make thy
way prosperous, and then thou shalt have good success. Have not I
commanded thee? Be strong and of a good courage; be not afraid, neither
be thou dismayed: for the Lord thy God is with thee whithersoever thou
goest. (Joshua 1:8–9)*

In 2007 Bob Jones University was invited to take a small student dele-
gation to the National Character and Leadership Symposium hosted
by the United States Air Force Academy in Colorado Springs. I accompanied our students as their sponsor. The symposium was hosted by the
AFA's Center for Character Development and is one of the annual ven-
ues whereby the academy keeps the issues of leadership and character
development before its cadets. The two-and-a-half-day conference was
filled with workshops and keynote addresses by leaders from industry,
government, and, of course, the military. I came away from the conference greatly encouraged by the level of commitment that our men and
women in uniform have to the founding ideals of our nation. I also
learned much about how courage is formed.

The words *character, commitment, courage,* and *leadership* were on the tip
of every speaker's tongue, and the cadets welcomed the challenge these
words call forth. They wanted to become men and women of character.
They wanted their four years in the academy to forge commitment and
courage into their very being. They knew they must possess these qualities if they are to be useful in the protection of the country they love.

FRONT-ROW SEAT IN A CAVE

In some ways I felt as if I were a participant in Plato's allegory of the cave.[1] In that allegory Plato speaks of men who are sitting on a bench in a cave, facing away from the cave's entrance. Behind them is a blazing campfire. Between their backs and the campfire are persons who are carrying out various duties. Rather than seeing these actions, the men on the bench can see only the shadows projected on the cave's wall. To them, this is all the reality they can know.[2]

As I sat in each session at the Air Force Academy, I saw speakers, most of whom probably do not profess a personal faith in Jesus Christ, who had a more clear understanding of character and leadership than do most believers. These were men and women who saw the "shadows" more clearly than those who are living in the "light" and who have an unveiled view of Christ and His ways. My heart rejoiced at their clarity but was grieved that more believers do not grasp these important concepts.

My heart is burdened in my ministry as dean of students at Bob Jones University when I see some parents and their children who want to have the final *product* of a Christian character but reject the *process* of its formation. These parents continually give in to their children's demands since their offsprings' happiness—not their holiness—is their primary goal.

The permissiveness of the culture has badly infected the church producing cowardly believers ruled by the fear of man and by their own lusts.

Their children resist accountability for their actions, thus rejecting *self-control*, and bail out of adversity before it can produce *endurance*. These parents want a "soft" Christianity that speaks only of nurturing, and they pejoratively label any effort that holds someone accountable for his actions as legalistic and heartless. They do not understand that the formation of self-control, endurance, and godliness—the components of courage—*is* a heart issue. The permissiveness of the culture has badly infected the church with the inevitable consequence of producing cowardly believers ruled by the fear of man and by their own lusts.

I am thankful there are many parents of our students who do understand the biblical issues at stake, and though any of us who are parents hate to see our children undergo hardship, they know that a child must, as Paul, "discipline [his] body" and make it his slave so that he can become useful to Christ (1 Corinthians 9:27 ESV). They know that the child must "discipline [himself] for the purpose of godliness" (1 Timothy 4:7 NASB).

The men and women at the Air Force Academy understand courage. They understand how it is formed on the foundation of commitment and is forged on the anvil of adversity and testing. Like Peter, they know full well that the virtues of *self-control* and *endurance* are strategic in the forming of courage. Cadets are expected to restrain their passions, obey their superiors, and persevere under external pressure. They know as Paul did that they must "endure hardness, as a good soldier [in their case, airman] of Jesus Christ" (2 Timothy 2:3).

What they do not know is the necessity of commitment to and fellowship with Jesus Christ for these virtues to accurately reflect Him as the fruit of His Spirit.[3] They can possess only the shadow of the reality of true character. In this respect, as the Lord Jesus commented, "the children of this world . . . in their generation [are] wiser than the children of light" (Luke 16:8).

BRAVE-HEARTEDNESS

One of the workshop speakers was an inspiring Asian-American, Gus Lee. His biographical entry in the conference guide stated that he is a "nationally recognized ethicist, leadership expert, business author, and novelist. Raised by YMCA boxers, he has been a corporate VP, senior executive, lead trainer for California's prosecutors, senior deputy district attorney, acting deputy attorney general, assistant dean, JAG officer, ethics whistleblower, paratrooper and drill sergeant."[4] His book, *Courage: The Backbone of Leadership*,[5] reminds us of some important principles we have studied in part two of this book. Note these concepts in some excerpts below, keeping in mind the things we have studied in column two of the chart. Note as well that while he doesn't put all the concepts together in as clear a picture as the apostle Peter does, he does possess a better understanding of what constitutes courage and how it is built than most modern believers.

> [Courage] is the mental and moral strength to venture, persevere, and withstand danger, fear, or difficulty.

It comes from the Latin and Middle English word for "heart." Courage is the tip of the spear of integrity and the spark plug for principled conduct. It is integrity at its highest. This is because it faces fear, converts integrity into a habit, and gives enduring power and usefulness to leadership.

It is human behavior at its most admirable, selfless, and excellent. It is the stuff of epics, legends, and heroism. It is what we wish our children will possess and demonstrate. It is what we admire most in leaders, friends, and spouses.

Courage begins by facing strong negative, gut-wrenching feelings. It requires the direct and robust facing of fear.

Facing fear then becomes the correcting of internal wrongs and confronting, addressing, and correcting external wrongs in others. . . . The opposite of courage is indifference. Courage comes from commitment, care, and love, whereas allowing wrongs in others leads to others' mistreatment and suffering. That is why being courageous for rightness is superior to being "a good person" who keeps his nose clean.[6]

Courage is addressing wrongs in the face of fear, regardless of circumstances, of risks to self, or of potential practical gains.

Courageous leadership is about utilizing our brains, character, and spirit to advocate principles regardless of the odds, heedless of fear, apart from collateral impact, and independent of personal career needs.[7]

The good person is just that—someone who keeps his or her nose clean. But . . . the person of character is a completely different cat; this person does the right thing not only for himself or herself but for others. For the principle of the thing.[8]

Although Gus Lee has captured well the secular vision of what it means to have courage, the biblical model of courage has a sharper focus because of the Scripture's Christ-centeredness. The virtues of *self-control*, *endurance*, and *godliness* produce

a *brave-hearted* disciple who advances Christ and His ways and opposes evil in himself and others regardless of risk to himself.

We should be able to see by this time that *courage for Christ is nothing more than grown-up commitment to Christ.* People without courage have either failed to develop commitment by cultivating *aretē* and *knowledge,* or they have failed to cultivate *self-control, endurance,* and *godliness.*

WORLDLINESS MAKES COWARDS OF US ALL

Worldliness is extremely toxic to the development of Christian character. *Worldliness creates a culture of cowardice.* It lures the believer away from the appeals and ideals of Christ in exchange for the appeals and ideals of the pleasure-driven world. It, therefore, destroys *commitment* to Christ.

Even those believers who truly have a measure of devotion to Christ and His ways are short-circuited in their full Christian development by their failure to cultivate column-two virtues because they have been seduced by the world. When self-control, endurance, and godliness are hindered, it isn't long before column-one commitment is eroded as well. The result is a disillusioned, discouraged, and eventually, dis-integrating believer. It is therefore, exceedingly important that we understand how these virtues build upon one another and that we reject anything that erodes them.

Worldliness destroys courage for Christ by scorning self-control—the first essential virtue in column two. The constant cry of the sinful heart and of the world—the collective cry of many sinful hearts joined together against God—is to "do as you please, don't let anyone tell you what to do, be yourself, resist authority, and be your own person." Anyone who is not saying no to the internal lusts that demand self-rule will remain a coward.

One way the world especially undermines self-control is through its appeal to sensuality. Indulgence in sexual activity of any kind outside marriage—even in the mind—stops self-control dead in its tracks, and consequently, courage dies. Men and women who fill their minds with the sensuality of the world's entertainment offerings and pursue its sexually suggestive fashions will remain cowards because they will have no self-control.

A woman who dresses in a sexy fashion to attract a man erodes the character of every man who views her as her clothing seduces him to lust after her in his mind.[9] She may attract a man by her immodesty, but the kind of man she will get will bring her great disappointment because he will have no character, and she has helped to destroy it. He has to abort his commitment to Christ to lust after her, and his lack of self-control has thwarted any further development of moral strength or courage.

A man who has been seduced by the world into pornography, sensual entertainment—movies, electronic games, music—and sensual conversation has sabotaged any development of courage. He can never truly be a man of integrity; he is incomplete. He will always be less than a godly man because he lacks self-control—an essential virtue in godly manhood.

It is sad that so many believers defend their right to exercise their misapplied Christian liberty to indulge in activities that sabotage self-control. This was the problem that Peter was addressing in 2 Peter, as we have seen previously.

The popular idea that the Bible condemns only drunkenness ignores the major effect of today's undiluted and distilled alcohol: it impedes self-control. The issue is not whether a believer can control his alcohol; the issue is that even a couple of beers control him. Proponents of social drinking have argued for the *particulars* of whether the social use of alcohol is absolutely forbidden in Scripture while ignoring the *universal* of the essential virtue of self-control, which is clearly commanded in Scripture and which alcohol destroys.

It is ironic that in a time when science and sociology are becoming more concerned about the adverse effects of alcohol,[10] some conservative Christians are scrambling to justify its use under the guise of Christian liberty. Most have come to that position not by a careful study of their Bibles about how Christlikeness is formed but by a carefree indulgence in their culture. The issue isn't whether the Bible is clear about alcohol. The issue is that it is clear about the necessity of self-control and the effect of one's choices on others. The courageous Christian will not bend to the cultural winds infecting the church.

Christian liberty, as Paul taught it, does not give believers freedom to do anything they want as long as it is not forbidden in Scripture. It gives them the freedom to reject anything that does not advance Christ and His ways even if it is not forbidden in Scripture.

The same call to abstinence applies to any verbal or physical activity between the sexes that tempts them to sensuality.[11] We are commanded at all times to exercise a God-empowered mastery over internal desires. The old taboos of no physical contact between the sexes and chaperoned activities for young people in mixed company weren't exercises in legalism or outdated social constructs. They were the wise application of biblical principle by courageous people who knew there is no room for compromise in the command for self-control if essential virtues of character are to be developed.

The popular logic, born in the permissiveness of the sixties, goes like this: "If we never give people the opportunity to make these decisions for themselves, they won't develop the ability to make choices." What is missing is the understanding that every time a person faces a limitation, he has the opportunity to make a decision—a decision to control his passions and submit to the limitation or to indulge himself and ignore the limitation. A clear example of this even in the secular world is how the military academies forge character by this very process. *It is not the absence of limitation and demands that builds character; it is the exercise of self-restraint in the presence of limitations and demands that builds character.*

For example, a Christian believer who is in a Muslim or communist prison for his faith makes decisions every day though he faces severe limitations. Prison does not eliminate essential decisions. The Christian prisoner must frequently decide how he is going to respond to the situation God has placed him in, how he is going to treat his oppressors, how he is going to look out for the good of others around him instead of becoming self-focused, and so forth. Much of the Christian world has bought into the old Freudian concept that repression creates neuroticism. Repression without Christ can produce any number of unacceptable behaviors if the individual is living for himself, but self-restraint to advance the work of God in ourselves and others is virtuous—and essential. Worldliness destroys courage because it scorns self-control and restraint.

Worldliness destroys courage for Christ by scorning endurance—the second essential virtue in column two. The world encourages people to bail out when the going gets rough. People are encouraged by their flesh and by the world to abort their babies, divorce their spouses, quit their jobs, drop out of school, hop from one church to another, and change their personal standards—all based upon their personal feelings and social conformity rather than upon biblical principle. Consequently,

> What we call the "fear of man" is usually the lack of godly courage.

they never develop endurance. They are not used to saying no to themselves, so they have a hard time saying no to anyone else who wants them to go along (Psalm 1:1; Proverbs 1:10–19).

J. I. Packer makes some insightful parenting applications to this matter of self-control and endurance:

> If there are never any difficult situations that demand self-denial and discipline, if there are never any sustained pressures to cope with, if there are never any long-term strategies where the child must stick with an educational process, or an apprenticeship, or the practice of a skill, for many years in order to advance, there will never be any maturity of character. The children (who, of course, want life to be easy and full of fun, as children always do) will remain spoiled all their lives, because everything has been made too easy for them.[12]

Worldliness destroys courage for Christ by scorning godliness—the third essential virtue in column two. Furthermore, the world promotes the fear of man. It does so by promoting conformity to its values and practices through advertising, entertainment, the secular news media, secular education, and unprincipled court rulings (like *Roe v. Wade*) and legislation. It punishes nonconformity with rejection and ridicule. People are taught to please the crowd; they are not taught to please God. Godly people who draw a line in the sand for righteousness are caricatured as mindless or out of date.

The godly man is more conscious of what pleases God and of what God requires than of what pleases the world and of what the world requires. He fears God, and thus, does not fear man. What we call the "fear of man" is usually the lack of godly courage. Courage is skilled at saying no to internal lusts and desires that undermine commitment to Christ; it has self-control. Courage is skilled at saying no to external pressures that undermine commitment to Christ; it has endurance. Courage is skilled at saying no to evil because it has become skilled at saying yes to God; it has godliness.

The consequences of living without courage are staggering. People without courage run from challenges and conflict. They don't repair relationships; they don't ask forgiveness. They don't face hard tasks or new endeavors in which they may possibly fail. They form protective barriers of perfectionism to avoid having to make decisions in gray areas or become indifferent, lazy, and self-indulgent. They will not face angry people and won't give honest feedback. They avoid uncommunicative people.

People without courage will not speak up. Silence is the language of cowardice. They tolerate backbiting, gossip, revenge, and other relationally destructive evils in themselves and others. They never want to stand out and will never stand alone. They ostensibly don't want to be like everybody else, but their cowardice makes them exactly like everyone else. There seems to be comfort in the fact that no one else is saying anything, and the crowd has voted for conflict aversion—like Israel before Goliath.

If they finally do speak up, it is out of personal frustration and anger. They will boldly oppose anyone who is upsetting their paradise of personal comfort and pleasure. They are not responding out of principled values. They are responding because they will no longer tolerate interference with their personal self-serving agenda.

They conform to avoid anything uncomfortable. They are victims of and contributors to a culture of cowardice—within their families, their government, their churches, their workplaces, their society, and their personal friendships. *Tragically, any group without courageous individuals is on a path of self-destruction.* We must be clear, therefore, about how courage is formed and how it is destroyed.

CULTIVATING COURAGE FOR CHRIST

By now it should be obvious that courage is based upon development of the essential virtues in the first two columns. It should, therefore, be clear that anything that impedes the development of any of those essential virtues erodes courage.

What may not be clear yet is that courage will become second nature to the godly man. He doesn't have to mechanically think through every temptation and trial that comes his way in order to decide what to do. The godly man has faced many decisions requiring *self-control* and *endurance* before. He has become well-practiced in making right responses. When he faces a newer, larger challenge, he may not know exactly what he will immediately do, but there is no question in his mind that he will do the right thing when it comes time for the decision to be made. All he must do is weigh what is the best course of action that will keep him on the path of righteousness. Gus Lee once again weighs in on this aspect of courage and character, though from a secular perspective.

> [Character] derives from a Greek word that means "engrave, impress deeply and permanently." It is possessed by a person with fixed habits of moral firmness and excellence who acts spontaneously for what is right.[13]

What I want you to see is that even the secular mind recognizes that character has to do with cultivated habits and responses, according to a set of absolute standards.

In the summer of 2007 my wife and I toured Israel. Our sixty-year-old guide, Arie Bar David, was not only a Scripture-saturated believing Jew but also a courageous warrior in his own right. He had fought in every major war of Israel since he was a teenager. He took us to the eastern edge of the Golan Heights, where we visited a kibbutz featuring a documentary film of the tank battle at OZ77. Real footage from the Yom Kippur War in 1973 portrayed a fierce tank battle between the lone 77th Israeli tank battalion with outdated machinery against twenty-two battalions of modern Syrian tanks equipped with night vision.

The film was moving and sobering. Many lives were lost on both sides, but Israel won a strategic battle, repelling the Syrian battalion on the border plains, preventing further penetration by Israeli enemies. The documentary not only showed the courageous heroism of a small battalion of tank commanders and their crews but also demonstrated the obvious providence of God on their behalf—though that was never mentioned in the film. What impressed me most, however, about the visit were several comments Arie made about courageous leadership after the film was over.

He said wars like this were won by many "split-second decisions that make a difference," and cautioned, "if you wait too long to make the decision in war, you lose the opportunity to make a difference." I jotted down those comments and pondered them much over the next several days. He is right.

Leadership is about making many split-second decisions that make a difference: split-second decisions to encourage, to rebuke, to stand against wrongdoing, to initiate right actions. *A courageous person does not miss these opportunities because he has developed the habit of doing right!*

How did those tank commanders and crews learn to make split-second decisions that made a difference? They practiced! They drilled and drilled and drilled. Their lives and their nation depended upon instinctive, split-second reactions.

We develop godly courage as a lifestyle the same way. Godly courage requires that the believer make split-second decisions to look away from the sensual commercials on television, erotic billboards on the highway, and suggestive magazine covers at the gas station. A man who does *not* instinctively make split-second decisions that make a difference will be desensitized and more easily corrupted. If he is not "practicing" on smaller targets, he will not instinctively turn away when the temptation comes to give in to the advances of someone who is not his spouse or to click on an unsolicited porn ad on the Internet. The godly man does his practicing on smaller battlefields and targets so that he will not lose the larger battles. *Self-control becomes his norm.*

Godly courage requires that the believer make split-second decisions not to answer in kind when a coworker demeans him or to speak up when an unexpected opportunity comes to witness for Christ and His ways. He is ready for those battles because he has practiced the restraint of his tongue at home when his children are particularly irritating or disobedient. He hasn't lashed out at them in anger or removed himself from the situation to avoid conflict. He has intentionally looked for opportunities to encourage and instruct. He does not allow himself to belittle his wife in public—or private. He knows that his God-given mission is to improve her spiritually by the "washing of the water by the Word" and he "practices" loving her as he instinctively loves himself (Ephesians 5:25–31). He has faced his passions on the practice field of his home and is battle-ready for larger wars in the workplace.

Godly courage requires that the believer make split-second decisions not to pad his expense account, time records, or production results or to cover his mistakes and losses with deception. He is practiced at doing the right thing beginning with getting up in the morning. He doesn't fuss about having to get up. He rises, prepares himself spiritually and physically, and gets on with doing the kingdom business God has for him that day. He isn't looking for the easy way out or the cushy job for himself. He is grateful for any gains God gives him and takes responsibility for any losses. Doing right has become instinctive.

A Call to Courage

Please understand that I am not reducing godliness to a series of practiced actions. I have spent an entire book up to this point emphasizing the necessity of Spirit-enabled living and have written extensively on biblical change elsewhere. You have noted that each definition for the essential virtues is prefaced by phrases such as "God-taught," "God-empowered," "God-sustained," "God-fearing," "God-engendered," and "God-imitating." That is purposeful. I want you to see that God is not only the Object of all we do but also the Source of help to do it. All this growth is merely the outgrowth of God's gracious work in us. This likeness to Christ is the end to which He saved us.

My point in this chapter is to reinforce the fact that *committed, courageous, godly living can and must become our lifestyle.* It must become almost second nature and instinctive. This is what Paul calls us to in Romans 12:2. We are to reject being "conformed to this world" but are to be "transformed by the renewing of [our] mind." It is this transformation of our minds that I am illustrating and calling for.

If you have ever taken a foreign language in high school or college, you know something of this process. Suppose you have taken two years of French in high school. You are somewhat familiar with basic vocabulary and sentence structure. Though you have memorized a few French phrases, your "translation" work is largely mechanical. You have to examine every word you read or hear, think of its meaning in English, examine its placement in the sentence, and put all that together to understand the French statement. The process is pedantic, stilted, and burdensome—though necessary—if you are to learn French.

Suppose you take two more years of French in college. Following those two years, you spend several weeks in the summer on a mission team to France or Quebec. There you have to converse with people in French and live with a French host family. The "translation" process becomes more natural for you. You still think in English and instinctively write home in English, but you are becoming familiar with French.

Let's further suppose that upon graduation from college you return to France or Quebec to serve as a lifelong missionary. Within a couple of years you not only speak French fluently but also think and dream in French. You have to think twice sometimes about how to say something in English when you reply to an e-mail from someone from the States. You have been "transformed by the renewing of your mind." You think, speak, and dream in a new language.

Godliness is like that. At first, having to think through every action, reaction, and temptation is burdensome. You have to ask yourself, "What should I do now? What does God's Word say? How should I react?" Your responses feel rather unnatural and mechanical, but with God-dependent practice they become almost second nature to you. You "translate" every situation that comes up, every act of suffering, and every temptation through the grid of God's Word. After a few years you think and speak in a biblical paradigm.

This kind of godliness—well-practiced in cultivating commitment to Christ and self-control and endurance—is courageous for Christ. It knows almost instinctively what is right, chooses what is right, does what is right, and calls others to do the same. This is courage; this is loving God with all your heart.

This kind of godly courage must become something we highly value because God values it. There is no integrity without it. *Christlike wholeness requires the courage to do the right thing no matter what.*

It must become a core value of your Christian experience. It forms the guts, the virility, the backbone of your Christian character. It is the strength of the pillar of core values. Understand it and cultivate it with all your being. It is the stuff that made up the godly heroes of the past. You, too, can be a courageous believer—"a brave-hearted disciple who advances Christ and His ways and opposes evil in yourself and others regardless of the risk to yourself.

Chapter Thirteen

THE CORE VALUE OF
COMPASSION LIKE CHRIST

*So being affectionately desirous of you, we were willing to have
imparted unto you, not the gospel of God only, but also our own souls,
because ye were dear unto us. For ye remember, brethren, our labour
and travail: for labouring night and day, because we would not be
chargeable unto any of you, we preached unto you the gospel of God.
Ye are witnesses, and God also, how holily and justly and unblameably
we behaved ourselves among you that believe: as ye know how we
exhorted and comforted and charged every one of you, as a father doth
his children, That ye would walk worthy of God, who hath called you
unto his kingdom and glory. (1 Thessalonians 2:8–12)*

"OTHER MOTHER"—ONE PERSON
CAN MAKE A DIFFERENCE

The rebellious teens, runaways, unwed mothers, and battered wives
whom she took under her wing affectionately called her "other
mother." Ruth Morgan's husband was in the military, and while he was
away for protracted periods of time, she filled the hours with ministry
to her own four children—three girls and a boy—and to the needy
children around her. When her own children were preteens, she started
a Bible study for girls in a reformatory near the military base. Her love
for helping troubled girls never left her. She became the "other mother"
for scores of girls before the Lord called her home to heaven in 1998.

She had no education beyond high school and no formal Bible training.
She studied the Word diligently, taught it to others, and listened attentively to the faithful preaching of God's Word in the local assemblies
she and Bill, her husband, joined at each new military assignment.

When they settled in Greenville, South Carolina, in 1968, her own teens were starting college at Bob Jones University, and Bill had retired from the military. As usual she and Bill became active in their local church—the same one Patty and I attended. As her own children graduated, married, and left home, the Morgans opened their home to any girl who needed a family. Ruth would often keep one or two troubled teens in the upstairs bedrooms while a missionary family on furlough lived in the basement apartment.

She would often involve other women in the church in her individual counseling sessions and group Bible studies with these needy girls. She was in every respect a Titus 2 woman, who taught the younger women to love their husbands and walk with Christ. Her weekly Bible studies in her home not only taught the troubled women she was trying to help but also demonstrated to the church women how to minister the Word to others.

In fact, she was the one who started my wife on a lifelong ministry of teaching women by asking her to speak at a women's retreat. My wife and I admired Ruth as we saw her involvement in the lives of the girls she brought to church. Years later when I became dean of students at Bob Jones University, I got to watch her up close. Some of her girls enrolled, and Ruth continued to minister to them alongside us.

Her funeral was a tearful reunion of many of her girls—some with families of their own by then, others in ministry, but all touched by the life of one woman who knew the meaning of biblical compassion. She lived Jude's admonition to "have compassion, making a difference" (Jude 22). I will illustrate the points in this chapter with examples from her life of devotion to Jesus Christ.

Not every woman can have the ministry Ruth had, but every one of us must cultivate the compassion—the *brotherly kindness* and *love*—that so richly characterized her life. In order to write this chapter I interviewed one of her daughters, our former pastor, and two of her "girls," Becky and Debbie, now with families of their own. Ruth and I worked together with Becky and Debbie while they attended Bob Jones Academy during their high school years.

I want especially to show through Ruth's ministry how the blend of virtues Peter has been calling us to cultivate produce a robust compassion that is both tough and tender—both courageous and kind. Ruth exemplified this like very few people I have known. As a result, she made a difference in countless lives.

Is Love Tough or Tender?

Consider these scenarios. A wife thinks her husband is being too tough on the children, so when she can, she tries to balance his heavy-handedness with more leniency. She often doesn't discipline them because she thinks they get enough from their father. Consequently, the children play one parent against the other.

A pastor wants to show that he is trying to reach the heart of the students, so he overrules the Christian principal's disciplinary action toward a senior after the pastor hears the boy's tearful pleas for a second chance. The entire school staff is surprised—and confused—by the pastor's actions.

A single mom reads a book about tough love and realizes that her guilt over her divorce has motivated her to be too easy on her teenage son, who now, after years of permissive parenting, won't do his homework, won't come home by curfew, and won't lift a hand to help out around the house. She decides to show some tough love.

John's shift supervisor is creating enormous morale problems. Two men on the crew of ten that John leads have been written up many times for tardiness and breaches of safety regulations with no reprimands or disciplinary action taken. The supervisor has told John he wants to be compassionate to these men, yet the supervisor's brand of compassion isn't having any positive effect on the work performance of the men. Instead, it seems that they are becoming even more careless.

All these scenarios demonstrate the tension and resulting confusion of trying to decide whether love should be tough or tender, but our friend Ruth wasn't confused. She practiced the biblical truth that love moves freely between toughness and tenderness based upon whatever is needed at the moment to advance the mission of forming Christlikeness in others.

Our pastor relied heavily upon Ruth to minister to women in need in our congregation. He recalls that she had a gift of looking past a girl's outward appearance, whether she sported a black leather-studded collar, a shabby, well-worn hand-me-down, or a designer outfit. Ruth saw behind outward appearances the souls of girls Christ had died for and loved. For that reason, she loved them too.

Many of the girls she helped had been victimized in some way, but she had an uncanny ability to sort through the moral responsibility each girl had for her own responses to life's challenges. She had been "lied to by experts" and learned how to ask the right questions and not let an issue go if it was crucial to the young woman's spiritual progress. She was unrelenting in getting to the truth. She tolerated no deception. She was a warm-hearted comforter but could also be a penetrating "prosecutor." She poured the oil of encouragement on wounded hearts while at the same time ferreting out the infection of bitterness, deception, immorality, and stubbornness.

This blend does not come by trying really hard to be compassionate and then pulling back when one has to be tough. Biblical love is always compassionate whether it is addressing sin in someone else's life or comforting a hurting soul. Compassion is built by cultivating all that has gone before it—*aretē, knowledge, self-control, endurance,* and *godliness.* As we have seen, compassion rests upon the base of commitment to Christ and the strength of courage for Christ.

Squishy sentimentality and hard-nosed rigidity in the name of love are far cries from *agapē* love. Neither of these positions is willing to sacrifice for the true spiritual needs of others. The sentimental mother, who cannot bear to see her child hurt or deprived of something, will be overly protective and permissive because her goal is her child's and her own immediate happiness. The heavy-handed father who is overly rigid and unbending responds that way because his goal is the control of his child—and often his own peace and quiet. Both miss the mark because their goals are unbiblical. They are not aiming for the restoration of the likeness of Christ in their child—nor in themselves. They have not seen God's mission for themselves. Therefore, they do not see it for their children.

Love moves freely between toughness and tenderness based upon whatever is needed at the moment to advance the mission of forming Christlikeness in others.

What a contrast to Paul's ministry example to the Thessalonians. Listen to his testimony of his work in that city. Notice the amazing gentleness of a nursing mother, yet the stern exhortation of a father "charging" his children. Biblical compassion is both tender and tough—sometimes at the same time. Also, note why Paul was able to move so freely from one to the other: he did not seek to please men but God (Galatians 1:10)! *Man-pleasers have no courage for Christ. Self-pleasers have no compassion like Christ.*

> For you yourselves know, brothers, that our coming to you was not in vain. But though we had already suffered and been shamefully treated at Philippi, as you know, we had boldness in our God to declare to you the gospel of God in the midst of much conflict. For our appeal does not spring from error or impurity or any attempt to deceive, but just as we have been approved by God to be entrusted with the gospel, so we speak, not to please man, but to please God who tests our hearts. For we never came with words of flattery, as you know, nor with a pretext for greed—God is witness. Nor did we seek glory from people, whether from you or from others, though we could have made demands as apostles of Christ. But we were gentle among you, like a nursing mother taking care of her own children. So, being affectionately desirous of you, we were ready to share with you not only the gospel of God but also our own selves, because you had become very dear to us.
>
> For you remember, brothers, our labor and toil: we worked night and day, that we might not be a burden to any of you, while we proclaimed to you the gospel of God. You are witnesses, and God also, how holy and righteous and blameless was our conduct toward you believers. For you know how, like a father with his children, we exhorted each one of you and encouraged you and charged you to walk in a manner worthy of God, who calls you into his own kingdom and glory. (1 Thessalonians 2:1–12 ESV)

Who wouldn't admire this kind of tenderhearted disciple-making? This is the heart of a good shepherd; it is the heart of our Lord.

COMPASSION

Compassion like Christ is the crowning beauty of the pillar of core values. It is attractive and displays astonishing tenderness, boldness, and wisdom. Ruth, even through her final days on this earth, was a beautiful portrait of a woman full of grace and truth. Her daughter testified even on the day she passed into eternity another local pastor visited her. His wife was suffering physically at that time. Not once did Ruth talk about her own condition. She inquired with genuine interest into his wife's condition. Ruth slipped into eternity a few hours later. Her grace was abounding even in the time of her own impending death.

Understand, however, that the column capitol of compassion like Christ is nothing but a ruin on the ground unless it is resting upon the column base of commitment to Christ and supported by the column strength of courage for Christ. Nothing mattered more to Ruth than her Savior Jesus Christ. Her relationship with Him and her knowledge of the Word were uppermost in her mind. Her commitment to Christ was undeniable, and it fueled the fire of her courage for Christ.

She would not hesitate to sit down in the living room of a young husband mistreating his wife and let him know in no uncertain terms what God thought of his actions—and how God wanted to make him into the kind of man God could use. Her daughter recalls how *she fearlessly faced difficult situations because she knew that the right thing must be done and that God was with her.* Commitment, courage, and compassion were not mere window dressing to Ruth. They were values of paramount importance to her.

A value is something we care about, something that is worth preserving, and something that must characterize every interaction we have with others. None of these core values are optional because they are all manifestations of Christlikeness, our ultimate goal.

Integrity demands all three. *Commitment* serves as the fins of a rocket guiding the missile to its intended target, keeping it on track. *Courage* functions as the engine propelling it onward. The rocket would miss the target entirely without the strength that overcomes the resistance of gravity and airflow. When the whole rocket functions properly, the payload of *compassion* is delivered according to plan and on target. Without all three the mission will fail.

As our chart shows, the essential virtues of *brotherly kindness* and *love* "produce a tenderhearted disciple-maker who seeks the lost and who by

his example and effort disciples others to live a Christ-centered life."
According to Jesus Christ, this kind of love is the trademark of Christlike character (John 13:35).

MISSION-MINDED COMPASSION

Compassion is not mere sentimentality, nor is it only helping the down
and out with financial or physical needs. It is more robust than that.
We saw when we studied *agapē* love that love is always mission-minded:
seeking the redemption and restoration of fallen man to the likeness of
Christ to the praise of His glory. It always seeks the best interests of the
subject, and those best interests will be primarily spiritual.

What we really think is important is revealed by the content of our
prayers. Listen to the prayer requests at any church or small group prayer
meeting. Examine your own prayers. Do we not pray mostly for the
physical, financial, and emotional needs of others? While that would
seem to be the compassionate thing to do, are these requests what our
Lord thinks are the most important needs for these people and for His
kingdom?

When we examine what has been called the Lord's Prayer in Matthew
6:9–13 (ESV), we see a much different agenda.[1] Read it carefully. I have
numbered its components.

Our Father in heaven,
1. hallowed be your name.
2. Your kingdom come,
3. your will be done, on earth as it is in heaven.
4. Give us this day our daily bread.
5. And forgive us our debts, as we also have forgiven our debtors.
6. And lead us not into temptation, but deliver us from evil.

Only one petition of this model prayer is for "daily bread"—current
physical and financial needs. *Everything else is for spiritual matters.* We
are to have a burning concern 1) for the advancement of the reverence
of the name of God in the earth, 2) for the coming reign of Christ upon
the earth, 3) for the fulfillment of His kingdom purposes in our lives,
4) for the supply of our daily necessities, 5) for the forgiveness of our
sins, which hinder spiritual fellowship with Him, and 6) for our deliver-

ance from temptation and evil so that God's work and not Satan's is advanced.

These are inspired priorities. Spiritual issues always trump physical issues. We have seen this pattern before: universals trump particulars; eternal matters trump temporal matters. Without a commitment to this mindset of meeting spiritual needs the exercise of compassion will be severely malformed. It will be reduced to mere good deeds—not bad in themselves, but not complete.

The fact is that if our compassion is truly mission-minded, a lion's share of our compassionate demonstrations will be targeted at the spiritual needs of those around us. Men and women need to be saved, and believers need to be delivered from the self-centeredness that keeps them from spiritual maturity. Compassionately dealing with the greatest needs of others will often require the facing of our own fears; thus, we need the courage for Christ discussed in the last chapter. Listen to Barclay's comments about *agapē* love.

> If we seek nothing but a man's highest good, we may well have to resist a man; we may well have to punish him; we may well have to do the hardest things to him—for the good of his immortal soul.[2]

> But the fact remains that whatever we do to that man will never be . . . vindictive; it will never even be merely retributory; it will always be done in that forgiving love which seeks . . . his highest good. In other words, *agapē* means treating men like God treats them—and that does not mean leaving them unchecked to do as they like.[3]

> Love is not *sentimental* (II Cor. 2:4). Christian love does not shut its eyes to the faults of others. Love is not blind. It will use rebuke and discipline when these are needed. The love which shuts its eyes to all faults, and which evades the unpleasantness of all discipline, is not real love at all, for in the end it does nothing but harm to the loved ones [emphasis his].[4]

While biblical compassion is tender-hearted (it feels deeply the distress others are in), it is never sentimental (governed by emotionality rather than spiritual purposefulness). People who judge an action by its emotional effects rather than its spiritual purposefulness will be misled. In the end, those who care mostly about the emotional outcome of an action will not be compassionate at all, for they will fail to address the greatest needs.

Like a doctor who cannot stand the sight of blood, they will avoid the procedures that will bring genuine healing. Their actions, though well intended, will be superficial and temporary. In the end, shortsighted remedies may be fatal. Pain medication for a complaint of stomach pain may make the patient feel better at first, but he will die when his inflamed appendix ruptures. *Compassion doesn't gauge its efforts by emotional outcome, but by genuine spiritual need.*

That is not to say that compassion does not consider emotions. Someone has said, "People do not care how much you know until they know how much you care." The doctor who knows he needs to do painful and risky surgery takes into consideration the fearfulness of the patient and the patient's great physical distress at the moment. He speaks in reassuring and confident tones when he describes what he must do to genuinely help. A doctor's comforting bedside manner will have a great deal to do with the patient's frame of mind going into the operation—and, in many cases, in his recovery. A truly compassionate doctor sees both the physical needs and the emotional but is not content to deal with only the emotional.

The same is true for the compassionate believer. He must always minister to the spiritual needs as the most important, but his "bedside manner" must remove as much as possible the fears and suspicions of the person he is trying to help.

THE KIND OF PERSON GOD USES

No one, of course, exhibits integrity—completeness and wholeness—like the Lord Jesus. The people in Palestine marveled at His tenderness as He touched lepers, healed the blind and lame, fed the multitudes, and released those afflicted with demons. But they also grew to respect His toughness. His rebukes, whether to faithless disciples, debating lawyers, or arrogant Pharisees were penetrating and humiliating. He knew that a mission-minded Great Physician had more than one tool in His medical kit. He always chose the tool that would most effectively accomplish the mission. Not everyone needed "surgery." Some needed instruction and others needed an advocate. Still others needed a Comforter. They all received precisely what they needed.

So what kind of person does God use? He uses someone like Jesus Christ. Let's listen in on a couple of conversations the Great Physician has with patients. In the second and third chapters of the book of Revelation, Jesus Christ addresses the needs of His churches. He speaks to their pastors, diagnosing their problems and prescribing remedies. Take a few moments right now before continuing this chapter and read Revelation 2–3.

Our Lord always assures these churches that *He knows their true condition—the first duty of compassion.* He knows those in Ephesus who have labored for Him, have endured much affliction, and have resisted those who are evil. He knows those in Smyrna who have faced great "tribulation and poverty." He also knows they will soon endure unprecedented suffering and many will give their lives for Him. He knows that some in Pergamos have been martyred. He knows the deeds of love, service, and faith of those in Thyatira and the good works of those in Sardis.

But examining their true condition reveals that the commitment to Christ in the church at Ephesus is dying and that the other churches are being infiltrated with the deadly evils of false teaching and immorality because their courage to face evildoers has been waning. *The compassionate Christ gives encouragement where that is the greatest spiritual need and rebuke where that is the greatest spiritual need. He moves quite easily from tough to tender. Compassion is not one-dimensional.*

The instructions to the church at Laodicea are most instructive for us in revealing the compassionate methods of our Lord. He finds nothing to commend in this church. Instead He finds self-satisfaction, self-confidence, and self-justification. He states their true condition: "wretched, and miserable [pitiable], and poor, and blind, and naked" (Revelation 3:17).

"Other Mother" Knew Their True Condition

Ruth labored hard and long to get to know the true condition of the girls she ministered to. They often fought her questioning. Both Debbie and Becky told me that Ruth spent hours with them to determine where their real battles lay. Debbie said, "I tried to get her to hate me; I didn't want anyone to love me." Ruth would patiently reply, "Debbie, it doesn't matter how much you try to get me to hate you, you can't stop me from loving you."

Debbie stayed in one of the upstairs bedrooms next to Ruth and Bill's and said, "Somehow she could always tell when I got up at night. I'm sure she wanted to be sure I wouldn't run away, but also she knew that sometimes at night a girl's guard would be down more than it was during the day. She often got me to talk at night." The questioning times were often painful. Debbie remembers, "I would say, 'Please don't go there; I don't want to think about those things.' I was bitter at my dad and didn't want to think about my sin. But she would say, 'I have to take you apart so that I can put you back together right. You're not put together right, at the moment.'"

> Christlike compassion knows the true condition, but Christlike compassion also knows the true remedy.

Becky recalled that Ruth would pick her up from her home and take her to breakfast at a restaurant before school to try to get her to talk. She says, "I tried to be deceptive, but she was good at breaking through it. She would lead the conversation to expose the needs of my heart. She knew what I needed. No matter what answer I gave her, she would counter with questions that would make me come to the right conclusion. If I refused to acknowledge what I knew was right, she would let me stew on it."

One night Becky ran away from home. She walked several miles and then hitched a ride with a man going to work. Fortunately, he knew she needed to be with someone who could help and drove her to her pastor's home. Ruth picked her up and spent several hours with her, trying to discover what was going on in her heart. By then, it was time for breakfast, so Ruth took her into the kitchen and had Becky set the table while Ruth continued to listen to her. Ruth knew she couldn't genuinely help until she knew the true condition of the girl's heart.

Both girls commented that Ruth never was cross with them; never did she display frustration or anger. She was the most godly person they had ever met. Debbie commented that Ruth was the first person in whom she had seen God's love. She said, "In the past, God's love was too abstract. Ruth made it real. She kept loving me while I was trying to get her to hate me." It was this kind of caring love that allowed Ruth to learn the true heart condition of these girls. Our Lord in Revelation 2–3, of course, knew instinctively the heart condition of these churches. You and I do not have that ability, but if we are compassionate, people will open their hearts to us.

Christlike compassion knows the *true condition*, but Christlike compassion also knows the *true remedy*. The Lord Jesus admonishes the Laodicean church to come to Him for the remedies for their spiritual poverty, their nakedness, and their blindness (Revelation 3:18). Then Christ makes an astonishing statement—one that some people have a hard time understanding. He says,

> As many as I love, I rebuke and chasten [discipline]: be zealous therefore, and repent. (Revelation 3:19)

Biblical compassion is not afraid to rebuke and discipline those it loves. In fact, biblical love *demands* that rebuke and discipline be administered when needed. The testimony of Christ Himself with these seven churches is a powerful proof.

"Other Mother" Knew the True Remedy

Becky once stole some narcotics from a medical doctor in whose office she was working. Ruth knew something was wrong and got the truth out of her. She drove her to face her employer to make things right. It broke his heart that Becky had been deceptive. His loving concern for her touched her deeply.

Another time Becky was stubbornly fighting her parents and trying to get kicked out of her Christian high school. At church Ruth noticed the change in her countenance, took her into an office during the service, and told her they were not leaving the office "until something happens." Becky said, "I knew she meant it, so I talked. Not many people could have gotten away with that methodology, but I knew with her I'd better get serious." Ruth knew when a girl needed comfort and when she needed confrontation.

Biblical compassion, however, isn't even a matter of balancing comfort with correction. Biblical correction doesn't need to be balanced with comfort and vice versa. Biblical wisdom administers the right measures of correction and comfort for each situation. The Lord's ministry to the Revelation churches is a model of this dual responsibility. Some people need more correction; some need more comfort—just as these churches did. The spiritual need will determine the spiritual remedy. In all cases, *fleshly* correction and *fleshly* comfort are equally destructive. *Biblical compassion knows the true condition and administers the true remedy.*

Sometimes, as we saw in the cases of the churches in Revelation 2–3, it falls our lot to deal with someone about hard issues in his life. We are our brother's keeper (Genesis 4:9). If the sin in a brother's life is a personal sin against us, God has mandated that we follow the steps outlined in Matthew 18 to restore the brother to fellowship with us and with God. If he stubbornly refuses reconciliation, the procedures in Matthew 18 end in disciplining the sinning member out of the church. God does not take sin lightly—nor should we.

If the sin is not a personal sin, there are any number of tools God has put into the toolbox of edification to get the sinning brother back on track. As we saw in Revelation 3, rebuke and chastening are two. For more grievous matters of unrepentant sin, church discipline is the proper tool. Paul was adamant with the Corinthian church that "a little leaven leaveneth the whole lump" (1 Corinthians 5:6). Paul's instruction to the church was to "put away from among yourselves that wicked person" (1 Corinthians 5:13). Again, God does not take sin lightly.[5]

We all will sin after one fashion or the other, but the Scriptures do not permit us to ignore sin in our own lives or in the lives of others in the body of Christ. Notice the Lord's tone to the churches in Revelation who were permitting immorality or false teaching to go unchallenged. Notice as well that His tone was strong even though many of those churches had many things right! The fact that Christ died on the cross to deal with sin is a statement about God's hatred for sin, not just a statement about the love of God for sinners.

We must confront in a "spirit of meekness, considering [ourselves], lest [we] also be tempted" (Galatians 6:1; 1 Thessalonians 5:14; James 5:19–20). We must remove the log from our own eye in order to be able to see clearly to remove the speck of dust from our neighbor's eye (Matthew 7:3–5). We do not have the option of doing nothing.

Those who have seen the depths of their own sinfulness and have also tasted the wonderful mercy of God upon repentance will, indeed, approach the sinning brother, not as a district attorney, but as a hopeful yet persistent fellow traveler on the pathway of reconciliation and sanctification.

PUTTING IT TOGETHER

My point in using this extended testimony of Ruth Morgan is to give you a picture of what full-bodied compassion looks like. Biblical compassion does not ignore problems; it seeks to address the genuine needs—especially spiritual needs—whenever possible. Jesus did not leave people as He found them. Everywhere He went He was alert to genuine needs and did something about them. He was on a mission of redeeming and restoring fallen man to the likeness of Himself for the glory of His Father. This is our mission as well.

So, is compassion like Christ tough or tender? Notice the two responsibilities Solomon commands. We must exercise both.

> Do not let kindness and truth leave you; Bind them around your neck. Write them on the tablet of your heart. So you will find favor and good repute in the sight of God and man. (Proverbs 3:3–4 NASB)

Compassion like Christ completes the pillar of core values. It blends *brotherly kindness* and *love* into a beautiful crown for Christian character. It is the final component in integrity. A man isn't complete without it—just as he isn't complete without *commitment* to Christ or *courage* for Christ. These three core values testify that the essential virtues are maturing. A Christian character—the marks of the Christ-centered life—is forming, to the glory of God.

Peter says that this kind of character will not only withstand the false teaching of the day but will provide an "abundant entrance into the everlasting kingdom." It is the evidence of our "calling and election"—the proof that we do, indeed, possess Christ.

We, the people of God, are to grow together "unto an holy temple in the Lord" (Ephesians 2:21). Each of us is a "living stone" (1 Peter 2:5)—in our analogy a pillar. "Only through the supporting columns of individual, mature saints does the church stand as a magnificent edifice to the glory of God."[6] No wonder he vowed to make it his life-long responsibility to remind his scattered congregation of the truths of 2 Peter 1. So crucial are they that he promised to make sure they would be reminded of these things after he went home to be with the Christ he loved. Notice the urgency of his words.

> Therefore I intend always to remind you of these qualities, though you know them and are established in the truth that you have. I think it right, as long as I am in this body, to stir you up by way of reminder, since I know that the putting off of my body will be soon, as our Lord Jesus Christ made clear to me. And I will make every effort so that after my departure you may be able at any time to recall these things. (2 Peter 1:12–15 ESV)

We must take our cue from the apostle. We must continually remind ourselves and those to whom we minister that we must *explore the farm*, then diligently *work the farm* to cultivate *aretē*—the pursuit of the excellence of Christlikeness—the *knowledge* of the person, work, and ways of Jesus Christ, *self-control, endurance, godliness, brotherly kindness,* and *love*. These are not optional window dressings for those who would be super-saints; they are essential virtues for us all. May God help us to diligently cultivate them!

Epilogue

CAN VIRTUE BE TAUGHT?

P lato in one of his discourses has Meno ask Socrates, "Can you tell
me Socrates—is virtue something that can be taught? Or does it
come with practice? Or is it neither teaching nor practice that gives it
to a man but natural aptitude or something else?"[1] Socrates concludes
that virtue is primarily a matter of *knowing,* and that if a person knows
what is right, he will do what is right.

Aristotle disagreed and saw virtue as the habit of *choosing* what is right
once a man knows what is right. He proposed as the standard of excellence for any virtue "the golden mean"—the peak between extremes.
Of course, Aristotle too had his critics who rejected his views in favor
of some newer thought.

How blessed we are that God has not left us to wonder whether virtue
can be taught and what it looks like! From the opening chapters of the
Scriptures God has shown us *Himself* as the epitome of excellence and
has offered His divine aid in our quest to become like Him. He obviously believes virtue can—and must—be taught.

A VOCABULARY OF VIRTUE

Virtue is taught best when a *vocabulary of virtue* exists within a *culture
of virtue.* Second Peter 1 gives us a working vocabulary of virtue—words
that represent what must become God-empowered habits—*characteristics* of life.

My burden for writing this book is that you will be able to see more
clearly what Christlikeness looks like and be able to express that in the
vocabulary of Scripture—the pursuit of the excellence of Christlikeness, knowledge, self-control, endurance, godliness, brotherly kindness,

189

and love. These virtues themselves are the overarching qualities of which so many other virtues are subsets. For example, the requirements of Paul in Timothy and Titus for pastors have at their foundation the *essential virtues* God inspired Peter to write about.

A Culture of Virtue

God intended for families and other groups of believers, most notably the church, to create an environment in which the members—particularly the leadership of the group—intentionally make *character connections* out of the daily experiences of life. In short, it should be an *aretegenic* (virtue-producing) environment.[2]

In such a culture the believer is aware of how his own actions and reactions and the actions and reactions of others measure up against a clear pattern of Christlikeness. Because he knows what virtue looks like, it is obvious to him when he or someone else lacks dedication to the pursuit of Christlikeness, a proper knowledge of Christ and His ways, self-control, endurance, godliness, brotherly kindness, or love. And when he sees the deficiency in himself, he sorrows over his condition, seeks his Lord's help and, if necessary, His forgiveness, and fortifies himself with scriptural wisdom to meet the challenge correctly the next time it comes around.

If he sees an absence of a certain virtue in a brother, his *commitment* to Jesus Christ demands that he *courageously* yet *compassionately* align himself with God's mission by restoring and edifying that brother so that he can become more like Christ.

This is how the Christian family should function; this is how God intended the Christian church to function. May God use *this book* to instill in you a *vocabulary of virtue*. May He use *you* to create a *culture of virtue* wherever He places you so that you can join Him in His mission of "redeeming and restoring fallen creatures to the likeness of His Son to the praise of His glory."

APPENDICES

Appendix One

FOOLS BY DEFAULT[1]

We need to be reminded that becoming wise is not an automatic matter. All of us are born fools (Proverbs 22:15) and will continue to become "better" fools unless we submit ourselves to the disciplines of wisdom. The fact that we are *fools by default* should not surprise us if we understand the depravity of man. Neither should it surprise us that unless we take specific measures to counteract that default status, we will progress only to become increasingly useless as servants of God.

Proverbs, the parental training manual for wisdom, goes to great lengths to acquaint us with the ways of the fool so that we can avoid his path and his end. Solomon describes for us three grades of fools in Proverbs 1:22. He says, "How long, *ye simple ones*, will ye love simplicity? and the *scorners* delight in their scorning, and *fools* hate knowledge?"

THE SIMPLE MAN

The simple man is the budding fool. The word *simple* means "open, wide, and spacious." The simple man is one who is open-minded and, therefore, vulnerable to all kinds of enticement. He has not developed a discriminating judgment about what is right or wrong (1:22; 9:13, 16–18; 14:15). He is gullible to temptation and is naive—not about sin, but about sin's effects on him. Because he is undiscerning, he easily drifts into moral corruption. He is aimless, but his tempters and temptresses are not (1:10ff.; 7:6ff.; 22:3). Apart from godly tutelage, he is on the road to death (1:32; 7:7, 27; 22:3). If he refuses to learn, he will graduate to a fool (14:18). In the end, along with the other types of fools, he will be judged because he has rejected God's wisdom and discipline (1:22–25, 32).

THE FOOL

The fool is the common, ordinary, generic, garden-variety fool. The word *fool* means "dullard" or "one who is obstinate." He is slow, but not in mental capacity. He is slow in his willingness to obey and has an inclination to make wrong decisions because of his stubbornness.

Proverbs describes him as self-confident (12:15; 14:3, 16; 18:2; 26:12; 28:26), unreliable (26:6), and a grief to his parents (15:20; 17:21). He is restless (17:24; 20:3), deceptive (10:18; 14:8; 17:7), resentful of correction (15:5; 17:10), and unteachable (1:7, 22; 13:19; 17:10; 18:2; 23:9; 26:11; 27:22). He does not prepare his heart for wisdom (17:16), often appears illogical (26:7, 9), and delights to speak of evil (12:23; 15:2, 14; 19:1). In addition, he makes light of sin (14:9), slanders others (10:18), is known as a mischief maker (10:23; 26:11), has an anger problem (12:16; 14:16; 27:3; 29:11), and will eventually fall (1:32; 3:35; 10:8, 10; 11:29).

A young person who is weak in discernment exhibits characteristics of the simple man. He seems easily swayed by peers and seems to end up in trouble unintentionally. These characteristics should certainly raise concerns on the part of his parents and leaders. There is much that can be done to counter his simple-mindedness, as the following chart points out. The concern should escalate greatly, however, if his life is moving from this state of impressionableness to a state of stubbornness. If he now defends his actions and deceives others to cover his actions, he is fast becoming a common fool. If those actions and attitudes become his lifestyle, parents should have serious doubts about whether he knows Christ as his Savior. There is yet another level of fool, however.

THE SCORNER

The scorner is a deliberate, mean-spirited troublemaker. He is not content to be evil himself but is bent on corrupting others. He rejects rebuke (13:1), hates those who correct him (15:12), mocks justice (19:28), and enjoys despising good (1:22). He is hotheaded and arrogant (21:24) and is, therefore, odious to society (24:9; 29:8).

Satan himself is the master scorner—the ultimate fool. He was characterized by Jesus as destructive (i.e., a murderer) and a deceiver (John 8:44). Those two characteristics are dominant elements in this fool's life. He is becoming conformed more and more to the image of his master, Satan.

The progression of evil in these classes of men, and Proverbs' instruction about how to deal with each one, can be summarized in the following chart.

	THE SIMPLE MAN (THE BUDDING FOOL)	THE FOOL (THE COMMON FOOL)	THE SCORNER (THE FULL-BLOWN FOOL)
CHARACTERISTICS	• Unguarded • Defenseless • Weak • Impressionable	• Unrestrained • Disobedient/ deceptive • Stubborn • Involved (in evil)	• Uncontrollable • Devilish/destructive • Mean • Incorrigible
METHODS OF CORRECTION	• Appeal to him about the consequences of his actions (8:5–7; 9:1, 4, 6). • Strike the scorner and the simple will be warned (19:25; 21:11).	• Appeal to him about the consequences of his actions (8:5–7). • Rebuke him (26:5) but don't debate with him (23:9; 26:4; 29:9). • Restrain him (7:22). • Punish him (19:29; 26:3). • Don't honor him (24:7; 26:1, 8). • Avoid his companionship (13:20; 14:7).	• Punish him (9:12; 19:25; 21:11). • Give him strong judgments (19:29). • Expel him/cast him out (22:10). • Expect God to mock him (3:34).

THE PURITAN VIEW OF SIN[2]

There is a growing trend within evangelical circles to view the sin nature differently than has been historically taught from the Pauline epistles. Increasingly the sin nature is viewed as merely a weakened condition of unredeemed humanity. Its pull is thought to come only from the residual sinful propensities of the formerly unredeemed body and its mind—its memories and habits. Such a truncated view of indwelling sin calls for less watchfulness, less dependency, and far less severity when dealing with sin in our own lives and in the lives of others. The remedy for these sinful propensities when viewed in this fashion is to apply more nurturing even though the Scriptures call for mortification.

In order to help set the record straight about how biblical theology has historically viewed the nature of indwelling sin, I include here an article by J. I. Packer, an authority on the history of theology. Packer's ecclesiastical decisions of recent years are regrettably unbiblical, but his grasp of the history of doctrine, particularly of the Puritans, is unparalleled in evangelicalism. Here is Packer's summary.

> The Puritans as a body manifested an acute awareness of the holiness, righteousness, hatred of sin, and judicial severity against sin that marks the great, gracious, omniscient, and omnipresent God of the Bible. Their sharp-eyed discernment of the pervasiveness, repulsiveness, and deadliness of sin sprang directly from this deep sense of God as holy. Their sensitivity to sin as an inner force, devious and wily, tyrannizing the unconverted and tormenting the saints, was extraordinary. They remain Christianity's past masters in this particular field of understanding. They saw sin as a perverted energy within people that enslaves them to God-defying, self-gratifying behavior, and by distraction, deceit, and direct opposition weakens and overthrows their purposes of righteousness. They perceived sin as the moral equivalent of a wolf in sheep's

clothing, presenting itself to us again and again as good, desirable, and a necessity of life, thereby corrupting our conscience so that we lose the sense of its guiltiness, and cherish it as if it were a friend rather than an enemy.

In *The Great Divorce* C. S. Lewis pictures a man with a lizard on his shoulder, representing lawless lust. The lizard whispers in his ear about how essential it is to his continued well-being. When the angel asks, "Shall I kill it?" the man's first response is to say no. (One thinks of Augustine's prayer: "Give me chastity, but not yet.")

The Puritans would have applauded Lewis's lizard as a perfect projection of the way sin entrenches its various forms of expression in Christians' lives. Puritan theology affirmed that in Christians, sin has been dethroned but not yet destroyed. Now sin takes on, as it were, a life of its own, seeking to re-establish the dominion it has lost. Its power appears both in bad habits, which are often deep-rooted and linked with temperamental weaknesses, and in sudden forays and frontal assaults at points where one thought oneself invulnerable. Of itself sin never loses its strength. The most that happens is that with advancing age, ups and downs of health, and shifting personal circumstances, indwelling sin finds different modes of expression. But wherever it appears, in whatever form, Christians are charged not just to resist it, but to attack it and seek to do it to death—in other words, to mortify it, in the biblical sense of that word (see Rom. 8:13; Col. 3:5).

Puritan teaching on mortifying the lusts that tempt us is businesslike and thorough. It includes the disciplines of self-humbling, self-examination, setting oneself against all sins in one's spiritual system as a preliminary to muscling in on any one of them, avoiding situations that stoke sin's boiler, watching lest you become sin's victim before you are aware of its approach, and praying to the Lord Jesus Christ specifically to apply the killing power of his cross to the particular vicious craving on which one is making one's counterattack. "Set faith at work on Christ for the killing of thy sin," wrote the greatest Puritan teacher, John Owen. "His blood is the great sovereign remedy for sin-sick souls. Live in this, and thou wilt die a conqueror; yea, thou wilt, through the good providence of God, live to see thy lust dead at thy feet."[3]

The Puritans have always had a bad press. Their emphasis on each Christian's lifelong war to the death with "besetting" (habitual) sins has sometimes been dismissed as Manichean (denying the goodness of created human nature), morbid (denying the joy of natural behavior), and morally unreal (obsessed with self-flagellation, in disregard of everything else). But all of this is factually incorrect, and the idea that fighting sin was all the Puritan saints ever thought about is quite wrong. Love for God, joyful assurance, spiritual-mindedness, honesty and public spirit, quiet acceptance of God's will, the pathway of persistent prayer, and the power of the hope of glory, are among the many themes that are greatly developed in Puritan teaching about holiness. It was not all harping on a single note. Yet it is true that a drumbeat stress on detecting, resisting, and overcoming sin's down drag appears everywhere. This obtrusive emphasis has kept many in the past from seeing that Puritan holiness is fundamentally a cheerful affair of peace, joy, worship, fellowship, and growth. The solemn business of self-scrutiny and suffering, inward and outward, as one strives and struggles against sin is only one side of it. But in an age in which self-ignorance, secular-mindedness, moral slackness and downright sin are as common among Christians as they are today, it is doubtless from the stern side of Puritanism—the side that forces on us realism about our sinfulness and our sins—that we have most to learn.

Appendix Three

DISCOURSE ON TEMPERANCE (SELF-CONTROL)[4]

The apostle's third direction to the Christian as to how he was to make his "calling and election sure," is—"Add to knowledge temperance." Temperance, according to the current use of the English language, signifies freedom from excess in the gratification of the appetites, those principles of our nature which we possess in common with the lower animals, the humblest part of our complex constitution. It is opposed to all epicurism, gluttony, drunkenness, and incontinence. The temperate man abstains from all forbidden, sensual pleasures, and is moderate in the use of even lawful enjoyments of this kind. Christians are required to be thus strictly temperate. They are forbidden to "make provision for the flesh to fulfil the lusts thereof." They are commanded by their Master to "take heed lest their hearts be overcharged with surfeiting [dissipation] and drunkenness." "Be not filled with wine," says the Apostle Paul, "wherein is excess." "Walk honestly"—respectably— "in the day, not in rioting [carousings, orgies] and drunkenness, not in chambering [sexual immorality] and wantonness [sensuality]." "Mortify your members which are upon the earth, fornication, uncleanness, and inordinate affection." "The time past of our life," says the Apostle Peter, referring to the unconverted state of those to whom he wrote, "may suffice us to have wrought the will of the Gentiles, when we walked in lasciviousness [sensuality], lusts, excess of wine, revellings [carousing, orgies], banquetings [drinking parties], and abominable idolatries." One of the very first things, which "the grace of God, that bringeth salvation to all," teaches those who receive it in truth is, "to deny worldly lusts," and "to live soberly."

This species of temperance, however, can go but a short way, or rather no way at all, towards making a man's "calling and election sure." Habitual intemperance, in any of its forms, clearly proves that a man has not been called of God. Even occasional acts of intemperance, must

199

make a man's calling very doubtful to himself as well as to others. But the strictest temperance is no proof of conversion. It may, it often does, originate in bodily constitution, in education, in natural good sense, in a clear apprehension of, and delicate sensibility to what is decent and honest, becoming and honorable in moral feeling and conduct, without any reference whatever to religious principle. The want of it degrades a man almost to the level of the brutes [the animal kingdom], or even below that level; but the presence of it, even in its most perfect form, by no means gives a man ground to conclude that he has a place among "the called and chosen."

The word "temperance"—ἐγκράτειαν—here and in the New Testament generally, includes this, and a great deal more. It has a deeper root, and a much wider sphere of influence. The word properly signifies "self-command," and denotes the right state of the mind, heart, and life, in reference to those objects in the world which naturally call forth our desires, whether it be pleasure, profit, power, or reputation. It is just another word for moderation or self-control, and is descriptive of the right state of the thoughts, affections, and behavior, in reference to "things seen and temporal."

The foundation of temperance, in this extensive sense, lies in the just estimate which the faith of Christian truth leads a man to form of the intrinsic and comparative value of "all that is in the world—the lust of the flesh, the lust of the eyes, and the pride of life;" that is, all that the eye or the flesh desires, and all of which living men are apt to be proud. The Christian does not consider the wealth, the honors, and the pleasures of the world, as things altogether destitute of value; but he sees that that value is by no means so great as the deluded worshippers of Mammon suppose it to be. He sees, with equal clearness, that the possession of them cannot make him happy, nor the want of them make him miserable. They cannot obtain for him the pardon of his sin; they cannot pacify his conscience; they cannot transform his character; they cannot give him strength in weakness, consolation in sorrow; they cannot save him from the pit of corruption, or the deeper pit of perdition; they cannot give life in death, or secure happiness for ever; and the want of them, though it may—in some cases must—give him severe uneasiness, cannot deprive him of the favour of God, of the testimony of a good conscience, or of the hope of glory, honour, and immortality, beyond death and the grave. The views which, as a believer, he has obtained, lead him to look on the prosperities of life with some measure of alarm. They appear to him polluted with sin, replete with temptation, pregnant of danger to his highest interests.

With these views, he is temperate in all things. "He is temperate in his desires of earthly enjoyments; not setting his affections on the things on the earth. He is temperate in his pursuit of them; he does not *labour* so much for the meat that perisheth, as for that which endureth unto eternal life." He is temperate in his attachment to them, while he enjoys them; he does not say, "Soul, take thine ease; eat, drink, and be merry; thou hast good laid up for many years." He is temperate in his regrets when he is deprived of them; he does not feel as if he had lost his all, or say, "My gods are taken from me, and what have I more?" He does not allow his natural desire of such things to interfere with his convictions and obligations. He keeps the body, and all the desires connected with things seen and temporal, in subjection. The world has not dominion over him: he is master of himself; and, being possessed of a far better inheritance than it can give him, he does not expect or seek on earth real, perfect happiness, which he believes to be in heaven and secured for him there. This is the Christian temperance, which the apostle says, must be added to an energetic, enlightened faith,[5] in order to the making of our "calling and our election sure." It is for those who have earthly relatives to be as if they had them not; for those who weep, as though they wept not; for those who rejoice, as though they rejoiced not; for those who use this world, to use it as not abusing it,—knowing that "the fashion of this world passeth away" (1 Cor. vii. 29–31).

Now, this temperance is to be *added* to "faith, virtue, and knowledge." It cannot exist without these; it naturally results from them. It is what the Christian believes that makes him temperate in this world. Never were there more temperate men, in the sense we have explained, than the Christian apostles: in the world, they were not *of* it. How were they formed to their temperate, their unworldly character? We shall allow them to answer the question themselves. One of them says, "The cross of Christ"—i.e., the faith of the truth about Christ—has "crucified the world to me, and me to the world." "This is the victory," says another, "which overcometh the world, even our faith." The man who believes that he has an inheritance laid up for him in heaven—that he is rich in faith—the heir of a kingdom; that there is reserved for him a crown of life, and that rivers of pleasure are awaiting him at God's right hand for ever more—is not likely to be intemperate in his estimates, desires, attachments, and regrets, in reference to worldly wealth, honors, or pleasures; especially as he believes, also, that an inordinate regard to the latter is inconsistent with the enjoyment of the former.

And it is not a *dead* faith—it is not merely speculation about Christian truth which will suffice to produce this temperance; it must be such a faith as has had energy [*aretē*] added to it. The world has a strong hold on the human heart, and it requires nothing short of "the power of the world to come" brought in the heart by believing, to enable the Christian to keep attachment to it in due subjection.

Moreover, the faith, to which temperance is added, requires to be enlightened as well as energetic. Where knowledge has not been added to an energetic faith, a bastard kind of temperance is in danger of being produced. To escape the temptation, an energetic but unenlightened faith has led men to go out of the world, to become hermits and monks; and availing themselves of this tendency of unenlightened energy, men of corrupt minds have "forbidden to marry, and commanded to abstain from meats which God hath created to be received with thanksgiving of them that believe and obey the truth;" as if "every creature of God were not good, and any of them to be refused if it be received with thanksgiving: for it is sanctified by the word of God and prayer." Knowledge is profitable, even necessary, to direct where, and how, and when, self-denial is to be exercised; when pursuits and pleasures, lawful in themselves, are to be followed and indulged, and when they are to be abstained from—when and how the world may and ought to be used without being abused.

The manner in which this temperance—which is just the opposite to the love of the world—the manner in which this disposition, and the conduct to which it naturally leads, make a Christian's "calling and election sure," is so obvious, that it does not require more than a word or two to point it out. For what is the Christian calling? It is this— "Come out from among them," that is, from among "the world lying under the wicked one," "and touch not the unclean thing, and I will receive you, and ye shall be My sons and daughters, saith the Lord Almighty." And what is the Christian election? The Saviour has chosen all His people out of the world that they may be like Him, "not of the world." The man, then, who makes things seen and temporal the principle subject of his thoughts and object of his affections—who is not temperate in the sense we have explained—makes it plain, whatever profession he may make, that *he* has not been thus called and chosen; he is still of the world. On the other hand, he whose faith, energetic and enlightened, is overcoming the world—in whose heart, affections, and pursuits, the world has its proper, that is, a very subordinate place— has the evidence in himself that he is among the called and chosen ones, and his unworldly dispositions and conduct silently, but expressively, confess before the world that he is a stranger and a pilgrim on the earth, and plainly declare that he is seeking a better country—that is, an heavenly.

Appendix Four

THE MAP METHOD OF MEDITATION

Find a portion of Scripture relevant to your problem or find one that deals with a Bible truth you wish to master. Always meditate on Scripture that God's Spirit "highlights" as you are reading His Word.

MEMORIZE THE PASSAGE

Memorizing often occurs automatically if the passage is studied intensely enough in the next step. During temptation you must know exactly what God has said word for word. Merely having a general idea about what is right is not enough when dealing with the deceptive nature of your own heart. A man who cannot remember God's exact words is in danger of leaning to his "own understanding" (Proverbs 3:5).

Many people memorize verses by writing the first letter of each word in a verse. For example, Psalm 119:105 says, "Thy word is a lamp unto my feet, and a light unto my path." The first letters are

T w i a l u m f, a a l u m p.

The first letter of each word (include the punctuation just as it appears in the text) gives enough of a prompt so that you can recall the word, but since the whole word is not present, you do not find yourself merely reading the words mindlessly.

ANALYZE THE PASSAGE

Study the passage, asking the Holy Spirit to give you a thorough understanding of its message. You can do an intensive study on the passage by listing the major words of the verses and then using an English dictionary to find out the meaning for each word. If possible, look up each word in a Greek or Hebrew dictionary or check the meaning of each word in *Strong's Exhaustive Concordance*. Once you are sure of each word's meaning, put the passage in your own words (i.e., paraphrase it).

A more extensive study would involve using a commentary or good study Bible to help you understand more about who wrote the passage, to whom it was written, and why. Most importantly, pray that God will illumine your understanding. Ask Him to teach you what He wants you to know from the Scriptures.

Personalize the Passage

Plan concrete changes in your life that are consistent with your understanding of the passage. Such plans would include schedules, steps, and details. Ask yourself, "When have I failed to obey this truth in the past? When am I likely to meet a temptation again? What should be the godly response the next time I am tempted?" Think through this "game plan" thoroughly and in advance of the next temptation. Use the passage in a personal prayer to God. For example, a person meditating on James 4:1–11 may begin a prayer this way: "Lord, You tell me here in James 4:1 that the conflict I am having with John is the result of my own lusts—my desires to have something my way. I know that isn't pleasing to You. Instead of responding in anger to John, I need Your help and grace, which You promised in James 4:6 when You said that You resist the proud but give grace to the humble. Help me to humble myself instead of proudly insisting on my way. I want to allow You to lift me up in Your time. . . ."

SECTION ONE: ESSENTIAL VIRTUES MATERIALS

The discussion to follow will refer to these components available from JourneyForth.

- *Essential Virtues: Marks of the Christ-Centered Life*—296-page book of thirteen chapters with included study guide. After he reads a chapter in the text, the reader answers questions in the study guide to help him apply the material to his life.

- *Essential Virtues Video Series*—DVDs containing thirteen thirty-five-minute sessions by Jim Berg. The thirteen inspirational sessions correspond to the thirteen chapters of *Essential Virtues* and provide an effective way to teach the truths of Christian character development to large groups, small-group discussion classes, or individuals in one-on-one discipleship opportunities.

SECTION TWO: PRESENTATION AND STUDY FORMATS

The components mentioned above can be used in a variety of ways, as discussed below, to fit your circumstances and ministry goals. The greatest impact occurs, of course, when all components are used together.

INDIVIDUAL USE OF ESSENTIAL VIRTUES AND THE ACCOMPANYING STUDY GUIDE

An individual can systematically study through the truths of *Essential Virtues*. After reading each chapter, the reader will answer questions in the study guide to apply the material to his own life. A good pace is to cover one chapter per week.

One-on-One Discipleship

A person discipling someone else can have him work through one chapter of *Essential Virtues* and the study guide per week. For additional impact, the person being discipled can watch the video session on that chapter before he begins his weekly study. Counseling and discipleship can then deal with issues that were raised by the study guide application questions.

Adult Elective Training Courses

Pastors can offer the videos for interested adults in a Sunday training hour, before the evening service, or on a given night of the week for thirteen weeks. This latter option will fit the weekly Bible study classes that many churches offer for their people.

Small-Group Discussion Sessions

Adult Sunday school classes can be broken down into small groups of eight to ten participants. If groups consist of only men or only women, the members are more likely to share what they have learned with others. Each class member will study through a chapter of *Essential Virtues* and answer the questions in the study guide each week. When the members come to the small-group class, one class member can lead a discussion of what the members have learned that week about the Scriptures and about themselves.

The leader needs to do little more than ask the questions in the study guide and go around the class allowing each member to share answers. More complete help for small-group leaders is given in the next section of this Leader's Guide, "Information for Small-Group Leaders."

Entire Church Congregations Using Weekly Video Series Combined with Small-Group Discussion Sessions

This option provides the most saturation for your church congregation and integrates *Essential Virtues*, the study guide, and the *Essential Virtues Video Series*. Of course, the videos can be viewed without follow-up small-group discussion sessions, but the greatest impact will come when the viewers are made to personally apply the truths by using the book and study guide in conjunction with the video series.

A pastor can show the video series on a weekly basis to the entire congregation on Sunday evening for thirteen weeks. For example, a pastor could show session 1 on a Sunday evening and then have the adults read chapter 1 of *Essential Virtues* and work through the corresponding questions in the study guide during the following week. The next Sunday the adult small-group Sunday school classes would spend the entire time in application and discussion. This format has the advantage of providing an extended, unified instruction time for the whole congregation.

Home Bible Studies

Essential Virtues and its study guide may also be used in a two-hour home Bible study in conjunction with the video series. The first session would consist of showing the first video (about thirty-five minutes), taking time for a fifteen- to twenty-minute fellowship break, and then spending forty minutes to an hour covering the material in "The First Week" of section three in this Leader's Guide. Throughout the coming week, the participants would go through chapter 1 of the book and study guide on their own.

When the group members assemble a week later, they would discuss during the first forty to forty-five minutes what they learned during the week as they studied through the text and study guide. They could take a fifteen- to twenty-minute fellowship break and then reconvene to watch the next video (about thirty-five minutes) in preparation for chapter 2 the following week.

The group can be as large as ten to twelve participants or can be as small as one or two people you are personally discipling.

Concentrated Staff Training

The videos can be viewed in a concentrated time frame as part of a weeklong staff training program for church, school, or camp staffs.

SECTION THREE: INFORMATION FOR SMALL-GROUP LEADERS

If you are a small-group leader using the study guide, the following information will help you get the most out of your time with the group. These methods have been used very effectively during the Sunday school hour in local churches. The comments below will be geared for that situation but can be adapted for use in Bible studies at home or in one-on-one counseling situations.

Each member of your group should have his own copy of *Essential Virtues*. It is important to stress to the group that character development takes time.

Though it is not essential that you do so, if you have read through *Essential Virtues* yourself before you begin this responsibility as a group leader, you will be able to speak with great conviction about the necessity of taking time. You will then have an overview of how the group should progress and why taking time is such an important matter in the development of Christian character. Of course, if you cannot read through the entire book before beginning, do not despair; work on one chapter at a time with the group.

THE FIRST WEEK

The first week's lesson will be an introductory session for chapter 1, which your small-group members will be studying throughout the following week. They will not have completed the study guide questions this first week, so there will be no discussion time during this first session. You can use this first week's discussion time to pass out the books and to have each member of the group introduce himself.

Once everyone is acquainted, you can briefly survey the materials for the participants. Tell them that before they leave this first meeting, they will have watched the video session for the first chapter, which they will be studying during the coming week.

SUBSEQUENT WEEKS

After your first week together, once you have opened in prayer, you will begin a group discussion time.

Small-Group Discussion

Small-group discussion is one of the most effective means for helping your group members think through the personal implications of a lesson. Remember the following guidelines as you facilitate group discussion:

1. Small-group discussion is most productive when there are ten or fewer participants and when the participants are arranged in a circle rather than in rows. Each participant can then make eye contact with everyone else in the group.

2. Begin discussion by reading to the group the introductory paragraphs in the study guide for that week's chapter and then asking group members to relate to the group one of the most significant truths they learned in the chapter during the past week. Going around the group one person at a time, in the order in which they are seated, helps the participants feel more at ease in giving public feedback. This is where some of the greatest benefits of the class time will come—as believers share with each other what God is doing in their lives (1 John 1:3). A participant hearing someone share the same idea or principle that God has taught him can be greatly encouraged that God is working in his life and that he is on the right track. You may even spend your entire discussion time on this one aspect of discussion.

3. If you have time, you can then move on to the discussion questions in the study guide, asking the participants whether there were any questions that were unclear or for which they couldn't think of an answer. If someone points out a certain question with which he had trouble, ask other group members what they put down for an answer and why.

4. Carefully guide the flow of the discussion. You should not dominate the conversation, but you must motivate group members by restating contributions made, expressing appreciation for all input, and asking follow-up questions.

   If the discussion gets sidetracked, you will need to refocus it tactfully. You may also need to keep dominant group members from monopolizing the discussion, or you may need to privately encourage quiet participants to become involved. Going around the group asking each one to state what God has spoken to him about as mentioned above is often enough to get some measure of response from everyone—including those who are naturally withdrawn.

5. Draw the discussion to a close by asking the group members to summarize the conclusions they have reached together. You can write the conclusions on a flip-chart pad, chalkboard, or overhead transparency. Stating clear conclusions helps participants feel that the discussion time was productive.

6. If your group exhibits a high level of involvement and interest, you will find that the Sunday school hour is not enough time to cover the material to everyone's satisfaction. Offer an extended time of discussion at another time during the week at your home or at the home of one of the group members. This will allow for a greater measure of discipleship of your group members.

ADDITIONAL IDEAS

Atmosphere

Try to cultivate a warm, informal atmosphere throughout each group session. This will motivate participants to be responsive when the time comes for them to participate or for you to challenge them. Unless it is desirable to have a clearly defined teacher/student relationship (as it might be in a Bible institute or college setting), do not view yourself as the authority in the group but as a colearner and facilitator of your group's learning. Take time in private conversation to ask about what is happening in the lives of the participants and to develop a genuine concern for them.

Your small groups will be much more open if you have the men meet with the men and the women meet with the women. Your applications can be much more pointed and the interchange freer if group members feel they are interacting with people who face similar challenges.

Late Starters and Stragglers

You may have people come into your small-group class—especially if it is an adult Sunday school class—who have not had the benefit of the previous weeks of study. If they are going to be a permanent part of your class, they should be assured that they can begin right where the class is even though the chapters you have studied build one upon the other. They can catch up in the text if they would like to do so, but encourage them to start studying the same chapter the rest of the class is studying.

There are enough stand-alone truths in each chapter that they can still benefit from the study.

If you have people who have been part of the group all along but are not doing the work, try to speak to them outside the class context and ask them whether you can be of any help to them. Perhaps they aren't good readers or don't think they can do all the work. Encourage them to try at least to read the chapters and pick out two significant sentences even if they think they can do nothing more.

Of course, if they have not read the material and then try to take part in the discussion by presenting merely their own opinions, they should be asked privately not to participate in the discussion if they have not studied what the rest of the class has studied.

Building Up One Another

You will learn in chapter 9 of *Essential Virtues* about the importance of building up one another in the body of Christ. Small-group discussion times led by a tactful and well-prepared leader are one of the most effective ways of ministering to each other. May God make it a profitable time for you and your group as you study *Essential Virtues*.

Study Guide for

ESSENTIAL VIRTUES

The Portrait of the Christ-Centered Life

☐ Take Time to Read

Begin this study by prayerfully reading the preface and chapter 1 of *Essential Virtues*.

☐ Take Time to Reflect

While traveling with the family in an automobile, the favorite question for children is often "Are we there yet?" We adults, too, like to see if we are making progress in an endeavor, whether it is checking the scales to see if our weight is down, watching the mile markers on the road to see if we are near our exit, or checking investments online to see if our portfolio is growing. We like to know how we are doing.

Our study in this book is about the progress we are making in the development of a Christian character. As you might guess, character is a little harder to measure than weight, mileage, or investments. There are no numbers to track. God has, nonetheless, provided seven character markers for us in 2 Peter 1 that reveal our progress toward Christlikeness. Combined, they form one of the most complete pictures of Christlikeness in the Bible.

This study guide will help you evaluate your progress on each marker. Mile markers on a highway help us only if we look at them. Therefore, take the time to reflect prayerfully and carefully on each study question throughout this study guide. Your answers to the questions will give you a good idea of how much progress you are making and where you need to improve. So let's get started.

1. In your own words, explain the concept of simultaneous yet sequential.

The following questions apply to The Harvest section of the chapter—the results of pursuing a Christlike character.

2. The Cure for Apathy—Would you say that you are a "self-starter" in your spiritual growth (i.e., you have a regular, daily time with God in His Word, seek Him daily in prayer, fellowship regularly with believers, listen carefully to the preaching at a local church, etc.)? Or do you have to be "pushed" or "pulled" by someone else continually because you are "stalled" in your progress? Are you involved in "pushing" and "pulling" others who need to make progress? Explain your answers.

3. The Path to Intimacy—Describe your relationship with your heavenly Trainer before you started this study. What instructions has He been giving you for improvement? What areas of your life does He have you working on? Are you really engaged in His training program for you, or are you "staying home from the gym" by being lazy, resistant, or inattentive? Again, explain your answers.

4. The Key to Discernment—The text said, "The near-sighted believer can't see anything beyond the present draw of the world—neither does he want to. Furthermore, when he faces a trial or temptation, he is focused only on the immediate situation and how he can get relief. He cannot see beyond the trial or temptation to what God wishes to do through it in perfecting Christlikeness—the essential virtues." How attentive are you to qualities God is trying to develop in you through the trials and tests of life? Explain your answer.

5. The Basis for Assurance—Can you truly say that the seed of salvation has been sprouting in your life? What evidences can you cite?

6. The Requirement for Stability—Christian character acts like a rudder on a boat. It keeps the believer heading in the right direction rather than "being driven by the wind and tossed" (James 1:6). How prone are you to emotional ups and downs as your circumstances change? How well do you weather temptations? Are you known to be a stable person—an anchor to those around

you—or are you one who frequently has to be "anchored" by someone else because you easily drift off course when facing difficult circumstances and temptations? Describe your stability level.

7. The Cause for Expectancy—Peter tells us that we can expect the Lord to prepare an "abundant entrance into the everlasting kingdom" to the same degree that we have been purposefully and diligently cultivating our likeness to Christ. On a scale of 1 to 4 how would you rate your diligence in cultivating these qualities in your life up to this point (1 being lowest and 4 being highest)? Explain your answer.

Don't get discouraged if your answers to these questions indicate that you have much work to do in cultivating Christlikeness. The whole purpose of our study of Peter's admonitions is to evaluate ourselves and then learn how we can indeed develop these marks of a Christ-centered life. Give diligence to this study, asking God to produce the fruit of His Spirit in you as you study His Word and obey it.

☐ TAKE TIME TO RENEW YOUR MIND

Throughout this study you will be challenged to memorize the passage under discussion in this book—2 Peter 1:1–15—and some pertinent parallel passages. Look up the verses in your Bible, copy them on note cards, and review them several times throughout the day. Try to memorize them word-perfect so that you can easily meditate upon them during free times when you do not have the cards with you. Each week continue to review the verses from previous weeks so that you do not lose the recall of these important passages.

- This week memorize 2 Peter 1:1–2.

☐ TAKE TIME TO RESPOND TO GOD

To build a relationship with God, you will need to respond to Him about the things you have learned from Him in your Bible study. Strengthen your prayer time by "PRAYing." Jot down some topics you wish to include in your conversation with God so that you are not speaking without thinking.

Praise—What have you seen about Who God is or what He has done that you can praise Him for?

Repent—What has God shown you that needs to be confessed to Him and forsaken?

Ask—What do you need God to do for you in order for you to become more like Him?

Yield—Where do you need to humble yourself before God and give up something you are stubbornly holding on to?

Study Unit Two

THE PROVISIONS FOR THE CHRIST-CENTERED LIFE

☐ TAKE TIME TO READ

- Begin this study by prayerfully reading chapter 2 of *Essential Virtues*.

☐ TAKE TIME TO REFLECT

When our children were young, we vacationed annually at a log cabin I had built in a wooded area about an hour's drive from our home in Greenville, South Carolina. The times we spent at our "little cabin in the woods" built a wonderful family unity and many warm memories of special times together.

While our daughters had only to get into the minivan when we were ready to leave, Patty and I—especially Patty—had an enormous amount of work to do to get everything ready and into the van. Patty had to plan the menu, pack the necessary supplies she didn't want to purchase locally, gather the clothing and toiletries for all of us, and make sure the girls had the necessary crayons, coloring books, dolls, and books for us to read to them.

There was always something to be repaired, finished, or improved so I packed the tools and materials and then loaded everything into the back of the minivan. Forgetting to pack diapers, toilet paper, or some hardware item would mean a long drive into the nearest town. Forgetting to bring swimsuits or a circular saw would mean a change in plans altogether.

Patty developed a "cabin packing list" of routine items while I kept a running list of materials and tools I would need as I thought of projects to be done at the cabin. The vacation would be more pleasant and stress-free if we remembered to take all the provisions we would need.

How blessed we are that God has provided "all things that pertain to [eternal] life and godliness [in this life]"! He has not forgotten anything for our journey of Christian growth. Our failures in Christian growth and experience are, therefore, the result of our ignorance of His provisions, our laziness that prevents us from using them, or our refusal to utilize them as we handle life on our own terms.

As you answer the questions, be very much aware of Who Jesus Christ is and what He has done for you, and be alert to the astonishing promises He has made to us as provisions for our Christian walk.

1. God reveals His provisions for us in His Word. Everything we need is "stored" in the Scriptures. You have to "unpack the minivan" to use the resources He has "packed for the journey." We are often quite optimistic about the time we really spend in God's Word. This week track the actual time you spend reading and meditating upon the Scriptures and write down the number of minutes you spent each day. Also, write down the passages you read or studied that day.

Day 1 Minutes: Passage:

Day 2 Minutes: Passage:

Day 3 Minutes: Passage:

Day 4 Minutes: Passage:

Day 5 Minutes: Passage:

Day 6 Minutes: Passage:

Day 7 Minutes: Passage:

2. This week find and write down both the reference and the text of five promises from Christ in His Word that will help you through the tests and trials you are facing. Write these on a card or sheet of paper that you can carry with you this week and can look at when you need to be reminded of how to handle difficulties. A good daily devotional source for promises is Stewart Custer's book *God's Promises New Every Day* (BJU Press, 2004).

3. The church today is characterized by people who are "lovers of pleasures" more than "lovers of God" (2 Timothy 3:4). What are three pleasures that can easily capture your affections this week and turn you away from Christ and His Word?

4. Would you rate your relationship with Christ as casual or seriously intentional? Explain your answer.

5. Explain what it means for you to "cultivate the conditions" for your Christian growth. What is your part in this partnership in discipleship and what is God's part? How are you doing on your part?

☐ Take Time to Renew Your Mind

- This week memorize 2 Peter 1:3–4. Continue to review the verses from last week.

☐ Take Time to Respond to God

Praise—What have you seen about Who God is or what He has done that you can praise Him for?

Repent—What has God shown you that needs to be confessed to Him and forsaken?

Ask—What do you need God to do for you in order for you to become more like Him?

Yield—Where do you need to humble yourself before God and give up something you are stubbornly holding on to?

Study Unit Three

CULTIVATING THE EXCELLENCE
OF CHRISTLIKENESS

☐ TAKE TIME TO READ

- Prayerfully read chapter 3 of *Essential Virtues* and appendix 1, "The Puritan View of Sin," in order to see what we are up against as we try to become like Christ and why we so desperately need God's grace to grow.

☐ TAKE TIME TO REFLECT

In college I heard a man say, "You are not ready to live until you know what you want written on the tombstone." I do not recall his name, but his statement made a profound impact upon my life.

I went back to my room, drew a crude tombstone on a blank sheet of paper, and contemplated what I wanted my life to have counted for when it was all over. I scoured the Scriptures for days seeking God's direction and purpose for my life. God eventually directed me to a passage that became my life's verse, and from it I crafted a statement I wrote on the tombstone I had sketched. (I won't tell you what I wrote so that you won't be distracted by it in your own personal search for your life's purpose.)

Have you seriously decided what you are going to live for? Have you given this any serious consideration? If not, are you willing to get started? Because Peter tells us that we must first cultivate *aretē*, the purpose you ultimately decide on must have something to do with that overarching concern.

Most believers who are stalled in their Christian growth are stuck right here, not yet having decided to wholeheartedly pursue God's purpose for their lives. Consequently, they are frustrated and defeated and blame their circumstances, their family background, or their genetic heredity for the lack of progress they have made toward spiritual maturity in Christ.

To be sure, difficult circumstances and family issues can make life harder, but the Bible is clear that all of us are personally responsible for our growth in Christ. Hebrews 11 is a powerful testimony of this. Many of these heroes of the faith endured incredible hardships and setbacks, yet it did not deter them from staying in the race (Hebrews 12:1–3).

You must decide to "develop and display the excellencies (character) of Jesus Christ." If you set out on a trip and don't pick where you are going, every road is the wrong road. The journey starts with deciding where you are going to end up. What do you want written on your tombstone?

1. Define *aretē*.

2. Take some time this week to seriously reflect on the Scriptures and the question "What do you want written on your tombstone?" Write out that statement.

3. What means does Satan use today to conform people to his image?

4. Where are you on the continuum below? Put an X on the line below, that indicates your position. Explain your choice.

Weak/Worldly   Willful/Wild   Wicked/Wasted

5. What influences keep you in this position and what must you do about them if you are to move to Christlikeness?

6. Write your own personal purpose statement that will greet you with your alarm clock every morning. If you have seriously considered what you want written on your tombstone, this purpose statement might reflect those thoughts.

☐ Take Time to Renew Your Mind

- This week memorize 2 Peter 1:5–7. Continue reviewing the verses from previous weeks.

☐ Take Time to Respond to God

Praise—What have you seen about Who God is or what He has done that you can praise Him for?

Repent—What has God shown you that needs to be confessed to Him and forsaken?

Ask—What do you need God to do for you in order for you to become more like Him?

Yield—Where do you need to humble yourself before God and give up something you are stubbornly holding on to?

CULTIVATING KNOWLEDGE

☐ TAKE TIME TO READ

• Prayerfully read chapter 4 of *Essential Virtues*.

☐ TAKE TIME TO REFLECT

The importance of a daily, purposeful intake of the Word of God cannot be underscored enough if you are to become like Christ. Peter emphasizes that Christian growth is dependent upon nourishment from the Word just like newborn babies crave milk (1 Peter 2:2). Believers who intend to grow in Christlikeness need daily intake of the Word. No one has ever become godly without consistently reading and studying God's Word. If you have not yet established a habit of spending daily time with God, consider the following helps.[1]

1. Establish a regular time. Many Christians find that early morning is best since their first thoughts can be of spiritual things (Psalm 5:3).

2. Get alone. Shut yourself up in a room away from the distractions of people and technology if possible (Matthew 6:6).

3. Have a pen and notebook ready. Proverbs 10:14*a* says, "Wise men [store] up knowledge." Write down anything that God points out to you from His Word.

Include the following elements in your quiet time.

1. Bible Reading—Before you begin, ask God to show you something just for you (Psalm 119:18). Follow a Bible reading schedule so that your reading is not haphazard. Some believers find that including the chapter of Proverbs that corresponds to the day of the month is helpful. Read until God points out something especially for you. Jot down the verse and your immediate thoughts about it. As you read, God will convict you of sin. Write down your decision to forsake these sins, confess them to God, and ask for power to overcome them in your prayer time. God uses His Word to cleanse us (John 15:3). Thank Him for what He has shown you in your reading and share these special verses and insights with others (1 John 1:3).

2. Meditation—Use the MAP Method found in appendix 4 for one way to help you concentrate on God's Word to learn its truths.

3. Prayer—Keep a personal prayer journal, using the PRAY acronym introduced in the Taking Time to Respond to God sections. We tend to forget the times of praise. Without them, however, our prayer life becomes a shallow "give me" time. Your times of praise will become easier as you see God answer your requests. Every prayer won't include all four elements, but none of them should be missing from your regular prayer life.

If you have a hard time getting started, consult with your pastor or another mature Christian who spends daily time with God. That person will be more than willing to help you and encourage you in your daily pursuit of Christlikeness through the study of God's Word.

1. How would you describe the consistency and effectiveness of your personal daily devotional time with Christ?

2. How would you describe the consistency and effectiveness of your response to the preaching of God's Word in your local assembly? In other words, are you profiting from the preaching, and if so, how?

3. Write out two concrete examples of how you wrestled through the temporal versus the eternal matters of an issue.

4. Define Christian liberty in terms of temporals versus eternals. In other words, what eternal truths must govern our participation in temporal matters?

☐ TAKE TIME TO RENEW YOUR MIND

- This week memorize 2 Peter 1:8–9. Continue reviewing the verses from previous weeks.

☐ **TAKE TIME TO RESPOND TO GOD**

Praise—What have you seen about Who God is or what He has done that you can praise Him for?

Repent—What has God shown you that needs to be confessed to Him and forsaken?

Ask—What do you need God to do for you in order for you to become more like Him?

Yield—Where do you need to humble yourself before God and give up something you are stubbornly holding on to?

Study Unit Five

Cultivating Self-Control

☐ Take Time to Read

• Prayerfully read chapter 5 of *Essential Virtues*.

☐ Take Time to Reflect

In the text of this chapter David DeWitt said, "A man is a male who has taken on the responsibility for establishing order for his life." A key word in that statement is *responsibility*. While we are not responsible for our upbringing and for the things other people do to us, God holds each of us personally responsible for our current spiritual condition and character.

As we have seen, we must decide to pursue the excellence of Christlikeness (*aretē*), decide to study the Word (knowledge), and then decide to order our lives by God's priorities as outlined in the Scriptures (self-control). Those decisions are made daily and by the enablement of God's Spirit as we submit to His will as revealed in the Word.

No one can make those on-going, daily decisions for us. They are our personal responsibility to make. Others can encourage us, reward us, warn us, and even chasten us, but in the end, we must by the grace of God decide ourselves that we will become like Jesus Christ and be useful to Him in His kingdom work here on the earth.

The world fosters self-indulgence and a victim mentality, which stymie the development of Christian character because they destroy any sense of personal responsibility. Cultivating self-control means rejecting the flesh's habit of sidestepping personal responsibility through deceit, laziness, blame-shifting, and excuse-making, evidences of a weak and worldly character.

Self-control accepts personal responsibility, confesses sin, bows before God in submission, and obeys His Word and will by His grace. This week as you study this chapter, reflect seriously on these issues because the church today has largely bought into the world's mindset on these matters. We must return to the biblical view that we are personally responsible for our spiritual condition and character. God has given us everything we need. Our responsibility is to explore the farm and then with His help work the farm.

1. What is your present reaction to the concept of "order" and the necessity of self-control? What intentional practices in your life show that you consider order and self-control important issues to develop?

2. Is taking personal responsibility a high priority in your philosophy of life? As you reflect on that question, keep in mind that the practices of deceit, laziness, blame-shifting, and excuse-making are polar opposites of taking personal responsibility. Be sure when considering this question that you take full responsibility for whatever failures you have in this area.

3. In the student's prayer (page 59), how does the gospel itself fuel his commitment to his studies?

4. Rate yourself on the order continuum below? Put an X on the line below that indicates your position. Explain your choice.

Pursues chaos	Pursues order for himself/herself	Disciples others to order their lives

5. Read "Discourse on Temperance" by John Brown in appendix 2. Write five significant statements from that article that had specific application to you and explain why they apply to you.

☐ Take Time to Renew Your Mind

- This week memorize 2 Peter 1:10–11. Continue reviewing the verses from previous weeks.

☐ Take Time to Respond to God

Praise—What have you seen about Who God is or what He has done that you can praise Him for?

Repent—What has God shown you that needs to be confessed to Him and forsaken?

Ask—What do you need God to do for you in order for you to become more like Him?

Yield—Where do you need to humble yourself before God and give up something you are stubbornly holding on to?

Study Unit Six

CULTIVATING ENDURANCE

☐ TAKE TIME TO READ
- Prayerfully read chapter 6 of *Essential Virtues*.

☐ TAKE TIME TO REFLECT

When the world praises a military hero, firefighter, police officer, or government official for his character, they usually are admiring his integrity under great pressure or his bravery under great threat. The common element in either case is endurance. The honored individual has remained faithful to his principles and to his mission no matter what the external pressures. When speaking of such a person, people used to say things like, "He has backbone. He has something to him. She isn't spineless. She didn't take the short-cut. He remained faithful to his duty."

It is sadly obvious that such men and women are in short supply today. The popular culture prevalent today does not produce men and women of character. Sadly, neither does much of the church since it is widely influenced by the world's self-indulgent, pleasure-seeking mindset. Consequently, people today are given to mood swings, discouragement, moral failures, quitting, and cowardice. All these demonstrate a lack of endurance—a lack of "God-sustained faithfulness under external pressure."

You and I can become men and women of Christlike character! We can by God's grace cultivate the endurance that puts backbone into our lives. But, as we have seen in the previous virtues, it is developed intentionally. Demonstrating endurance must be a goal of your life. You must want it and work for it. You must let God bring situation after situation into your life that will demand right responses from you each time until those responses are *character*istic of your life—until they are your character.

To remind yourself of how endurance is developed over the long haul, reread the section of this chapter about the mother of teenagers who is dying with cancer and the story of Joseph. Notice how they consistently made the right responses with God's help to become people of endurance. That can be your testimony, too. Why not start today with that as your goal?

1. What "external pressures" make it hard for you to do the right thing? What are you doing about them? What can you do about them that you are not yet doing?

2. Are your "external pressures" from "outright persecution" or from the threats of the "moral degradation" around and within you? Explain.

3. For each of the "Do I Stop..." questions (pages 74–75), rate yourself in the blanks below on a scale of 1 to 5 (1 being never and 5 being predictably).

1. _____   4. _____   7. _____

2. _____   5. _____   8. _____

3. _____   6. _____   9. _____

4. How does your handling of injustices and temptation differ from Joseph's? Explain your answer.

5. Why is your having a ministry outlet so critical to developing endurance?

☐ Take Time to Renew Your Mind

- This week memorize 2 Peter 1:12–13. Continue reviewing the verses from previous weeks.

☐ **TAKE TIME TO RESPOND TO GOD**

Praise—What have you seen about Who God is or what He has done that you can praise Him for?

Repent—What has God shown you that needs to be confessed to Him and forsaken?

Ask—What do you need God to do for you in order for you to become more like Him?

Yield—Where do you need to humble yourself before God and give up something you are stubbornly holding on to?

CULTIVATING GODLINESS, PART 1

☐ TAKE TIME TO READ

- Prayerfully read chapter 7 of *Essential Virtues*.

☐ TAKE TIME TO REFLECT

Carefully reflect on these statements describing godliness from this week's chapter, then answer the questions that follow.

Godliness: "A God-fearing lifestyle that promotes righteousness and opposes evil" (page 89)

Godliness: "A vibrant, personal relationship with God that manifests itself in actions consistent with Who God is and with what He is doing in the earth" (page 89)

Godliness: "All that makes up the 'engine' of loving God with all our heart" (page 89)

Godliness: "Keeps" the horses of devotion and discipline "together and hitched to the cause of being salt and light for Christ in the world" (page 90)

Godliness: "To have a lifestyle that is distinctive from the world and useful to Christ" (page 90)

1. What is your initial response to these statements? Do they seem beyond your reach? Do they discourage you or do they challenge you and motivate you to greater devotion and discipline so that you can become everything God wants you to become? Write out your answer below.

Whether those statements discourage you or motivate you reveal a great deal about the current state of your walk with God. A believer who is still struggling with *aretē*, knowledge, self-control, and endurance may be easily discouraged when he sees the bar on the hurdle set that high. The believer who, however, has developed a sincere devotion to Christ and has much experience in disciplining his life toward godliness will see those statements as motivation to continue and to grow even more. He is not discouraged because He has seen God reveal Himself in the Word as he has diligently sought Him day after day in his private devotions. He has also seen God give Him increasing victory over his internal passions and lusts as he has learned to deny the expression of his sinful nature in the face of temptation.

If you were discouraged by these statements, read the previous paragraph over again and note that you do not have to stay in that same spiritual condition. You can go back to chapters 3 and 4 of *Essential Virtues* and study them until you begin to see consistent progress in your walk with Christ.

Everyone can grow! But no one will grow who will not take personal responsibility for where he is and for what he must do to cultivate these essential virtues. We have the promise of God's grace and all the provisions of God's promises at our disposal.

2. Write out five significant statements from all the Wilberforce quotations in this chapter.

3. Explain how the virtue of godliness is the crown and summary of the previous virtues.

4. Explain the effects upon a person's life (see the train illustration) if he has "devotion" without "discipline." Explain the effects if he has "discipline" without "devotion."

5. Why is it important for the person pursuing godliness to never stray from the doctrines of the gospel?

6. What are three concrete things you can put into place to move your weekly quiet time "minutes" to "hours" this week?

☐ Take Time to Renew Your Mind

• This week memorize 2 Peter 1:14–15. Continue reviewing the verses from previous weeks.

☐ Take Time to Respond to God

Praise—What have you seen about Who God is or what He has done that you can praise Him for?

Repent—What has God shown you that needs to be confessed to Him and forsaken?

Ask—What do you need God to do for you in order for you to become more like Him?

Yield—Where do you need to humble yourself before God and give up something you are stubbornly holding on to?

CULTIVATING GODLINESS, PART 2

☐ TAKE TIME TO READ

- Prayerfully read chapter 8 of *Essential Virtues*.

☐ TAKE TIME TO REFLECT

Discipline. The word can sound harsh, cold, even legalistic. It certainly can be, but it must never be abandoned because it is wrongly developed or wrongly used by some. Like fire, it can be a wonderful help or a destructive force. Like fire, it must be properly regulated and wisely used.

Our culture scorns discipline because it scorns the ways of God. It promotes either self-indulgence or self-serving discipline. Both are destructive.

A proper devotion to Jesus Christ will motivate a believer to discipline himself for the purpose of godliness and will keep that discipline from being deployed selfishly. Christ-centered devotion fuels Christ-centered discipline. Conversely, those without Christ-centered discipline lack Christ-centered devotion. They go hand in glove.

Godliness, as we saw in the text, harnesses both devotion and discipline for the cause of Jesus Christ. This is mature Christianity; this is loving God with all your heart.

Do you see this kind of godliness developing in your life as you cultivate column-one devotion and column-two discipline? Or do you find that your life is riddled with the corruption experienced by Lot? Is your soul being worn down with the filthy lifestyle of the wicked as you see and hear their unlawful deeds? You must give yourself wholeheartedly to devotion and discipline if you are to become godly.

1. What are twenty "menial jobs" that Christ has placed in your life to help you mature in personal discipline (think of David's harp and slingshot practice)?

2. If the "tourist mentality" has crept into your thinking, where can it be seen in your life?

3. What evidences are there that you are not just "being good" but are "doing some good" for the kingdom of God?

4. Explain in your own words (from Lot's example) what it means for a soul to be "tortured/vexed" by what it tolerates.

5. What are you "seeing and hearing" in your daily routine that "wears down" your soul and causes it to be spiritually insensitive? What response of your will in those situations would minimize the negative effect upon your soul and would cause others to know that God has other ideas about how life should be lived?

6. Describe three situations within the last three months in which you took God's side of an issue against other people. If you did not step out in that way, tell what you should have done in three such situations.

☐ Take Time to Renew Your Mind

- This week memorize 1 Timothy 4:7b–8 (7b means begin with the second part of the verse). Continue reviewing the verses from previous weeks.

☐ Take Time to Respond to God

Praise—What have you seen about Who God is or what He has done that you can praise Him for?

Repent—What has God shown you that needs to be confessed to Him and forsaken?

Ask—What do you need God to do for you in order for you to become more like Him?

Yield—Where do you need to humble yourself before God and give up something you are stubbornly holding on to?

PART THREE: THE TRADEMARK OF
CHRISTIAN CHARACTER

Study Unit Nine

CULTIVATING BROTHERLY KINDNESS

☐ TAKE TIME TO READ
- Prayerfully read chapter 9 of *Essential Virtues*.

☐ TAKE TIME TO REFLECT

Industrialized nations today show most of the marks of advanced civilization—a highly developed spoken and written language, stable social and economic structures, cultural and artistic refinement, and scientific progress. While technology and science continue to improve, however, social, cultural, and artistic conventions are declining to the primitive, uncivilized norms of violence and immorality.

Humor today is reduced to inflicting pain and embarrassment on others, participating in crude and vulgar locker-room antics, and worse yet, watching or engaging in illicit sexual activities. All of this "fun" comes at the expense of others. People are mistreated and abused—whether the actions are simulated or actual—for the pleasure of the audience. What many do not realize is that this violation of others is essentially violence. Innocence, purity, reputation, sensibilities, property, manners, and lives are destroyed rather than preserved and improved. The message today is clear: "Others exist for my pleasure."

When this twisted entertainment mindset is wed to greed and materialism, business and social relationships are characterized by backstabbing, manipulating, dog-eat-dog, ill-mannered, and often profanity-filled exchanges. These are the exact opposites of the command of God for His people to "esteem other better than themselves" (Philippians 2:3).

Popular culture, rooted in and reinforcing self-centeredness, destroys the very foundations of the kind of character that builds advanced civilizations—personal self-restraint and sacrifice for the good of the whole. The consumer mentality consumes first its surroundings and then the individual himself. A biblical stewardship mentality, on the other hand, sees the individual as a caretaker: one who takes care of something and must give an account of his stewardship before God. Rather than using everything for his own pleasure, a steward guards everything for the pleasure of his Master.

If you and I are to escape being victims of our culture and are to become people of Christian character, we must see and resist the world's mindset and cultivate attitudes and qualities that are counterculture. Self-centeredness must be rejected; the ways of Christ must be embraced. We must "give all diligence" to cultivate the personal virtues of the excellence of Christlikeness, knowledge, self-control, endurance, and godliness if we are to have the foundation and strength of character to display the social virtues of brotherly kindness and love.

1. Would you say you have a reputation for brotherly kindness or does your life reflect the pop culture mindset described in the paragraphs above? Explain your answer.

2. In what ways does your lifestyle reveal that you are more tuned in to the people who are like you in superficial ways rather than sensitive that all believers are your brothers and sisters because of your unity in Christ? Think carefully about this; this is not a trivial question. Does your life tend to be exclusive or inclusive? There is a strategic difference and does not apply only to relationships with peers but with those younger and older than you.

3. Create a ten-point checklist of "one another" commands and the supporting Scriptures that will be the filter you use to determine what Christian blogs and/or social networks you will view. The ten-point checklist (your cyberspace ten commandments) will also become the determiner of what you will say should you choose to participate in any online communication—including e-mail and text messages. Of course, these commands should regulate your verbal communication as well. God doesn't see our words differently whether spoken or written.

Commandment One:

Commandment Two:

Commandment Three:

Commandment Four:

Commandment Five:

Commandment Six:

Commandment Seven:

Commandment Eight:

Commandment Nine:

Commandment Ten:

4. How do you rate yourself on the commands to "don't badmouth others" and "don't grumble about others"? Explain your answer.

5. Of the "one another" passages mentioned in this chapter pick the five you most need to cultivate. Write out supporting Scriptures and begin meditating upon them.

☐ Take Time to Renew Your Mind

• This week memorize James 3:13–15. Continue reviewing the verses from previous weeks.

☐ Take Time to Respond to God

Praise—What have you seen about Who God is or what He has done that you can praise Him for?

Repent—What has God shown you that needs to be confessed to Him and forsaken?

Ask—What do you need God to do for you in order for you to become more like Him?

Yield—Where do you need to humble yourself before God and give up something you are stubbornly holding on to?

Study Unit Ten

CULTIVATING LOVE

☐ TAKE TIME TO READ

• Prayerfully read chapter 10 of *Essential Virtues*.

☐ TAKE TIME TO REFLECT

Our purpose to be like Christ aligns precisely with God's own mission and purpose "to redeem and restore fallen creatures to the likeness of His Son to the praise of His glory." It is what Christlikeness is all about: "cultivating a God-imitating mindset that scripturally and sacrificially meets the spiritual needs of others." It is, in a word, love.

How are you doing? Is it your purpose to join God in His mission? Are you single-minded about being like Christ and about bringing others to increased Christlikeness? Is it your purpose to actively and diligently cultivate the virtues we've studied? If that is your purpose, how much progress are you making?

If this isn't your mindset, you cannot say that Christlikeness is your purpose. Something else has your attention. If this isn't your mindset, you will experience frustration, angst, and eventually, the despair of meaninglessness and purposelessness. This is the reason for the prominence of those internal disturbances in today's teens—who reflect what they have been taught by and seen reflected in their parents and their peers. George Barna summarizes their situation:

> Three out of four teenagers (74 percent) concur that they are still trying to figure out the purpose or meaning of their life. This journey is affected by the fact that most of them—63 percent—admit that they do not have any comprehensive and clear "philosophy of life that consistently influences their lifestyle and decisions." Every day remains a period of discovery for them, a time to try new ideas, new behaviors, and new relationships in their quest to solve the puzzle of life.

> One of the disturbing finds, though, is that a majority (53 percent) contends that they have decided that the main purpose of life is enjoyment and personal fulfillment. In some ways this

outcome is not at all surprising: It is exactly the same conclusion drawn by most of the parents of teens and is a perspective that is modeled and verbally communicated to young people by their peers and elders. Most parents lack any motivation not to embrace such a perspective; the absence of spiritual depth and moral reflection and their own philosophical superficiality support such a perspective. Hearing or seeing their offspring adopt the same perspective is therefore not a cause for chagrin among most parents, but rather a welcomed sign that their youngsters are finally maturing. . . . The pattern is unmistakable: American teens are much more interested in what they own or accomplish in life than in the development of their character. Given the cultural context in which they have been raised, this is not surprising.[2]

They—and the adults around them—do not have "a God-imitating mindset that scripturally and sacrificially meets the spiritual needs of others." They have become consumers who take and use for their own pleasures rather than lovers who sacrifice and give for the spiritual good of others.

The results are predictable. No other purpose will ultimately satisfy. We must love because God is love and has loved us. "Beloved, if God so loved us, we ought also to love one another" (1 John 4:11).

1. What part does the cross play as a conscious "backdrop" for your life? That is, is it something you rarely think about or is it something that consciously stands behind the action happening on the "stage" of your life?

2. Since "God is on a mission," explain that mission in your own words and summarize the extent that your life is involved in His mission.

3. What "good deeds" characterize your lifestyle and how do they relate to God's mission?

4. Write out a one-sentence definition for each of the characteristics of love in 1 Corinthians 13:4–8.

5. Write out the five most significant sentences from Jonathan Edwards' pen at the end of this chapter.

☐ Take Time to Renew Your Mind

• This week memorize 1 John 4:9–11. Continue reviewing the verses from previous weeks.

☐ Take Time to Respond to God

Praise—What have you seen about Who God is or what He has done that you can praise Him for?

Repent—What has God shown you that needs to be confessed to Him and forsaken?

Ask—What do you need God to do for you in order for you to become more like Him?

Yield—Where do you need to humble yourself before God and give up something you are stubbornly holding on to?

THE CORE VALUE OF COMMITMENT TO CHRIST

☐ TAKE TIME TO READ

• Prayerfully read chapter 11 of *Essential Virtues*.

☐ TAKE TIME TO REFLECT

Jesus tells us that double-mindedness is the cause of instability in a believer (James 1:6, 8). Sometimes this double-minded man obeys Christ; other times he obeys his lusts. He is up and down. The only consistent thing in his life is his inconsistency in his commitment. Like a pilot who flies east for a while and then west, he never gets anywhere.

But a pilot who has committed himself to a destination stays on course. He rejects flying west when his destination is east because flying west does not fit his purpose. This is the mindset of the "wholehearted disciple who chooses the appeals and ideals of Christ and rejects the appeals and ideals of the world."

The biblically informed believer—the one cultivating knowledge—knows that his greatest enemies are the world around him, the flesh within him, and the Devil, who uses both as staging grounds for his war against Christ. The believer with knowledge knows what Christ is like and what He wants. He critically examines everything the world offers by way of entertainment, fashion, adventure, and convenience before he partakes of it. He knows that while most believers live without purpose, Satan does not. The God-taught believer suspects that hidden within the world's bait of a good time is a hook that will corrupt his soul by its appeal to his lusts (1 John 2:15–17). He will reject anything that will enslave him, wound another believer, or displease Christ.

Progress in Christlikeness has priority for him over personal pleasure and gain—though neither has to be wrong in itself. He is willing to "count all things but loss" to have more of Christ and for Christ to have more of him (Philippians 3:7–8). This is Christ-centeredness. This is adult (i.e., mature) Christianity. This is commitment.

If, by contrast, someone is rebellious and disobedient to Christ or lethargic and lukewarm about Him, he must see that God has drawn a line in the sand and he must "choose . . . this day whom [he] will serve" (Joshua 24:15). Jesus did not look upon indifference as a light matter. He takes it personally. He said in Matthew 12:30, "He that is not with me is against me; and he that gathereth not with me scattereth abroad."

Furthermore, none of the subsequent essential virtues can be fully developed without a firm commitment to Jesus Christ. You will never have integrity—wholeness—without this component as the groundwork. If you do have this commitment, you can expect God to forge the likeness of His Son in you. This is the starting place—the foundation.

1. How would you rate your commitment to Jesus Christ on a scale of 1–10 (1 being no commitment and 10 being total commitment)? Explain your answer.

2. As you look over the past month of your life, what are five ways/times you desired to "minimize suffering" that could have benefited you? What should your response have been?

3. What are five ways/times you desired this past month to "maximize pleasure?" What should your response have been?

4. Explain the connection and importance of lordship and integrity.

5. Provide four additional examples of wholeheartedness—two from the Bible and two from modern-day examples of believers. What is it about each of the four that merits your notice?

☐ TAKE TIME TO RENEW YOUR MIND

- This week memorize Romans 12:1–2. Continue reviewing the verses from previous weeks.

☐ TAKE TIME TO RESPOND TO GOD

Praise—What have you seen about Who God is or what He has done that you can praise Him for?

Repent—What has God shown you that needs to be confessed to Him and forsaken?

Ask—What do you need God to do for you in order for you to become more like Him?

Yield—Where do you need to humble yourself before God and give up something you are stubbornly holding on to?

THE CORE VALUE OF COURAGE FOR CHRIST

☐ TAKE TIME TO READ

• Prayerfully read chapter 12 of *Essential Virtues*.

☐ TAKE TIME TO REFLECT

Gus Lee taught us in this chapter that the courageous person does more than just "keep his nose clean." We cannot be content with being good. We must do some good. We must defend and promote what is good.

The apostle Paul was alarmed that the believers in the church at Corinth had not courageously addressed the corruption of immorality in their assembly. Commitment to Christ does not tolerate what Christ hates.

Many believers today are no different from those in Corinth. They condone sensual language, dishonesty, disobedience to authority, gossip, bitterness, immorality, sensual music forms, prayerlessness, and a lack of devotional, evangelistic, and church-assembling habits in themselves and in others. They lack the courage to take the hard stance against themselves, and, consequently, they tolerate the ravages of evil in others. They are cowards because they lack first-column commitment to Christ and have not cultivated the column-two virtues of self-control, endurance, and godliness.

They might even accuse those who do boldly address such issues in others as having no heart, when in fact, the man without courage is the one without "heart." God values wholeheartedness and brave-heartedness and wants to see both expressed with tenderheartedness—as we shall see in the next chapter.

Fellow believer, you must cultivate courage! Families, churches, and Christian schools, colleges, and organizations are floundering because of a lack of courageous, God-fearing leadership. You can become such a person, but you must practice, practice, and practice on the smaller battlefields of your own lusts and trials as we saw in this chapter. Godliness must become instinctive. It can be for you with God's help, and it must.

1. Write down your favorite one-sentence definitions for courage from this chapter.

2. On a scale of 1–5 (1 being lowest and 5 being highest), rate your courage to stand up for what is scripturally right in the following categories, even though no one else is standing with you. Under each rating, indicate whether your rating is moving towards 1 or 5 and why you would say that.

| Immodesty | 1 | 2 | 3 | 4 | 5 |

| Unbiblical Communication | 1 | 2 | 3 | 4 | 5 |

| Fleshly Entertainment | 1 | 2 | 3 | 4 | 5 |

| Attacks on Marriage | 1 | 2 | 3 | 4 | 5 |

| Greed and Materialism | 1 | 2 | 3 | 4 | 5 |

3. Explain when the presence of personal and/or institutional standards are, indeed, legalistic and when they are not.

4. Is there a time in your recent past when you should have stood against wrongdoing but regrettably demonstrated silence? Describe it. What should you have done and/or said instead?

5. In what areas of life do you need to cultivate self-control, endurance, and godliness in order to be biblically courageous for Christ?

☐ Take Time to Renew Your Mind

- This week memorize Joshua 1:8–9. Continue reviewing the verses from previous weeks.

☐ Take Time to Respond to God

Praise—What have you seen about Who God is or what He has done that you can praise Him for?

Repent—What has God shown you that needs to be confessed to Him and forsaken?

Ask—What do you need God to do for you in order for you to become more like Him?

Yield—Where do you need to humble yourself before God and give up something you are stubbornly holding on to?

THE CORE VALUE OF
COMPASSION LIKE CHRIST

☐ TAKE TIME TO READ

- Prayerfully read chapter 13 of *Essential Virtues*.

☐ TAKE TIME TO REFLECT

Christ-centered people are always other-centered people. They are on a mission—God's mission—to redeem and restore fallen creatures to the likeness of Christ to the praise of His glory. That mission requires the commitment and the courage to be both tough and tender with people. We saw this kind of biblical compassion modeled through the godly life and ministry of Ruth Morgan.

I hope that this kind of integrity—wholeness—is what you long to see in yourself and in those around you. It can be yours, as it was Ruth's. God wants it for you, Christ died to make it possible, the Bible teaches us how, and the Spirit enables us to carry it out.

Don't merely read these chapters once and go on—perhaps convicted, perhaps inspired and encouraged. Review and reread them, meditate upon the Scriptures they refer to, and stay at it until you see the fruit of those efforts in your own life. May God help you to become a committed, courageous, and compassionate disciple-maker!

1. What are five Christlike qualities that you saw in Ruth Morgan's life as you read this chapter that you know you must grow in?

2. Explain the relationship of tough and tender. What is one Bible text that demonstrates each from Christ's life and ministry? Discuss how this challenges your thinking and ministry.

3. Journal your prayer life for the next seven days and note the content. How does what you pray for match the categories of the Lord's Prayer in Matthew 6:9–13?

4. Can you say that your compassion has a definite *agapē* love mission-mindedness in that you are reaching out to others with a spiritual goal in mind for them? Explain your answer.

5. Has anyone like Ruth Morgan had an impact upon your life? If so, explain that impact. What do you need to do to become that kind of person?

☐ TAKE TIME TO RENEW YOUR MIND

- This week memorize 1 Thessalonians 2:8–12. Continue reviewing the verses from previous weeks.

☐ TAKE TIME TO RESPOND TO GOD

Praise—What have you seen about Who God is or what He has done that you can praise Him for?

Repent—What has God shown you that needs to be confessed to Him and forsaken?

Ask—What do you need God to do for you in order for you to become more like Him?

Yield—Where do you need to humble yourself before God and give up something you are stubbornly holding on to?

NOTES

PREFACE

1. Jim Berg, *Changed into His Image* (Greenville, SC: BJU Press, 1999). Learn more about this book at www.changedIntoHisImage.com.
2. Douglas J. Moo, *2 Peter and Jude* (Grand Rapids, MI: Zondervan, 1996), 11.
3. Libertines "assume that the grace of God revealed in Christ gives them the 'liberty' to do just about anything they want to do (2 Peter 2:19–20; Jude 4). They have no use for authority (especially spiritual authority . . . ; cf. 2 Peter 2:10–11; Jude 8–9). And so they engage in all manner of 'sins of the flesh': illicit sex, perhaps including homosexuality, excess drinking and eating, greed for money (2 Peter 2:13–16; 18–20; Jude 4)." (Moo, 19).
4. Richard J. Bauckham, *Jude, 2 Peter* (Waco, TX: Word Books, 1983), 156.
5. Charles, J. Daryl and Erland Waltner, *1–2 Peter, Jude* (Scottdale, PA: Herald Press, 1999), 206–7.

CHAPTER ONE

1. Throughout this book when quoting this passage from the King James Version, I will substitute the words *self-control* for *temperance*, *endurance* for *patience*, and *love* for *charity* for the sake of clarity.
2. D. Martyn Lloyd-Jones, *Expository Sermons on 2 Peter* (Carlisle, PA: The Banner of Truth Trust, 1983), 26.
3. Gary Inrig, *A Call to Excellence* (Wheaton, IL: Victor Books, 1985), 69–70.
4. The exact rhetorical literary form Peter uses is a sorites (sǝ-rē´-tēz). It was a popular rhetorical form in Stoic ethical lists of the first century "in which we have a step-by-step chain that culminates in a climax" (Thomas R. Schreiner, *1, 2 Peter, Jude* [Nashville: Broadman and Holman], 297).
5. J. A. Bengel, *Gnomon Novi Testament*, 1773, quoted in Michael Green, *The Second Epistle General of Peter and the General Epistle of Jude* (Grand Rapids, MI: Wm. B. Eerdmans, 1968), 71.
6. M. R. Vincent, *Word Studies in the New Testament* (McLean, VA: MacDonald Publishing Company, 1886), 324.
7. D. Edmond Hiebert, *Second Peter and Jude* (Greenville, SC: BJU Press, 1989), 52.
8. Stephen W. Paine, "The Second Epistle to Peter," in *The Wycliffe Bible Commentary*, eds. Charles F. Pfeiffer and Everett F. Harrison (Chicago: Moody, 1962), 1458, quoted by Hiebert, 55.
9. J. Daryl Charles, *Virtue Amidst Vice: The Catalog of Virtues in 2 Peter 1* (London: Sheffield Academic Press, 1997), 145–46.
10. Dad corrected us too but didn't need a stick. Somehow his hand did an adequate job of reinforcing his point. Both Mom's stick and Dad's hand were effective—and deserved.
11. Michael Green, 71.
12. In this illustration "dead seeds" refers to "dead faith." Don't confuse this with Jesus' teaching in John 12:24: "Except a [kernel] of wheat fall into the ground and die, it abideth alone: but if it die, it bringeth forth much fruit." Jesus in John's Gospel is clearly calling the disciple to self-denial as He did in Luke 9:23–24.

CHAPTER TWO

1. "Stock" on a farm refers to the animals. I grew up hearing the daily "stock report" on the radio at noon. It had nothing to do with Wall Street, however. The noon stock report was the day's going price at the local sales barns for various kinds of livestock.
2. Richard C. Trench, *Synonyms of the New Testament* (Grand Rapids, MI: Wm. B. Eerdmans, 1880, 1953), 285.
3. Paul makes this same connection between the experiential knowledge of Christ and the believer's full maturity in Ephesians 4:13.
4. *Godliness* here is a Greek word meaning "good worship," and "the biblical authors use it to summarize the behavior expected of Christians who have come to know the God of the Scriptures" (Moo, 41). We will look at it in some detail in chapters 7–8.
5. Moo, 44.
6. M. R. Vincent, *Word Studies in the New Testament* (McClean, VA: MacDonald Publishing Company, 1886), 325.
7. Michael Green, 66.
8. Moo, 56–57.

9. This is not semi-Pelagian; it is apostolic.
10. J. Daryl Charles and Waltner, Erland, *1–2 Peter, Jude.* (Scottdale, PA: Herald Press, 1999), 215.
11. Hiebert, 51.
12. J. Daryl Charles, *Virtue Amidst Vice* (Sheffield, England: Sheffield Academic Press, 1997), 162.
13. Jerry Bridges, *The Discipline of Grace: God's Role and Our Role in the Pursuit of Holiness* (Colorado Springs: NavPress, 1994), 133.

CHAPTER THREE
1. Michael Green, 67.
2. The Greek philosophers focused much of their thought and discussion on what constituted the man of excellence—the *aretē* man. Aristotle rightly linked the understanding of *aretē* with *telos*—the end state or purpose of something. Therefore, a man could not be considered an excellent—*aretē*—man if he did not fulfill his ultimate purpose. Of course, for Aristotle man was functioning at his most excellent manner when he was most controlled by his reason as opposed to when his reason was fueled by knowledge. *Aretē* was the fullest expression of the complete human being. While Aristotle was correct in saying that only the man who was fulfilling his purpose could be considered excellent, he was wrong in setting forth control-by-reason as the means of excellence. Source: Gary Inrig, *A Call to Excellence* (Wheaton, IL: Victor Books, 1985), 27.
3. Michael Green, 67.
4. Elisabeth Elliot, *The Shadow of the Almighty* (New York: Harper and Row, 1958), 108.
5. Diana West, *The Death of the Grown-up: How America's Arrested Development Is Bringing Down Western Civilization* (New York: St. Martin's Press, 2007), 1, 4, 5.

CHAPTER FOUR
1. John Brown, *Parting Counsels: An Exposition of 2 Peter 1* (pp. 75–76) quoted in Christopher Green and Dick Lucas, *The Message of 2 Peter and Jude* (Downers Grove, IL: Inter-Varsity Press, 1995), 59.
2. A. W. Tozer, *The Pursuit of God* (Camp Hill, PA: Christian Publications, 1993), 46.
3. Ibid., 56.
4. Ibid., 58.

CHAPTER FIVE
1. Bauckham, 186.
2. For an expanded discussion of this concept see *Changed into His Image* (BJU Press), 33.
3. For an expanded discussion of natural desires versus desires created by the mind see Jay E. Adams, *A Thirst for Wholeness* (Wheaton, IL: Victor Books, 1988), 77–84.
4. William Barclay, *Flesh and Spirit* (Grand Rapids, MI: Baker Book House, 1962), 123. While Barclay is not entirely orthodox, his handling of the Greek text is well-respected.
5. Hiebert, 53.
6. Charles and Waltner, 215.
7. For an expanded discussion of how a man ought to "talk to himself" see D. Martyn Lloyd-Jones, *Spiritual Depression* (Grand Rapids, MI: Wm. B. Eerdmans, 1965), 20–21.
8. David DeWitt, *The Mature Man: Becoming a Man of Impact* (Gresham, OR: Vision House Publishing, 1994), 9. Please note that while the first part of DeWitt's book presents some thought-provoking and accurate observations about the male culture of our day and how it compares to the biblical presentation of responsible leadership, the book falls short in some of its allowances for entertainment activities that destroy the very self-control he says is necessary for Christian character. Italics are his.
9. Ibid., 12–13.
10. Ibid., 16.
11. Ibid., 21.
12. Martyn Lloyd-Jones, *Spiritual Depression*, 210.
13. Please note that "and us by extension" is only a reference to the fact that God, according to 1 Corinthians 10:6, 11 intends for us to learn from His older covenant. It is by no means an endorsement of Replacement Theology or Christian Reconstructionism.

CHAPTER SIX
1. Examples cited from Ron Tagliapietra, *Great Adventurers of the Twentieth Century* (Greenville, SC: BJU Press, 1998).
2. "Few writings of the NT find more touchpoints to contemporary culture than 2 Peter, with its stress on virtuous living, Christian ethics, and passionate critique of moral skepticism

NOTES

that fuels religious apostasy. In 2 Peter we find reflections of a social environment in which the Christian tradition appears to be taken for granted, Jewish influence is negligible, and pagan Hellenistic cultural winds are pervasive. The letter contains similarities to what Francis Schaeffer has called a 'post-Christian' culture" (Charles and Waltner, 225).
3. Charles, 143.
4. Bauckham, 186.
5. William Barclay, *New Testament Words* (Philadelphia: Westminster Press, 1964), 143.
6. Patience—*makrothumē*—is the quality listed in the fruit of the Spirit (Galatians 5:23) and is not the same word translated "endurance" here. *Makrothumē* is translated "longsuffering" in the KJV and "patience" in the ESV and NASB. Trench says the difference is that "the man [*makrothumē*], who having to do with injurious persons, does not suffer himself easily to be provoked by them, or to blaze up into anger (2 Tim. iv. 2). The man [*hupomonē*], who, under a great siege of trials, bears up, and does not lose heart or courage (Rom. v. 3; 2 Cor. i.). We should speak, therefore, of the [*makrothumē*] of David (2 Sam. xvi. 10–13), the [*hupomonē*] of Job (Jam. v. 11)" (Trench, 198).
7. G. Kittel, ed., *Theological Dictionary of the New Testament*. (Grand Rapids, MI: Eerdmans).
8. Barclay, 144–45.
9. Michael Green, 69.
10. Victor P. Hamilton, *The Book of Genesis, Chapters 18–50* (Grand Rapids, MI: Wm. B. Eerdmans, 1995), 464.

CHAPTER SEVEN
1. William Wilberforce, *Real Christianity*, ed. James M. Houston (Minneapolis: Bethany House Publishers, 1982, 1997), xii.
2. Ibid., 23–24.
3. Ibid., 25.
4. Ibid., 54–55 (emphasis his).
5. Ibid., 128.
6. Ibid., 129–30.
7. Thomas R. Schreiner, *The New American Commentary, Vol. 37: 1, 2 Peter, Jude* (Nashville: Broadman and Holman Publishers, 2003), 300. Schreiner says that "the word 'godliness' is especially common in the Pastoral Epistles for *living the kind of life* that pleases God. (1 Tim. 2:2; 3:16; 4:7–8; 6:3–5, 11; 2 Tim. 3:5; Titus 1:1)." Bauckham (p. 178) concurs: "It denotes . . . the respect for God's will and the moral *way of life* which are inseparable from the proper religious attitude to God."
8. Barclay, 106–7. Barclay's summary is why I have included the word "lifestyle" in the definition for godliness. It is an attitude toward God that results in a lifestyle that reflects that attitude of respect, awe, and obedience.
9. John Brown, *2 Peter Chapter One: Parting Counsels* (Carlisle, PA: The Banner of Truth Trust, 1856), 93, 95.
10. Notice Brown's remarks on the placement of godliness in this list of virtues:

> Godliness . . . is introduced as at once giving a peculiar character to the Christian's temperance and patience, clearly distinguishing them from, and highly raising them above, the natural qualities which resemble them, and often pass under their name, and giving completeness to the view of personal, Christian excellence: for what more complete idea can you form of personal excellence, than the union of temperance, patience, and piety? [Brown here uses the nineteenth-century translations of temperance, patience, and piety for the Greek words we are translating self-control, endurance, and godliness.]

> There is not only, thus, an obvious propriety in making godliness the culminating point of personal excellence, there is also an important significance in making it the connecting link, as it were, between personal and social excellence. It looks forward as well as backward. It stands in the centre between the two leading forms of personal excellence, temperance, and patience, and the two leading forms of social excellence, brotherly kindness and charity. It is the soul of both. Without godliness, neither temperance nor patience, nor brotherly kindness nor charity, in the true meaning of these words, can exist.

11. Thomas Watson, *The Godly Man's Picture* (Carlisle, PA: The Banner of Truth Trust, 1966). This book by Puritan preacher Thomas Watson was first published in 1666.
12. Jerry Bridges urges that the believer "preach the Gospel to himself every day" in the way I am suggesting in these paragraphs. He says, "To *preach the Gospel to [yourself]* means that you

continually face up to your own sinfulness and then flee to Jesus through faith in His shed blood and righteous life. It means that you appropriate, again by faith, the fact that Jesus fully satisfied the law of God, that He is your propitiation, and that God's holy wrath is no longer directed toward you" (Jerry Bridges, 58).

13. Wilberforce, 30.
14. By the way, listening to the Word of God on a media player while driving or exercising on a treadmill is helpful for an overall grasp of the Scriptures or for memorizing a passage by playing it repeatedly but can never be the substitute for time spent with Bible in hand meditating upon single words and phrases, mulling over them while praying for God to illuminate your mind with an understanding of them so that you might be able to put them into practice. While surveying and memorizing the Word through audio means is helpful, relationship with God through meditation cannot be multitasked.
15. Wilberforce notes, "Christianity proposes not to extinguish our natural desires. It promises to bring those desires under just control and direct them to their true object" (*Real Christianity*, 65).
16. If you want more help in developing this kind of walk with Christ, study *Changed into His Image* and its accompanying study guide, *Taking Time to Change*, available from BJU Press. In that book I take thirteen chapters to develop what I have tried to summarize here in a few paragraphs. Its companion volume, *Created for His Glory* with its study guide, *Taking Time to Rejoice*, develops these themes even further.

Chapter Eight
1. Barclay, 113.
2. Wilberforce, 9.
3. Ibid., 81–82.
4. For a rich allegory of this battle, read John Bunyan, *The Holy War* (Greenville, SC: Ambassador, 1998), originally published in 1682. The summary on the back of the book reads,

> The story sets out to recall the fall and redemption of mankind under the guise of a besieged city. The city of Mansoul originally belonged by right to Shaddai or God, but was betrayed through Ear Gate and Eye Gate into the hands of Diabolus or the Devil, a besieging giant who takes control. In the hands of the enemy Mansoul loses its Major, Lord Understanding, and Mr. Conscience is dismissed from his post as Recorder. Lord Will-be-Will becomes the Lord of Mansoul—man's fallen will, selfwill, and ill-will combined in one unpleasant and anti-God character. Mansoul is recaptured by Emmanuel's army and Diabolus is driven out. There is triumph over sin and evil—one of the Bible's most comforting themes.

5. This is what "Sheckaniah the son of Jehiel, one of the sons of Elam" did when Ezra rebuked the men of Israel for taking wives of the pagan peoples around them. Sheckaniah said to Ezra, "Arise, for it is your task [to clean up this mess], and we are with you; be strong and do it" (Ezra 10:4).

Chapter Nine
1. Peter H. Davids, *The Letters of 2 Peter and Jude* (Grand Rapids, MI: Wm. B. Eerdmans, 2006), 182–83.
2. Green and Lucas, 60.
3. Leon Morris, *Testaments of Love: A Study of Love in the Bible* (Grand Rapids, MI: Wm. B. Eerdmans, 1981), 118–19.
4. This priority should have been established while pursuing columns one and two. One essence of maturity is the "well-orderedness" of a man's life as discussed in chapter 5. He lives by *God's* priorities, not by the priorities of the popular culture around him (Romans 12:2).
5. This passage demands some comment. The early church was made up increasingly of members who were saved out of pagan mindsets. Women and slaves in the first century were treated with contempt. These new believers were learning that they were one in Christ, and some did not think it was necessary then for them to submit to their husbands and masters who were also believers—since they were equal before God. Paul tells them this is not the case. They must submit themselves to these authorities in their lives as he outlines in the next several verses—wives to husbands, children to parents, slaves to masters—regardless of whether they are on an equal standing spiritually with God. That standing does not dismiss the necessity for them to obey authority. This passage is not teaching *mutual submission*. It is teaching exactly the opposite. The word translated *submission* here is never used for anything in the Scriptures but a subordinate response.

NOTES

It is true the Scriptures teach elsewhere a mutual *humility* toward each other, but Ephesians 5:21 is intended by the apostle to set the record straight—equal standing with God does not obliterate obligations to authority. He makes that clear by defining exactly how believers are to be submitting to one another in the verses to follow, which specifically state the correct response of submission to the various roles present in the church. Though generally *allēlōn* represents reciprocal action, it is not always so as is the case in 1 Corinthians 11:33 (i.e., only the one who has already arrived can tarry for another; the one who is yet to come cannot be tarrying for the one who is already there). Interpreting this passage correctly is a watershed issue when dealing with evangelical feminists who wrongly use Ephesians 5:21 to teach *mutual submission* to bolster their unscriptural egalitarianism, which rejects the concept of biblical headship.

The main point we must not miss in this passage is that obeying brethren who have authority over us is a mark of brotherly affection/kindness. We wrong our brethren who rule us—and disobey the Father—when we do not "submit to one another [in our subordinate roles] in the fear of God."

For more detail on the "myth of mutual submission" see either of Wayne Grudem's books: *Countering the Claims of Evangelical Feminism* (Colorado Springs: Multnomah Publishers, 2006) or *Evangelical Feminism and Biblical Truth* (Sisters, OR: Multnomah Publications, 2004). For additional help on the topic of evangelical feminism in general, see also John Piper and Wayne Grudem, *Recovering Biblical Manhood and Womanhood: A Response to Evangelical Feminism* (Wheaton, IL: Crossway Books, 1991).

Chapter Ten
1. An example is *The Four Loves* by C. S. Lewis.
2. Morris, 114.
3. D. A. Carson, *Love in Hard Places* (Wheaton, IL: Crossway Books, 2002), 13. See also his work, *Exegetical Fallacies*, 2nd ed. (Grand Rapids, MI: Baker Academic, 1996), chapter 1, "Word-Study Fallacies."
4. Though it is certainly not devoid of emotion.
5. Notice once again why the supporting virtues are needed for mature love to function properly.
6. Barclay, 21.
7. Morris, 214.
8. Meditate upon Isaiah 53, the last several chapters of each gospel, which record the final week of Christ before the crucifixion, and 1 Corinthians 15.
9. Barclay, 23.
10. See *Created for His Glory* (Greenville, SC: BJU Press, 2002), "Part One: Rejoicing in the Grand Reality of God."
11. See Jonathan Edwards, *Charity and Its Fruits* (1852; Carlisle, PA: The Banner of Truth Trust, 1969), Leon Morris, *Testaments of Love*; W. Phillip Keller, *A Layman Looks at the Love of God: A New Devotional Study of 1 Corinthians 13* (Minneapolis: Bethany House Publishers, 1984), Thomas Vincent, *The True Christian's Love to the Unseen Christ* (1677; Morgan, PA: Soli Deo Gloria Publications, 1993).
12. Edwards, 7–9.

Chapter Eleven
1. Throughout this chapter I will occasionally hyphenate this word to stress its opposing relationship to integrity.
2. *World Magazine*, December 29, 2007/January 5, 2008, p. 13.
3. J. Mark Bertrand, *(Re)Thinking Worldview: Learning to Think, Live, and Speak in This World* (Wheaton, IL: Crossway Books, 2007), 135–36 (emphases his).

Chapter Twelve
1. R. C. Sproul, *The Consequences of Ideas: Understanding the Concepts That Shaped Our World* (Wheaton, IL: Crossway Books, 2000), 34–35.
2. Plato in *The Republic* used this allegory to explain his belief that the universal, transcendental "forms" are the source of true knowledge. These "forms" lay behind the particulars of life that we see.
3. I was encouraged, however, by the numbers of men and women who did possess a vibrant relationship with Jesus Christ—both cadets and officers. The officers, unfortunately, are severely limited in their opportunities to speak of anything "religious" because of the wrongful interpretation by the courts of the idea of separation of church and state.
4. Participant guide for the 14th Annual National Character and Leadership Symposium, 20.

5. Gus Lee, *Courage: The Backbone of Leadership* (San Francisco: Jossey-Bass, 2006).
6. Ibid., 35.
7. Ibid., 110–11.
8. Ibid., 188.
9. A woman may not be dressing that way to attract a man, but to be thought of as "cute" among her friends. As long as what is deemed "cute" is "sexy," the effect upon the men who see her is the same though her intention may be different.
10. In his unpublished manuscript "Christians and Alcohol," Robert B. Fischer notes the following: "The State of California, in a leaflet issued with applications for renewal of vehicle registration, advises that just one drink increases five-fold the risk of having an accident."
11. The test of whether it tempts them cannot be "Does it bother my conscience or arouse me physically?" A believer can become so desensitized to evil that many things do not bother him which should bother him. Furthermore, whatever physical activity he is engaged in with a woman did have a sensual appeal to him at one time or he wouldn't have begun the activity. We don't need for Scripture to "give us a verse" about this when common sense should inform us. Today's reverse legalism (i.e., "Show me a verse or leave me alone"), instead of fostering discernment and common sense, has eliminated the practice of both.
12. J. I. Packer, *Rediscovering Holiness* (Ann Arbor, MI: Servant Publications, 1992), 215.
13. Lee, 36.

Chapter Thirteen

1. The same concern for the spiritual well-being of people is evidenced in Paul's prayers: Ephesians 1:15–23; 3:14–21; Philippians 1:9–11; and Colossians 1:9–12.
2. Barclay, 22.
3. Ibid., 22–23.
4. Ibid., 28.
5. For a lengthier treatment of the topic of confrontation and church discipline, see Jay E. Adams, *The Handbook of Church Discipline* (Grand Rapids, MI: Zondervan, 1986).
6. Stephen Hankins in personal correspondence.

Epilogue

1. Reginald E. Allen, ed., *Greek Philosophy: Thales to Aristotle* (Toronto: Collier-Macmillan Canada Ltd., 1966), 97.
2. *Aretegenic* is a term coined by Ellen T. Charry in *By the Renewing of Your Minds* (New York: Oxford University Press, 1997). I am indebted to my colleague Eric Newton for introducing me to this term.

Appendices

1. Jim Berg, *Changed into His Image* (Greenville, SC: BJU Press, 1999), 301–303.
2. Copied from J. I. Packer, *Rediscovering Holiness* (Ann Arbor, MI: Servant Publications, 1992), 107–9.
3. John Owen, *Of the Mortification of Sin in Believers: Works*, ed. William H. Gould (London: Banner of Truth Trust, 1966), VI. 79, quoted in Packer.
4. John Brown, *Parting Counsels: An Exposition of 2 Peter 1* (Edinburgh: The Banner of Truth Trust, 1856), 79–84.
5. *Energetic* is Brown's term for the effects of adding *aretē* to saving faith. *Enlightened* is his description for the heart that is seeking to cultivate *knowledge*.

Study Guide

1. Adapted from *Basics for Believers* by Jim Berg (Greenville, SC: BJU Press, 1978), 18–19.
2. George Barna, *Real Teens: A Contemporary Snapshot of Youth Culture* (Ventura, CA: Regal Books, 2001), 83, 87.

BIBLIOGRAPHY

Adams, Jay E. *Handbook of Church Discipline*. Grand Rapids, MI: Zondervan, 1986.

_____. *The Christian Counselor's Commentary: Hebrews, James, I and II Peter, and Jude*. Woodruff, SC: Timeless Texts, 1996.

Barclay, William. *Flesh and Spirit: An Examination of Galatians 5:19–23*. Grand Rapids, MI: Baker Book House, 1962.

_____. *New Testament Words*. Philadelphia: The Westminster Press, 1964.

Bauckham, Richard J. *Word Biblical Commentary: Jude, 2 Peter*. Waco, TX: Word Books, 1983.

Berg, Jim. *Changed into His Image*. Greenville, SC: BJU Press, 1999.

_____. *Created for His Glory*. Greenville, SC: BJU Press, 2002.

Bigg, Charles. *A Critical and Exegetical Commentary on the Epistles of St. Peter and St. Jude*. Edinburgh: T and T Clark, 1987.

Bridges, Jerry. *The Discipline of Grace: God's Role and Our Role in the Pursuit of Holiness*. Colorado Springs: NavPress, 1994.

Brown, John. *Parting Counsels: An Exposition of 2 Peter 1*. 1856. Carlisle, PA: The Banner of Truth Trust, 1980.

Buchanan, Mark. *Hidden in Plain Sight: The Secret of More*. Nashville: Thomas Nelson, 2007.

Carson, D. A. *Exegetical Fallacies*. 2nd ed. Grand Rapids, MI: Baker Academic, 1996.

_____. *Love in Hard Places*. Wheaton, IL: Crossway Books, 2002.

Charles, J. Daryl. *Virtue Amidst Vice*. Sheffield, England: Sheffield Academic Press, 1997.

Charles, J. Daryl and Erland Waltner. *1–2 Peter, Jude*. Scottdale, PA: Herald Press, 1999.

Custer, Stuart. *A Treasury of New Testament Synonyms*. Greenville, SC: Bob Jones University Press, 1975.

_____. *Biblical Viewpoint: Focus on II Peter* 36, no. 2 (Nov. 2002).

Davids, Peter H. *The Letters of 2 Peter and Jude*. Grand Rapids, MI: William B. Eerdmans, 2006.

Edwards, Jonathan. *Charity and Its Fruits*. 1852. Carlisle, PA: The Banner of Truth Trust, 1969.

Green, Christopher and Dick Lucas. *The Message of 2 Peter and Jude: The Promise of His Coming*. Downers Grove, IL: Inter-Varsity Press, 1995.

Green, Michael. *The Second Epistle General of Peter and the General Epistle of Jude*. 1968. Grand Rapids, MI: William B. Eerdmans, 1983.

Hiebert, D. Edmond. *Second Peter and Jude: An Expositional Commentary*. Greenville, SC: Bob Jones University Press, 1989.

Inrig, Gary. *A Call to Excellence*. Wheaton, IL: Victor Books, 1985.

Jowett, J. H. *The Epistles of Peter*. 1905. Grand Rapids, MI: Kregel Publications, 1993.

Kistler, Don, ed. *The Puritans on Loving One Another*. Morgan, PA: Soli Deo Gloria, 1997 (sermons by Ralph Venning, Thomas Manton, Joseph Caryl, and John Ball).

Kolenda, Christopher, ed. *Leadership: The Warrior's Art*. Carlisle, PA: The Army War College Foundation Press, 2001.

Lee, Gus. *Courage: The Backbone of Leadership*. San Francisco: Jossey-Bass, 2006.

Lloyd-Jones, D. Martyn. *Expository Sermons on 2 Peter*. Carlisle, PA: The Banner of Truth Trust, 1983.

_____. *Spiritual Depression: Its Causes and Cures*. Grand Rapids, MI: Wm. B. Eerdmans, 1965.

Lucas, Dick and Christopher Green. *The Message of 2 Peter and Jude*. Downers Grove, IL: Inter-Varsity Press, 1995.

MacArthur, John. *The Quest for Character*. Nashville: Thomas Nelson, 2006.

Moo, Douglas J. *2 Peter and Jude*. Grand Rapids, MI: Zondervan, 1996.

Morris, Leon. *Testaments of Love: A Study of Love in the Bible*. Grand Rapids, MI: William B. Eerdmans, 1981.

Packer, J. I. *A Quest for Godliness: The Puritan Vision of the Christian Life*. Wheaton, IL: Crossway Books, 1990.

_____. *Rediscovering Holiness*. Ann Arbor, MI: Servant Publications, 1992.

Schreiner, Thomas R. *1, 2 Peter, Jude*. Nashville: Broadman and Holman, 2003.

Trench, Richard C. *Synonyms of the New Testament*. 1880. Grand Rapids: William B. Eerdmans, 1953.

Vincent, M. R. *Word Studies in the New Testament*. McLean, VA: MacDonald Publishing Company, 1886.

Vincent, Nathaniel. *A Discourse Concerning Love*. Morgan, PA: Soli Deo Gloria, 1684.

West, Diana. *The Death of the Grown-up*. New York: St. Martin's Press, 2007.

INDEX